More Praise for *Lost on Earth*

"I hope many people will be touched — as I am — by the human tragedies *Lost on Earth* conveys with such emotion and talent."
—Elie Wiesel

"It is a rare bit of luck these past 10 years that put a writer as gifted as Mark Fritz at most of our world's historic venues . . . a remarkable blend of history, analysis and humanity."
—*Detroit Free Press*

"This is an unpretentious book, but it brings out lucidly the moral and political problems caused by one of mankind's greatest migratory upheavals. *Lost on Earth* is a series of vivid dispatches from this shadowland of outlanders, and at their best they are the premier reports about the contemporary refugee."
—*Boston Globe*

"*Lost on Earth* is an enjoyable read, not least because of Fritz's eye for details."
—*Washington Monthly*

"Recommended reading. Helps put the new refugees (from Kosovo) in a larger context by examining the world's new homeless."
—*USA Today*

"Unfolds like a series of loosely interconnected short stories. Fritz writes with streetwise empathy for his dislocated subjects."
—*Publishers Weekly*

"An arresting eyewitness account of the end of the Cold War."
—*Cleveland Plain Dealer*

"This is a book about travel, but the travelers have no home to leave behind, their destination is nowhere, and the reason for the trip is anything but pleasure. The fact that our nation of immigrants (and tourists) has its borders closed to them is terrible and humiliating."
—P. J. O'Rourke, author of *Eat the Rich* and *Holidays in Hell*

"A vivid account and thoughtful examination of history's largest human migration. . . . All too often, these are the stories that go ignored by the American media; one must praise Fritz for bringing them to light."
—*Kirkus*

"This is inspired reporting — a trek through a world of dislocation and distress, a microscopic look at the human consequences of poor leadership and ignorance among our so-called family of nations. Mark Fritz focuses upon individual lost souls, then makes the connections to the reverberating waves of displacement that are slowly, but steadily, coming away."
—Arthur Kent, Emmy Award-winning war correspondent

"These are not just touching stories of poor refugees caught in a world gone mad. They are stories that starkly demonstrate just how interdependent the world has become."
—*St. Petersburg Times*

▶ lost on earth

lost on earth

▶ nomads of the new world

mark fritz

routledge
new york

Published in the United States of America in 2000 by
Routledge
29 West 35th Street
New York, NY 10001

Printed in the United States of America on acid-free paper.

10 9 8 7 6 5 4 3 2 1

LIBRARY OF CONGRESS CATALOGING-IN-PUBLICATION DATA

Fritz, Mark.
    Lost on earth: nomads of the new world / by Mark Fritz.
    p.   cm.
    ISBN 0-415-92609-2 (pb)
    1. Refugees—History—20th century. I. Title.
HV640.F75 2000
362.87'09'04—dc21   99-088060

To Karyn

There is no greater sorrow on earth than
the loss of one's native land

EURIPIDES

contents

◗ lost on earth

introduction

WHO says the Berlin Wall has fallen? What do we *mean* the Berlin Wall has fallen? Did we *see* the Berlin Wall fall? Is there a big hole there?"

Frank Crepeau was holding a little slip of paper. It was a dispatch that had just come in from Berlin. It was filed with what was known as a flash priority, which was pretty much reserved for, say, the assassination of an American president or an invasion from outer space. It was a single sentence, unattributed, too remarkable to be real. It simply said that the Berlin Wall had fallen.

I was a copyeditor on the foreign desk of a wire service, The Associated Press in New York. Frank Crepeau was the assistant foreign editor. He'd worked in Moscow and Berlin and Prague, among other places, back in the days when nations were constructed to keep their citizens caged. I sat in the slot, the center of a horseshoe-shaped collection of desks, and he sat off to the side, waiting to pounce on the mistakes that the rewrites and the filers like me inevitably made during the chaos of deadline.

So when something akin to science fiction popped up on the little printer at my right elbow, I handed the printer slip to him. And he looked at it with the incredulity of someone who had personally felt the chill winds of the Cold War.

He called the bureau in Berlin. East Germany's government had, indeed, lifted travel restrictions. The wall, technically, was open. Frank was satisfied. I pressed a key on my computer and put a bulletin on the wire. It was November 9, 1989. The Berlin Wall had fallen, and nobody could quite believe it.

Five months later, mostly by coincidence, I was sent to East Germany, and from there I took assignments to Moscow, the Persian Gulf, Somalia, Liberia, Rwanda, Bosnia and many other places. And it seemed like most of the stories I wrote in some way included a large number of people who had been forced to leave their homes, their jobs, their countries, their particular place in the world. Whether it was a Tutsi teenager on the road in Rwanda or a Togolese computer expert fleeing across the Sahara, every event seemed to have a sizable population of displaced people attached to it. But it wasn't until I came home five years later, after I'd left behind the little pieces of different places, that I realized how much all of these people were part of the same story.

In September 1995, during one of the many events held to mark the fiftieth anniversary of the United Nations, a group of diplomats, writers and humanitarians convened at Columbia University in New York to discuss a phenomenon that policy analysts refer to as forced migration. The purpose was to bring together people with a knowledge of the topic to discuss what to do about the multitude of refugees spawned by the porous borders, ethnically retooled homelands and overhauled ideologies that emerged when the Soviet Union quit the Cold War.

At one point, the discussion turned to the apathy that people in the wealthy West in general and the United States in particular had for what seemed to be the same faceless mass of wanderers, distant and anonymous and perpetually in need of a handout. And it dawned on me that perhaps *that* was the overlooked element that should have made their stories compelling: the shared voyage, their participation in a phenomenon so large and complex that most people can see it only as small pieces that look wearisomely alike.

An estimated 50 million people were either driven from their countries or uprooted within them by the mid-1990s, roughly one out of every hundred people on earth. Counting those who emigrated for what were viewed as dire economic reasons, the figure more than doubles. The impact of this great migration has been enormous. It has compelled U.S.-led armies to intervene in faraway wars. It has led to a reactionary wave of restrictive immigration laws around the world. And it has planted the seeds of countless future conflicts.

This book doesn't seek to join the sometimes insular debate about the future of U.S. policy in the post–Cold War era, but to perhaps move some aspects of it to slightly broader precincts, to put a few faces on the aftermath of one era and the rough beginnings of another, to detail how individual lives have been changed forever by abstract events. This book is a visit to a misunderstood world, a veritable refugee nation, a shadowland of outlanders that overlaps uncomfortably with our own world, but which exists very much in a different dimension governed by its own rules for survival. The inhabitants are motivated by varying degrees of two basic impulses: a desire to escape danger and a yearning for a life that comes closest to the one that we live. If we take a big enough step backward to see this world, if we study its contours, it is clear we are moving through one of mankind's greatest migratory disturbances, one with the power to shape our future.

On the surface, this book is a collection of character sketches about ordinary people who just happened to be standing in the way when history got made. Some of them make it back home, some of them find new places to live. Some simply disappear, back into the fog. Mostly, though, I've tried to use the pieces of these lives — from the running woman in the first chapter to the running woman, older and wearier, in the last — to create a single character to symbolize the twentieth century's stunning last decade. This is the tale of the contemporary refugee, an ordinary human being forced to cross a crumbling bridge between two eras. It is a chronicle of escape and pursuit, pilgrimage and exile. It is a postcard from oblivion.

1 portal

THE Gypsy opened the trunk of his car and Michaela got inside. She crouched sideways, hugged her knees and watched the lid come down on a sunny day. She didn't think about the danger. She didn't think about anything. She just gave herself up to this very strange moment. "Get in the trunk," he'd said. Yeah. OK.

The Gypsy got in the car and drove away. It was very hot inside the trunk. There was a little rust hole in the middle of the trunk lid, and Michaela peered through it, watching layers of forest fall away. After a few minutes, the car slowed to a stop, and Michaela heard the Gypsy talking to somebody, probably a soldier. She felt the car move again, then stop once more a few minutes later. The trunk flew open and the Gypsy looked into her wide green eyes.

"Run!" he shouted.

Michaela scrambled out of the trunk and saw she was in a field surrounded by forest. The Gypsy was pointing to a barbed-wire fence fifteen feet away. Beyond the fence was a low hill covered with brush. Michaela ran like a crazy woman. She got to the fence and climbed over it as carefully yet as quickly as she could. Then she ran up the hill, through the brambles that scratched her bare legs and snagged her black silk blouse, which had looked so pretty with the checked shorts she'd worn that day. Gradually, she realized that she was running through a vineyard.

She saw a woman standing in the distance. Michaela ran toward her, hoping.

"Is this Austria?" Michaela gasped.

"Yes," said the woman. "Are you from East Germany?"

"Yes!" Michaela said.

Michaela could barely think. She'd cleared the threshold. This woman seemed happy to see her. It was almost as if she'd been expecting her. It was like a dream.

COMMUNISM meant different things to different people, but to Michaela Woike, it was simply boring. There just seemed more to do in the West, at least from what she could see on West German television, one of the few outside influences the authorities couldn't filter out. Life seemed more, well, colorful, unrestrained. The fashions, the music. Of course, the political freedoms were nice, too.

Michaela had thought about escaping for years. Not just from East Germany, but from home. She had been born and raised in a beautiful little village called Zella-Mehlis, a postcard of a place snuggled high in the lush green mountains of Thuringia. Even when she was a child, Michaela had dreamed of fleeing its infuriatingly pastoral monotony.

And why not? Her father had abandoned the family when she was just three years old for reasons that never were quite clear. All she remembered was a tall man with a black beard, and the cryptic admonitions of her mom: "I forbid you to see him." Not surprisingly, Michaela didn't have a very good relationship with her mother. And she wasn't particularly close to her sister, who was seven years older.

All she asked out of life was the chance to live an exciting one, to travel to fantastic places, to have a career as an artist. But she knew even when she was a little girl that such a life was unattainable in her gingerbread village, which lay on the wrong side of the Fulda Gap, the strategic mountain pass that separated one superpower army from the other.

Still, Michaela experienced the sensation of freedom when she went off to nursing school after she turned seventeen. Her high school graduating class had been so tiny — thirty people — that only the top three students were given opportunities beyond a limited range of vocational choices. East Germany needed more workers than artists, it seemed. Since she wasn't one of the top students, her options were quite limited, which drove her crazy.

But at least nursing school got her out of Zella-Mehlis and into Suhl, a slightly bigger town a few precious miles from home. And then a year of nurse's training got her a job in a psychiatric hospital in a much more distant village, called Biesdorf, which just happened to be on the outskirts of the big city itself, Berlin.

Unfortunately, it was *East* Berlin. Life in a big Communist metropolitan area turned out to be just as static as life in a small Communist town. She lived in an apartment on the hospital premises and the work was quite dreary. Many of these patients were truly insane, while others seemed little more than chronic complainers and mere nonconformists, like herself. She worked all sorts of shifts, night and day. If she wanted to go into Berlin, it would take thirty minutes by train. It was hard to have an outside life, though she tried. She acted occasionally in community theater, because it was fun and she was pretty. She wrote and illustrated a children's book, though she couldn't find anybody to publish it.

But it wasn't enough. She wanted to travel. She wanted to go West. And it seemed like a lot of people her age felt the same way.

One day, a friend told her some rather amazing news.

"Have you heard? The Hungarians aren't shooting people at the border anymore."

Michaela got excited. East Germans had always been able to travel to Hungary, a favorite holiday spot. And now, Hungary had apparently sprung a leak. It had relaxed its border controls. There was almost a hole to Austria, to the West. She told her friend, Thorsten, who lived in her building, that she was thinking of going to Hungary and making a break for the border. It was quickly becoming a thing to do among young people.

Michaela began to lay the foundation for her plan. She told her coworkers that she was going to take a vacation to Czechoslovakia and, ahem, Hungary. Another nurse, her friend Katrin, became suspicious immediately. In certain circles, a "vacation in Hungary" was becoming almost a code for escape.

"Are you going to defect?" Katrin asked.

"No," Michaela said. "No. I can't say."

Katrin asked Thorsten, "Is Michaela going to defect?" and he said, yes, he thought she was.

This made Katrin very determined. She invited Michaela to her parents' home in Weimar one weekend, and when nobody was looking she dragged her into the bathroom. One never knew what homes or rooms were bugged, so it paid to be careful. Katrin turned on the faucet full blast, then told Michaela that she knew she was going to defect, and that she wanted to defect, too. Why not do it together?

It was amazing how easy it had been to get visas to Hungary. The two women figured the authorities would be suspicious. After all, it seemed as though everybody knew somebody who had taken advantage of this new hole in Hungary. But there wasn't a problem at all. Trying to cover their tracks, they also got visas for Czechoslovakia and decided to spend a week there first. They packed lightly, like they were going on a short trip, not leaving forever.

Michaela didn't say a word to her mother, who was a member of the Communist Party. The less she knew, the better for everybody. Michaela and Katrin took the train to Prague. Needless to say, they played the part well. Katrin was tall and lean with a leonine mane of long black hair; Michaela was small and sassy with a reddish brown bob. They hit the bars, met people, tried to have some fun. They had been dreading the scary adventure ahead, and partying among the Bohemians in Prague was the perfect release. For a while.

They finally decided it was time to begin hitchhiking to Hungary, a method of travel that was pretty safe in the Stalinist world. They caught a few rides, but didn't dare tell anybody what they were up to, until the last guy, a Hungarian. He was driving and Katrin was sitting up front, chatting away, and it just sort of came out that they were planning to cross over to the other side. The Hungarian told them exactly where to go, outside a town called Sopron, right on the border, right where he was headed. Katrin wrote the directions down and the Hungarian drew a little map.

The city sizzled in the August heat and the tourists wore their skimpiest clothing. Sopron was filled with Gothic and baroque buildings that drew visitors from all over, but Michaela and Katrin were too nervous to notice. They were so paranoid that they even bought T-shirts with Hungarian writing on them — who knew what they said? — so they would look like tourists. Of course, they couldn't bring themselves to actually wear T-shirts with slogans. It just wasn't them.

At dusk, they went to the outskirts of town and began to hitchhike. An old man on a tractor stopped and offered them a lift. They told him they wanted a ride to the border. If he suspected something, he didn't let on. He just dropped them off on a stretch of forest road, the starting point on their homemade map. Katrin studied the directions in the twilight and away they walked, into the woods, terrified by their courage. They crept through the brush for a few minutes, then heard rustling in the distance. Then voices.

Michaela and Katrin dropped to the ground. They stayed there, absolutely motionless in the itchy weeds, for maybe half an hour, long after the muffled voices had drifted away. The weather was miserably muggy and the mosquitoes were ravenous. It was soon pitch dark. They got up and began walking again. They came to the edge of the woods and saw a huge field in front of them.

This wasn't right. The landscape wasn't matching the description that the Hungarian had given them. There was no way they could cross this field without being spotted. While they whispered about what to do, signal flares sailed over their heads. The young women froze.

"Halt!" somebody shouted.

Soldiers with dogs, big Alsatians, jogged up to them. Michaela and Katrin were petrified. But the soldiers, looking at the two pretty young things quaking with fear, could not have been nicer.

"Oh God," one said. "Why did you go this way? If you would have gone a little to the right, you would have made it."

"Why did you stop?" asked another. "Now our superiors have seen you and we have to take you with us."

The Hungarian soldiers put them in a truck and drove off. They stopped several more times for other soldiers who had seized other East Germans. The truck was full by the time it reached the military base, where another forty East Germans who had been caught that night were being held in a stockade. The soldiers put Michaela and Katrin in a cell with another young woman from East Germany. Katrin and Michaela were scared and started to cry, but the Hungarian guards were extremely nice. One of them brought Cokes and stayed around and smoked with them. He said it was his last day in the army. He figured what the hell, and told them how they could get into Austria. He told them to wait three days, then try again at a certain spot. He said if people were caught twice in three days, they were sent back to East Germany. But if you staggered your escape attempts, you were merely set free in Hungary to try, try again.

The next morning, Michaela and Katrin were interrogated by an officer. Nicely interrogated. Then, the Hungarians just let them go. Just like that, the two girls walked off the base to the main road. They were relieved but still somewhat rattled, not to mention terrified of attempting another escape. They decided to go to Budapest because they needed to get their visas extended. So they began hitchhiking. And the first driver knew right away what these two East Germans were doing in a Hungarian border town.

"Do you want to escape to the West?" he asked.

"No!" Michaela said.

"Yes!" Katrin said.

Both women were under considerable stress, and they weren't exactly getting along at this point. But Katrin was adamant about getting this escape over with and the man in the car — who was a Gypsy — was quite convincing. He said he knew a good place at the border. He would take each of them — one at a time — in the trunk of his car. Then, all they had to do was run a little.

"Let's do it!" Katrin said.

Michaela reluctantly gave in.

"Get inside the trunk," the Gypsy had told her.

"Yeah," Michaela had responded. "OK."

MICHAELA was sweaty and panting and scratched by brambles that had snagged the black-and-white shorts that matched her blouse. She was disoriented, almost delirious with adrenaline. The woman in the vineyard led Michaela to another woman, a farmer named Marie, and Marie got her car and drove Michaela back to the border to wait for Katrin. Finally, Katrin came running through the brambles, up the hill, into the vineyard.

Apparently, the Gypsy had tried to get a little something from Katrin after he'd dropped Michaela off.

"Come over here, sweet baby," he'd said, putting his arm around her shoulder.

Katrin was a very tall woman, really strong, and she had gone a little crazy.

"Stop it! What have you done with my friend, you bastard!"

The Gypsy had backed off immediately, apologized profusely and then drove Katrin to the border and dropped her off. The two women would talk about it later, about how insane they had been to have accepted his offer in the first place. After they thought about it even longer, they didn't blame this Gypsy for making a pass at Katrin. He was just giving it a try.

The Austrian named Marie took Michaela and Katrin to her house, gave them lunch with wine. Two other East Germans were there, too. The village was full of them. A couple of days before, a crowd of them had simply stampeded through the fence. There was a new refugee camp in town and it was absolutely full. In fact, the government had set up daily shuttle buses to take East German refugees into Vienna. The refugees were like heroes.

Michaela and Katrin got on one of these buses and went to the West German embassy. They were given one hundred marks each — the standard amount that West Germany paid East Germans with the courage to defect — and put up in a hotel for the weekend. The place was full of refugees just like them, and they all swapped stories about their narrow escapes, the people they left behind, the amazing days ahead.

From Vienna, Michaela and Katrin were sent to a camp in West Berlin, the side of their city they'd never seen. It was overwhelming. Especially the little things. In East Germany, for example, if you ordered pizza, you got a little circle of tasteless dough with a couple of baked tomatoes on top. But when Michaela and Katrin ordered pizza here, it was a *wheel* of food so plentiful they couldn't have hoped to finish it. And the bathrooms, with the water that came on automatically when you stood over the sink. More than once Michaela drenched her handbag.

The West Germans were sort of amused by the people they dubbed, sometimes derisively, the *Ossis,* or "Easties." Michaela was in a supermarket once, trying to figure out how these people selected produce. They were putting their vegetables in plastic bags and then weighing them on a machine that spat out a sticker that they then affixed to the bags. Michaela was watching this one older woman when suddenly she swung around.

"Are you from the East? Do you want me to show you how this works?"

Michaela was mortified. Being out of sync like this was not a pleasant feeling for a twenty-one-year-old woman with a self-assured sense of style. It didn't take long to adapt, however. She found a flat in Berlin's Kreuzberg district, a charmingly blighted pastiche of ethnic restaurants, offbeat art houses, counterculture clothing shops and bars so progressive that they held special nights for lesbians, including people who were lesbians just on special nights. Michaela dyed her auburn bob a raven black and slipped into Berlin's bohemian underbelly. She also got a job as a nurse.

Meanwhile, the exodus of East Germans quickened and huge demonstrations broke out in the streets. Dissent was erupting all over Eastern Europe. Each regime reacted differently to the demands for the type of reforms that Mikhail Gorbachev had introduced in the Soviet Union. East Germany, for example, became even more doctrinaire. Poland gave up after a while and held a democratic election. And Hungary began cutting down the 160 miles of fence that separated it from Austria, from the West.

By the autumn of 1989, tens of thousands of refugees were racing for the widening hole in Hungary. Many were East Germans, but humanitarian agencies began noticing Soviets, Romanians, even Somalis fleeing something or other.

Then Hungary dropped all pretense at controlling the outflow of people. It announced that East Germans wouldn't need visas to transit Hungary into Austria. In other words, people like Michaela no longer had to cut through the woods. They could stroll through the checkpoint without any paperwork at all. Hungary transformed itself into a wide-open portal to the promised land. The border became a vortex. The entire region, the entire world, was put into play.

The coup de grâce was delivered by Gorbachev himself. He came to East Germany on October 7, the fortieth anniversary of the day the Soviet Union had forged the nation from the rubble of World War II. East Germany was hemorrhaging people. Huge crowds were marching in the streets to denounce party chief Erich Honecker. These same people turned out to cheer Gorbachev. "Gorby!" they shouted. "Help us!"

And Gorbachev was there for them. He admonished those who wouldn't change with the changing world. "Life punishes those who come late," Gorbachev told Honecker.

Honecker wouldn't listen. Nearly three decades before, as a party functionary, he himself had supervised the building of the Berlin Wall to halt the same sort of exodus, to imprison an entire people. Communism's gatekeeper was not about to let his people go. He was not about to give them the little freedoms they demanded.

So the escapes continued. Those who couldn't make it to Hungary flooded West German embassies in Poland and Czechoslovakia to plead for asylum. Within East Germany, the protests grew larger and spread to more cities. "We . . . are . . . *the people!*" the people roared, louder and louder. Less than two weeks after Gorbachev's visit, Honecker was deposed by his own Politburo.

His successor, Egon Krenz, tried to placate the people with a new law born of desperation. He decided to relax the travel ban on East Germans so they, like the Hungarians, could travel West and, presumably, return home again. A Politburo member read the resolution at a news conference. Radio stations broadcast it immediately. People who heard it poured out of their homes and moved toward the barriers. Could it be?

Michaela was having dinner with her roommate. She had actually come to regret her decision to slip through Hungary. She was missing these amazing demonstrations, this incredibly inspiring and rather stylish revolution against the old guard. And she never regretted it more than that day in November 1989, when she sat down for dinner. One of her roommate's friends, a West German, burst into their apartment.

"Turn on the TV!" she shouted. "The wall has fallen!"

They turned on the television set and there it was: Michaela's countrymen, joyous and disbelieving, pouring over and around and *through* the wall, heading West, heading right for the television cameras, right for their living room. The border guards had merely stepped aside. Michaela stared with disbelief at the ecstatic faces from her old world, crashing like a wave into her new one.

"Shit!" hissed her roommate's friend, either speaking without thinking or thinking far ahead. "The *Ossis* are coming!"

Then she looked at Michaela, embarrassed.

"You're not an *Ossi,* of course," she said.

Michaela just shrugged. Of course she was. She just hid it well.

She'd be gone from Berlin in just a few months. Romance and art school and a thrilling new world beckoned in London. But she was still, in her soul, an *Ossi,* an outlander, a seeker of asylum, a woman who had disappeared into a forest one day and emerged as a refugee on the other side. She had merely been a few steps ahead of the rest, as usual. She had been selected by circumstance to help unlock the gates, broaden the breach a bit, make it easier for the millions who would follow.

2 return of the gypsies

THEY came by train, mostly. At first, only the conductors and ticket clerks noticed them, the big families lugging their bundles and bags lashed with cooking pots and bedrolls. They would tumble out of the cars and wander the station, disoriented, gathering in big groups, muttering among themselves in that indecipherable language. Then they'd disappear into the city for the day. At night they would come back, not to wait for the train back to Bucharest — no, not to go home again — but to sleep. Sleep, and wait for their relatives to come in on the next train, the next day. In a week there were seven hundred of them, all of them living in the train station, sleeping in the corners, sprawling on the benches, eating their sausages, smoking their cigarettes, begging for money, oblivious to the chaos they caused for the travelers who stumbled around them in bug-eyed disbelief. After a while, as the weather grew warm in the spring of 1990, everybody in East Berlin noticed the newcomers.

Hannelore Gensch watched them on television. She was particularly struck by one young couple who showed up in the station with their four children, one just nine days old. They were dirty and dressed in rags — here in Berlin! These poor people, these poor *Roma,* what a horrible life they must have fled in Romania to come here, to live in that dismal train station, to beg for coins to buy food for their children. She saw the report on the local news and thought: We've got to help them.

Hannelore knew why these people were running. She saw that on television, too. Like most people, she felt the revolt against the despot Nicolae Ceauşescu was the beginning of better times for Romania. But the end of communism was followed by economic collapse and a new style of nationalism, one that couldn't accommodate the large minority of *Roma* and their different clothes and different language and different ways. The people who considered themselves real Romanians turned on the *Roma,* whom they considered beneath them. Homes were burned, people beaten. Politicians agitated against them. It was no wonder the *Roma* were coming here. Our revolution had a much happier result, Hannelore thought. To them, East Germany must seem like the promised land.

"This incredible poverty," she mused as she watched the television with her husband. "There seems to be no solution to it."

The footage focused on the *Roma* who were making themselves at home in the sepulchral old train station in Lichtenberg, a grayly decaying neighborhood that seemed to collect more soot than the rest of the city. Lichtenberg was known as the foreign quarter of East Berlin; many of the guest workers that the East German Communists had imported to help work the coal mines and factories lived there. Most came from Vietnam, Angola, Mozambique and other Third World outposts of Soviet ideology. Some of the poorest East Germans lived there, too, in decrepit prewar tenements and numbingly utilitarian clusters of blocky apartment buildings. They constituted the lowest caste in a supposedly classless society. And now, like an underground water main with a sudden rupture, a new population of even poorer people was bubbling up among them, pouring out of the train station and spreading out into the city, the country, the continent.

The men stood in groups and smoked cigarettes, the women with their bright shawls and long peasant dresses sat mournfully on the floor, their backs to the wall. The children darted everywhere, sometimes stopping travelers to flash little cards, written painstakingly in German, that said I AM ROMANIAN. PLEASE HELP ME WITH MONEY.

The Germans called them *Roma* now, a more respectful name reflective of the desire to put distance from the days when the Gypsies were second only to the Jews as objects of hatred. The Gypsies had migrated from India to Europe sometime around the fifteenth century, and many Europeans had been trying to get rid of them ever since. Hitler slaughtered half a million of them. Because of their close-knit communities, separate code of law and behavior, itinerant culture and often colorful peasant dresses and baggy pants straight out of central casting, Gypsies were blamed for a host of social ills. They were stereotyped as beggars, thieves, mystics and, mostly, shiftless nomads.

With the ouster and execution of Ceauşescu and his wife in December 1989, along with the removal of the Communist hard-liners throughout Eastern Europe, the Gypsies found themselves even more marginalized in the nations where they were most concentrated. In Romania in particular, the campaigns for upcoming elections had become a spawning grounds for virulent nationalism and anti-Gypsy sentiment. There was no doubt the Gypsies were being victimized, just as there was no doubt they were drawn to East Germany because Cold War borders had dissolved and the nation was suddenly a doorway to the West.

Ironically, many had traveled through Hungary into Austria first, following the path that East German refugees like Michaela Woike had blazed less than a year earlier. But Austria, now swamped with refugees, toughened its visa requirements in March 1990. So the tide quickly changed direction, opening a direct channel from Bucharest to East Berlin.

It was hard not to have sympathy for these people. After all, not too long ago, it was the East Germans who had been the refugees, who had poured out of the country and into the West. While hundreds of thousands of people had marched in the streets, demanding freedom, hundreds of thousands of others made an even more powerful statement by packing their bags and simply leaving. Just last year, Hannelore had sat in her living room and watched East Germans carrying their bags and bundles into West Germany, asking for shelter and sanctuary.

Like most people, Hannelore had watched the revolution from the sidelines, transfixed. She was a middle-aged woman who toiled rather anonymously for the Berlin city government. She had spent many years deep in the viscera of the Communist bureaucracy, dully aware that each new day was as predictable as the previous one. When the demonstrations broke out, she found herself both rooting for the revolutionaries and fearing for their lives, hoping for their success but dreading quite morbidly their bloody downfall. She'd wanted to participate in the demonstrations, to stand in the square with all those brave young protesters and shout: "We are the people!" But she had been afraid. She'd thought each rally would end with soldiers lined up, firing away, igniting a civil war.

One evening, at the height of the tumult, she couldn't resist anymore. She went to one of the evening services at the church where the pro-democracy protesters always gathered, where the ministers spoke allegorically about the revolution, where secret police informants surreptitiously memorized faces, where people lit candles and prayed for victory. That evening, she'd felt the pulse of the movement, the power of the moment. She had been both frightened and thrilled.

Then, like magic, startling and unexpected, the wall was breached, almost by accident. A harried official told a roomful of reporters that the government was finally going to ease restrictions on travel abroad. This official, reading from a piece of paper that had been handed to him just before the news conference began, said the new regulation would go into effect at midnight. Presumably *this* midnight. But he said people would still need to apply for visas. Probably.

This official would realize much later that he was badly misinterpreting a vague, ambiguously written draft of a *proposed* regulation, not an existing one.

Too late. Radio and television stations extrapolated the announcement to its most outrageously simple extreme: The Berlin Wall is open. Thousands of people gathered at the crossings.

The secret police, who were in charge of security at the border, grew frightened of the large crowds pressing against the wall with a collective ferocity that transcended individual courage. They merely stepped aside, and the wall with its sniper nests and booby traps and razor wire was transformed into a gateway to the West.

Hannelore had been stunned, naturally, and a little worried. She had been certain they would close it again, seal off the city once more. But it never happened. Four months later, the first free elections in history were held. The dreamers who had led the revolution, who had promised a "third way" between capitalism and communism, finished last, behind the Communists themselves. The party that won promised quick unification with wealthy West Germany. It promised that East German marks, which were worthless outside the Soviet Bloc, would be exchanged for West German marks. It promised wealth and freedom and one paradisiacally prosperous nation, together again.

So many things were happening that Hannelore's thoughts didn't linger for long over these mysterious refugees seeping into the city. Their arrival was just another one of those unfathomable events that seemed to happen too fast and too frequently to fully grasp. Amazing things happened so often that nothing really seemed to register anymore.

When the *Roma* arrived in the spring of 1990 — six months after the wall had fallen and six months before reunification — East Germany was floating in a gentle, loopy sort of anarchy. There was unlimited freedom to say or do or buy anything, to go absolutely anywhere. Yet the free market approached like a cold front, abstract yet inevitable. Cheap food, cheap housing and guaranteed jobs supposedly would soon disappear. The state-run factories and farms would frantically slash their workforces in a rite of passage into the new world of competition. And then they would collapse. East Germany reeled like a drunk on a bender, totally broke, yet about to be cared for by a beneficent relative. It was nervous and giddy and staggering home, sort of happy, like a prodigal son counting on the strong arms and deep pockets of powerful kin.

The newly elected East German government was trying to negotiate the terms and timing of unification to get the best deal it could, to preserve the perks of the past and minimize the pain of transition. It also was seeking to undo the ideological damage of the previous regime with a series of proclamations. It apologized for the Holocaust. It issued its regrets for helping the Soviets invade Czechoslovakia in 1968. It promised not to invade Poland. Tipsy with equanimity and the desire to be liked by the community of free nations, this neophyte collection of fairly elected democrats even invited Jews from around the world to return to East Germany, where only about three hundred remained. Applications for asylum immediately began to trickle in, almost all from Jews anxious to leave an unstable and increasingly anti-Semitic Soviet Union.

Despite the good intentions, the inchoate government became a seriocomic sideshow. Newly appointed ministers were fired or resigned in disgrace because of incompetence or evidence that they had been informers for the Communist secret police. The governing coalition quarreled hilariously over which historically significant date in the autumn of 1990 should be the precise moment of German unity. Carpetbaggers and

Communists-turned-crooks took advantage of the lack of oversight by inept and inexperienced new leadership. Functionaries cleaned out the tills, property traded hands illegally, the savvy and the simply unscrupulous used the chaos as cover to orient themselves for the new order. Squatters from West Berlin's iconoclastic anarchist scene moved into East Berlin, taking over vacant tenements and creating surreal communes that seemed to exist solely as canvases for elaborate graffiti. There was no real authority. You could park your car on the sidewalk and the cops, once scary but now unsure of their place in this new world, were more likely to just look away than write a ticket. American tobacco companies dispatched smiling and scrubbed young people to pass out samples of Camels and Marlboros on the streets. Currency traders lined up outside international hotels to buy or sell the East German marks that would soon be magically transformed from worthless Communist money to coveted West German cash. Pieces of Berlin Wall were sunk into chunks of clear plastic and sold as souvenirs. Companies from the West sold ice cream to stores without refrigerators, and hair conditioner to women who'd never heard of such a thing. West Germans who had fled East Germany before the wall went up in 1961 were coming back to reclaim their old homes, regardless of who lived there now. Young West German men hopped into their expensive cars and drove across the border, trolling the cafés of East German villages for beaming young women who seemed happy to discard their local men for a fling in the backseat of a BMW. Everywhere, everyone caught a scent of something — prosperity, pop culture, maybe — and went a little loony.

Though people generally were optimistic, the little signs of the hard times ahead began to pop up. One day, Hannelore's husband, Klaus, was told that he would be among the many employees at his firm who would have to take an early retirement. Hannelore wondered about her own job security, particularly since the two halves of Berlin would form a single city, with the West Berlin city government likely to whittle the Eastern municipal departments down to little or nothing.

"We'll manage somehow," she told her husband one evening. "Even if I have to work as a cleaning lady."

For the time being, however, Hannelore worked for the East Berlin Magistrate for Social Affairs. She worked in the personnel department, which meant processing job applications for all the hospitals and social service agencies in Berlin. Personnel was a curious field under the Communists, since full employment was guaranteed. And so it was interesting when the wall came down, how some jobless people from West Berlin showed up at her office, looking for work. Hannelore and her colleagues marveled at this. They'd heard about unemployment, but they'd never seen actual evidence of it.

Unfortunately, full employment also meant that every field and factory was pretty much overstaffed. And the word from the West was that the employee rolls in the East were going to have to be slashed pretty significantly. When the two cities finally merged their administrations in May 1990, Hannelore came to work one morning and found 120 people waiting outside her office to apply for the *one* job opening she had available. It got to the point where she had go in at 7 A.M. every day, skip lunch and work sometimes until 10 o'clock at night just to process the applications and conduct the interviews. Usually, there were only one or two openings at any given time in a given department, but every day there were more than a hundred people, freshly laid off from other departments, looking for what had once been a right of citizenship. Hannelore sat at her desk all day and much of the evening, listening to one sad story after another, all the time worrying about her own job, which was under review.

It was a taxing time. And then, on top of all that, her boss came into her office one day and asked her whether she could work some extra shifts, whether she could volunteer to help some of these refugees from Romania.

East Germany wasn't used to dealing with refugees. In the old days, when East Germany was more prison yard than nation, refugees were the people who escaped the country and went to West Germany, where they were welcomed as heroes. Now that all the border restrictions were relaxed and all these refugees were pouring in, the bureaucrats didn't really know how to respond. The whole system had been designed to keep people *in*. So they looked at what the people in West Berlin were doing, since a lot of these *Roma* were quickly finding their way through the fresh holes in the Berlin Wall. The Senate for Social Affairs, which was the western counterpart of the department in which Hannelore worked, was making plans to feed and clothe and house the *Roma*. So the East Berliners figured they'd better do the same.

"Do you mind volunteering some time? We need people to deal with the refugees," her boss asked her.

Hannelore remembered the television report just the other day, so she had no qualms about helping.

"Of course," she told her boss.

The refugees at the train station were all rounded up and taken to a military base just outside Berlin, in a village called Biesdorf. They were lodged in the only empty barracks on the base, one that had belonged to a special unit of the *Staatsicherheit*, the all-enveloping state security apparatus known as the Stasi. When the reformers took power, the first thing they did was to dissolve this vast network of spies and enforcers who had kept the Communists in power. Since the Stasi had been everywhere, its dissolution created little gifts of space.

The refugees filled every nook of Biesdorf barracks. Government social workers gave them blankets, clothes, hot meals. Even average East Germans, touched by the televised reports, donated household items to their unfortunate old comrades. Nobody noticed, at least not right away, that as soon as those seven hundred people were picked up at the train station, hundreds more took their place in the days that followed.

Hannelore worked in the refugee home once a week, sometimes more, depending on how much time she had. It wasn't easy. There was no time to think. One of her jobs was to register new arrivals, and at the end of her shift she would write a little report about the number of people who had come that day. One day, she realized that she had processed five hundred new arrivals in a single shift.

The city hired some Romanian immigrants as interpreters, and she noticed that these so-called regular Romanians spoke to the *Roma* in a harsh and demeaning way. Hannelore began to realize that this was the only way to get a response out of these people. They were beginning to test her patience. Their hygiene, for example, was horrible. The workers would give the refugees food, cans of fish and vegetables, yet these people would stick them half-eaten under their beds, then go into West Berlin and beg for money. It got to the point where the soldiers at the base refused to clean the rooms. After a while, meals were served only in the dining hall. No food was to be taken away.

And the clothing distributions. People would keep getting in the lines, over and over. And then the *Roma* would be spotted out on the streets, selling armloads of clothing. One day a woman came to Hannelore and begged for a skirt. Hannelore knew this woman already had been given new clothes. But the woman was so relentless, she begged so urgently and convincingly that Hannelore relented and unlocked the room where the clothes were kept. And out of nowhere forty women burst inside and grabbed what they could. Hannelore had no chance.

It got to the point where she even got irritated when they apologized. They would kiss her hand and then peck quickly all the way to her elbow. Hannelore found herself washing her arms after such apologies.

There were fights among the refugees almost every day, sometimes even a woman or a child would get hurt. People would come in with cuts and refuse to say how they happened. And the theft. In the beginning, the rooms had been left open. But many things were stolen, and all the offices and supply rooms were locked up, even the room where the children's toys were kept. And the way these *Roma* treated their children. They would just hand them over naked and demand that they be clothed. Once, Hannelore took a woman with a sick child to the doctor. The doctor was getting ready to prescribe some medicine, but the mother just put the infant, naked, on the cold concrete floor and left, expecting the doctor to care for it.

East Germany had no real asylum laws, and many of these Gypsies were finding that if they just strolled through one of the holes in the Berlin Wall, they could declare asylum in West Berlin, which promptly set them up with a fifteen-mark daily stipend and a place to stay. Sometimes they registered as refugees in both sides of the city and drew double benefits. And they began to figure out that West Germany had a law that allowed foreigners to stay in the country while their asylum applications were processed, which often took years. Word got around. Soon, advertisements in poor countries around the world touted asylum in Germany as the key to success, the ingress to a dawning era of free markets. These advertisements offered package deals for routes and escorts into the country.

Something was happening, but nobody was quite sure what it was. Everybody focused on the Gypsies, since they stood out and traveled in large groups and filled the grounds of the barracks in Biesdorf. Reporters on the trail of this sudden and somewhat mystifying migration were regular visitors. Sometimes they got a quick tour from Major Henry Kretschmer, who would wistfully stroll the corridors of the gray stone barracks, oblivious to the squall of the children and the entreaties of the adults who tugged at his elbow, pantomiming hunger by rubbing their bellies or sticking their bunched fingers in their mouths.

Kretschmer was a commander in the National People's Army, a veteran of the Cold War, and now his command had come to this: overseeing a barracks full of refugees. He was philosophical about this. Nothing surprised him anymore. He went along, moving with the changes, spinning his feet on the rolling log his country had become. These reporters expected him to talk about the refugees, but he'd find himself thinking about the old days, which weren't quite a year old, when he and his men weren't simply soldiers stationed in Biesdorf, but soldiers based on the brink of Armageddon.

"We kept weapons in there, but we had to clear them out," he'd tell his guests, pointing to a room now packed with tots and cots, clumps of clothes, toys and tins of food.

He'd lead his charges to the mess hall, where hundreds of people were finishing off a dinner of something resembling sliced meat in a thick, beige gravy surrounded by little round potatoes. The army cook would peel and slice and stir and serve, a look of high-speed torment on his face. And Kretschmer would point out that each act of charity had a rather interesting exponential impact: The number of refugees seemed to expand in direct proportion to the amount of aid extended to them.

"Every day there are more. Every day," Kretschmer would say, musing, tired. "They come here, see the free food and the free housing. And call home. Then more come."

He'd speak without rancor, only observation. "We do not know what to do with them," he'd say. "We are filled to capacity."

And the Gypsies would tell their stories, steeped in misery and usually not in need of the inevitable embellishment. They were fleeing political persecution, they'd say. Yet others would say simply that they wanted what the East Germans had: a running start. A spindly nineteen-year-old named Tain Neacscu showed up one day and was gone in two. He was leaning insouciantly against a wall when Kretschmer came strolling by, leading a newspaper reporter and a photographer. "And why are you here?" they wanted to know.

Neacscu didn't have a job, didn't have any sort of education, didn't have any sort of skill that he cared to talk about. He was moving ahead, though. He knew where the new holes were. "I want to go to West Germany, and then I want to go to America," he said. And then he was gone.

After a while, many people forgot they were supposed to be refugees. Maria Caldarau showed up with her six kids. She came simply because a son had broken an ankle and she figured it would get fixed faster and better here than in Romania, where the horrific hospitals often sickened and maimed more people than they cured. And she was right. They fixed the kid's ankle and she moved into the barracks. Dinner at 7.

Sometimes a Mercedes-Benz would pull up to the gated camp and neatly dressed men would get out. Then they would pull old and tattered clothes from the trunks of their cars, change into the rags and come inside and ask for help. They would take donated items — tools, toys, all sorts of things — and sell them on the black market.

Needless to say, the various civil servants who had agreed to work with the refugees began to feel bitter and exploited. And Harry Kretschmer would inevitably conclude his tour by dropping the local journalists off at the desk of one of these ranking civil servants, because he was just a soldier and they were the administrators with the facts and figures needed for a news story about refugees in Berlin.

"This is Frau Gensch," he would sometimes say. "She can help you."

And the short, square woman with severely cut black hair would be quite candid in assessing the problem and the ability of her department, her country, to deal with this great influx.

"At first we were ignorant about this problem," she would say. "They come here and say they are escaping the government. They don't have enough money, they don't have enough to eat, they don't have enough work. And so they come here. Because it is free."

It was clear to her that the East Germans had to help them, had to house them, had to share their opportunities with them. No matter how different they were or how much her patience was taxed, she understood very much why they were persecuted back home. Yet the numbers. Is anybody counting?

And then Hannelore would finish her shift in the evening and head outside, toward her husband's beige Lada. She didn't take the bus anymore. She was too afraid to walk off the grounds of the base at night. But that boxy old car, her husband waiting inside, it was the most beautiful sight in the world.

And then the next morning, Hannelore would get up and go to her other job. She would see the lines of people waiting in the corridor outside her office, waiting to plead for jobs. As the weeks went by, it got worse and worse. Factories would close and many people would have to be retrained, re-educated, so they could fight for the fewer jobs in a free market. Every day, people would beg her for work, even threaten to kill themselves if they didn't find work. Many of them wanted to work at the refugee camps, the only operation in the country that seemed to be growing.

Some of them got their wish. In June 1990 the city began hiring full-time workers to process and care for the refugees. Both East and West Germany began building an infrastructure of aid and housing to accommodate an influx of outlanders that everyone figured would eventually have to ebb. It didn't. The newcomers leaped from freight trains, waded through rivers and bolted across fields. They surfaced in cities, palms out, faces pleading.

Caring for these people was no longer a part-time job. Hannelore's boss told her thanks, thanks a lot for helping out these past few months. New people had been hired to take over. So Hannelore left the crowded barracks at Biesdorf, picked her way through the crowds on the trampled grounds and got into her husband's beige Lada, relieved to be finished, satisfied that she'd done her best for these people and, as always, awed by the sheer number of them.

3 mergers and acquisitions

H E knew how to fit in. He knew how to look like a student. He wore faded jeans and crisp white shirts and designer glasses and a neat goatee. Of course, he had an accent, but he spoke the language fluently. He could be charming and personable, and he had Cimmerian good looks, chiseled and aristocratic, that women liked. It was a strain, sometimes, because he really didn't like living here. But he could be as Western as he wanted to be.

But now Semir Khemmas was embarrassed and a little ashamed. The city was filling up with foreigners, Gypsies and Yugos who looked vaguely Arabic, like him, and he was upset. They didn't know how to act. Some of them actually begged, or loitered in groups. No wonder nobody liked them. They stood out. He felt no sense of solidarity. He was even more anxious to finish his studies and get out.

He missed Kuwait. People here just weren't as warm. He'd have a problem with a woman, or with work or at school, but he couldn't talk to his male acquaintances about how he really felt about these things. Not like he could with his friends in Kuwait, the friends he saw every day, no matter what.

Not that Semir was some sort of transplanted pasha who expected his adopted society to accommodate his cultural preferences. He was simply homesick for Kuwait. He was born there, raised there. Though he would have preferred going to college in an Arab country, Semir had wanted to study computer science, and German universities had pretty good programs. He was just twenty years old when he came over, and studying abroad had been quite an adventure. He spent a year learning German. He got an apartment and found a job at a metal-finishing plant, making things like car door handles. And through it all, he took classes at the respected Technische Universität Berlin, a big and modern campus with a slick student quarter of galleries, bookshops, bars and cafés. It was in the heart of Charlottenburg, once a rich Prussian city, now a fashionable district engulfed by the basic bigness of Berlin.

The times got pretty turbulent. The Berlin Wall came down in 1989 and the town was plunged into a period of almost surreal celebration. The streets were saturated with people, but Semir wasn't among them. He was still homesick, and these scenes of people hugging and kissing were just too much to bear. Old friends, severed families, all of them came together in a single moment of frenzied affection. It made him miss his own family even more. On a day when two halves of a divided city made unbridled love to each other, Semir stayed home, depressed.

Needless to say, the joy over the opening of East Germany lasted as long as a beer in Bavaria. Everybody in the West had grinned condescendingly at the comical East Germans in their funny little cars and their shabby clothes, ogling the overstocked supermarkets and sneaker stores and TV showrooms that represented the consummation of capitalist cultural evolution.

Then the city filled up with a different sort of foreigner. People who dressed even more poorly, from Romania and Poland and Hungary, suddenly were gawking at the same elaborate pastries and overpriced watches in the windows of the fancy shops that lined the Kurfürstendamm, Berlin's fanciest boulevard. Then Arabs and Asians and Africans, staring into the same windows, maybe selling cigarettes on the street or asking for handouts or busting a car window to steal a stereo. Everybody was trying to crash the party, and it wasn't fun anymore.

The Germans became angry and resentful. Semir felt the change in the air, like humidity on his skin. He worked even harder not to stand out. It was funny, though; Germans often asked people who didn't look German where they came from. And Semir would tell them he was a Kuwaiti. Which, technically speaking, wasn't quite true.

Like a lot of people throughout the Arab world, Semir's family had spent so many years working and living in Kuwait that they considered it home. Foreigners, in fact, outnumbered the people who were card-carrying Kuwaitis by a four-to-one margin. The Kuwaitis mainly collected the profits on their limitless oil wealth, while the Palestinians and Egyptians and Lebanese and Filipinos and Americans and Britons and Pakistanis and whoever else roasted the lamb, engineered the oil rigs, fluffed the pillows, delivered the babies and processed the petrochemicals — all at wages much higher than they would have earned in their homelands.

Semir's father was a buyer for a big trading company. Good money, nice house. But he'd always put off applying for Kuwaiti citizenship. And when he finally did, it was right after some radical Shiites tried to kill the emir by bombing his motorcade. The emir responded by cracking down on everybody. He censored what had been a free press, dissolved the parliament and virtually ended the concept of naturalization. After that, if you weren't Kuwaiti by blood, you just weren't a Kuwaiti.

Semir and his family really only thought about it once every five years, when they had to renew their residency permits. They would have to get a stamp in their passports, which happened to be Iraqi.

"Well," his father would say, "it's not really important. It's just a piece of paper, anyway."

He just didn't care. He had been living in Kuwait for forty years and didn't even remotely consider any other country to be home. What he did insist upon was that his two sons and two daughters get a good education, even if it meant sending them around the world for several years. But after four years of little else but hard factory work and full-time studying and the unending upheaval of life in Berlin, Semir was thinking about leaving in the summer of 1990.

Kuwait and Iraq had become embroiled in one of their periodic disputes. Iraqis always felt that Kuwait was a stolen bit of their country, a concoction of British colonialists. And the two nations had a long-standing dispute over the exact location of their oil-rich border. These days, Iraq was contending that its economy was being hurt by the Kuwaitis' overproduction of oil. Talks on the matter were not going well. Foreign news reports said Iraqi troops were poised at the northern border of Kuwait. Semir had a friend, an Iraqi, who claimed: Hey, this is it. Maybe war.

Semir, rattled, wanted to be there, with his family. He called home.

"Don't worry, finish your studies," they told him. "Everything here is fine."

They tried to reassure him, since everybody knew how lonely Semir could get. They said the newspaper that very day had reported that the whole dispute had been all but settled during negotiations. Of course, most people had gotten used to the censored press by then. When the media said a crisis had been averted, people sort of accepted it. So Semir, in early August of 1990, decided to keep working and keep studying in Berlin and, almost immediately, had reason to regret it.

He was working a Thursday late shift when his Iraqi friend called him at the factory. It was the kind of message that seemed so unbelievable that it took a moment for his mind to fully embrace the magnitude of it.

"The Iraqis are in Kuwait," his friend told him.

Impossible.

Semir immediately went back to his apartment and began trying to telephone his parents. He tried for hours and finally got through around midnight. His parents said there were Iraqi troops in the streets, but so far not in their home. They were fine. He wanted to go to Kuwait immediately, but they said no, don't even think about it. Things were too unstable. Nobody knew what was going to happen.

The tether that Semir had to his family and his home suddenly felt very frayed. Semir tried to continue his normal routine of work and study, but it was hard to concentrate. The news reports about the occupation were frightening. People were getting robbed, raped, killed. Iraqis in an instant became the most unpopular people on the planet. Saddam Hussein tried to turn his annexation of Kuwait into some sort of emblem of Arab nationalism, a struggle as epic as Saladin's twelfth-century conquest of Jerusalem and expulsion of the Crusaders, and some of Semir's Arab friends in Germany bought into that.

Semir's friends made a conscious effort not to talk about the invasion because they knew Semir considered himself Kuwaiti. But it was hard. One evening the topic came up while a few of his friends, two Iraqis and a Palestinian, were visiting Semir at his apartment. His friends said quite calmly and with a certain logic that Iraq had a historical claim to Kuwait. Semir tried not to get too upset, and everybody tried to discuss the situation in a civil way, but you could feel the tension. As far as Semir was concerned, his country had been invaded.

At school, Semir fell into a conversation one day with a Palestinian student, a casual acquaintance, and this Palestinian also started talking about how Kuwait really was part of Iraq. Semir disagreed, much more forcefully than when he'd had the same conversation with his friends. The discussion turned into a shouting match.

"You are lucky that we are in Germany, because if we were in Kuwait or Iraq," the Palestinian hissed, "I would kill you."

But Semir wasn't in Kuwait. That was the problem. He wasn't even Kuwaiti, which was a bigger problem. Semir was adrift in the world, linked only to the place where his father was born, the only nation that would issue him a passport even though he'd never lived there and certainly didn't plan to start now. Linked only to Iraq.

And what a place to be adrift. Germany formally united in October 1990, but the moment was oddly anticlimactic. The place was gripped both by rising xenophobia and an anxiety over the hard times ahead. The East Germans had expected easy prosperity, but their euphoria evaporated when they saw how heavy-handed and hard-hearted the West German capitalists could be once they drove an economic stake into the former Communist land. More than eight thousand enterprises were snapped up by a huge trust company created to sell off all the state-owned enterprises. The country's livelihood was reduced to a six-hundred-page sales catalog packed with pickle makers, pubs, ice cream parlors and one badly built nuclear power plant, most of them so overstaffed and outmoded that they had no chance of competing in the free market. The people formerly known as East Germans suffered a collective loss of equilibrium and identity, and they took it out on what were perceived as the parasitic strangers in their midst.

This sense of uncertainty and antagonism certainly wasn't restricted to Germany. Oddly enough, Semir's sister found herself in an almost identical situation. She was studying in Yugoslavia, which was experiencing times even more tumultuous. All six republics had just elected new leaders, and most of them seemed bent on breaking away along furiously disputed boundaries. All these old Communists had transformed themselves into malevolent nationalists. Semir's sister was living in what was being referred to less as Yugoslavia and more as a severed piece of Serbia.

Most unbelievably, the rest of his family had wound up back in Iraq without even leaving home. It was all so strange. Semir felt very alone and disconnected. Like one of these refugees pouring out of the train stations, tumbling into Berlin.

SEMIR'S brother, Sammi, was selling Cokes on the street. The international embargo was strangling the economy; food and medicine were scarce. People, wealthy people, were willing to pay dearly for necessities, and some considered caramel-colored sugar water an essential commodity. The Coca-Cola plant was open only one day a week these days, and everybody was restricted to buying one case per person. Semir's brother would wade into this mob scene with a group of friends, buy seven or eight cases and then go sell it all on the street, bottle by bottle. Even in these days, especially in these days, you had to make a living.

So there he was, peddling soda pop, when a Palestinian girl came up and asked him how much he wanted for a bottle.

"Three dinars," Semir's brother told her.

"Iraqi dinars?" the girl asked.

"No, *Kuwaiti* dinars," Semir's brother said.

The young woman didn't like this. She must have been a collaborator.

"We are in Iraq now," she said.

She kept trying to pay in Iraqi money, but Semir's brother wouldn't take it. Lots of people were doing this, refusing to take Iraqi money, refusing to put Iraqi license plates on their cars, refusing to turn in their Kuwaiti residency cards for Iraqi ones. Some of these people were being sent to prison, some of them were just being shot in the head. But Semir's brother wasn't going to take any Iraqi dinars from this sassy Palestinian girl.

The Palestinian girl finally went away, but a little bit later she came back. She was with an Iraqi soldier.

"How much for a bottle of Coke?" the soldier demanded in a way that was more inquisitional than inquisitive. There could be only one correct answer.

Semir's brother thought: What the hell.

"Three Kuwaiti dinars," he said.

The soldier stuck his gun in Semir's brother's chest. People on the street stopped to watch.

"You better sell it for Iraqi dinars," the soldier said.

Semir's brother was going to ride the pony of principle only so far, of course. So he sold the smug young Palestinian woman her bottle of Coke for Iraqi dinars, the currency that occasionally featured a picture of Saddam Hussein, an unfinished smile on his face.

After the guard and the girl went away, victorious, a Kuwaiti came out of the crowd that had gathered around and spoke to Semir's brother.

"Try to remember their faces," he whispered. "When we have Kuwait back again, they will get what they deserve."

This was how it was in the new nineteenth province of Iraq. The Iraqi army, supported by fighter jets and helicopters, had moved in to only scattered resistance from the surprised and outgunned Kuwaiti army. The Iraqis put up posters of Saddam in the street, selected pretty girls to rape, shot people for imagined infractions and took what they wanted. They tortured people with cattle prods to the testicles, perforated them with electric drills, dipped them in acid baths, shot them in the groin or kneecaps or plucked out their eyes before they executed them. They ordered everybody to get new identity cards that reflected that they now were living in Iraq. They jailed thousands and sent thousands of others to live in Iraq, and brought thousands of Iraqis to live in the new nineteenth province. They didn't trust many of the Iraqis who lived near the Kuwaiti border, so they forced them to move deeper into Iraq.

The army stole many things, dismantling radio stations and even traffic lights and sending them back to Iraq. Many Kuwaitis were rich and pampered, fat and lazy. They hired house servants with money made from the labor of others. The Iraqis were poor. They resented the fact that oil was not the source of wealth for the 40 million Iraqis that it was for the 600,000 Kuwaitis. This invasion was an opportunity for some Iraqis to wolf down a big helping of this other world.

Many people fled. Great torrents of refugees were unleashed, more than a million and a half in the beginning. Many of them were Kuwaitis who had been on vacation abroad, or who fled their country before the Iraqis could lock up the borders. More than 400,000 sought refuge in Saudi Arabia, Bahrain, Egypt, Europe and the United States. Their wealth, actual and assumed, opened many doors, particularly in oil-poor Arab states that had grown dependent on Kuwaiti aid. Most of the royal family, about a thousand people, went into luxurious exile. They paid $10 million to Hill & Knowlton, the big public relations firm that China had hired after its murderous repression at Tiananmen Square, to lobby Congress and the American public for support for a U.S. invasion. They flooded the media with propaganda about atrocities that needed no embroidering. After many of these refugees were caught living in five-star hotels and dancing in discos in London or Cairo, they became known as the jet set of the displaced.

Hundreds of thousands of much poorer Arabs and Asians who had worked in the country for many years, from Filipino housemaids to Egyptian construction workers, also fled in the weeks following the invasion. With the southern border to Saudi Arabia sealed off, most were forced to flee into Iraq, traversing eight hundred miles of dangerous territory to get into Jordan. Jordan, overwhelmed with hundreds of thousands of people from both Kuwait and Iraq, shut its border until the world community began pouring money into the country to accommodate the influx. By October, nearly half a million people were flown out of the tiny country back to their homes. It was the biggest human airlift in history.

But the biggest single group disrupted by this invasion was not even near the theater of conflict. They were Yemenis living far away, and quite quietly, in southern Saudi Arabia. Saudi Arabia and Kuwait had been quite close. They were both run by pampered royal families of Sunni Muslim faith. They were both big suppliers of American oil. And when Iraq took over Kuwait, there were deep fears that it was poised to invade Saudi Arabia next. Saddam tried to turn his invasion of Kuwait into a struggle of Arab autonomy against Western influence. Some of the poorer Arab nations cheered Saddam. Places like Mauritania and Libya and the Islamic lands in the Soviet Union. Places like Yemen.

Yemen, the ancient land of Sheba, had seemed like one of the success stories of the Cold War's end. Just a few months before Iraq invaded Kuwait, the Islamic government of North Yemen and the Communists of South Yemen reunited after more than two decades of ideology-driven division. The transitional government's tacit support for Saddam — many Yemeni parents

named their newborns after the dictator that year — angered
the Saudi sheiks. They retaliated by driving out 850,000 Yemenis who had lived along the ill-defined desert border between
the two countries. Some had been there for generations, farmers
and herders and grocers and mechanics with years invested in
their villages. No single nationality was more disrupted, or more
unnoticed. The money these people made in Saudi Arabia was a
major source of foreign exchange for the Yemeni economy. The
loss of this income and the forced return of all those expatriates
destabilized the newly reunified country so badly that it once
again collapsed into civil war, which created yet another largely
ignored refugee crisis.

Events were so intertwined that even staying put had its
consequences. Not everyone was able to escape Iraqi-occupied
Kuwait, of course, and not everyone wanted to. In fact, many
Palestinians who supported Saddam's repositioning of the dispute as a battle for Arab pride embraced the new Iraqi regime
and collaborated enthusiastically. Many of the Asians remained
in Kuwait in the hope they could continue to do their jobs
and draw their paychecks, which usually supported a small
army of impoverished family members back home. And perhaps
200,000 Kuwaitis stayed behind, many of them forming cells of
a frequently lethal resistance campaign. They set off car bombs,
faxed and phoned intelligence to the outside, assassinated Iraqi
soldiers whenever they could. Sometimes they shot people they
suspected were collaborators, in one case a couple of teachers
who went to school after the resistance had called for a boycott
of the classrooms.

In the southern town of Ahmadi, in the heart of Kuwaiti
oil country, industry executives tried to befriend the invaders.

The Kuwaitis knew that the Iraqis had planted mines in the oil fields and attached bombs to the well heads. So they cajoled and pretended to cooperate with the soldiers, plying them with cash and food and television sets so they wouldn't incinerate the emirate's main source of income. And then, at night, these seemingly affable Kuwaitis would get in their luxury cars and go cruising the highways, looking for Iraqi soldiers to run down.

Outside the country, envoys from everywhere sought to make peace while their military counterparts prepared for war. Five days into the invasion, President George Bush began dispatching American troops to protect Saudi Arabia and, if necessary, liberate Kuwait. Saddam responded quickly by rounding up as many Americans and other Westerners as he could find. Not everyone had managed to get out of the country.

American hostages were an established currency in the radical Muslim marketplace, of course. But Saddam would go one step further. He would have his men knock on their doors, take them from their homes and incorporate them into his civil defense system. They would be matériel, just like radar or artillery. They'd serve the same purpose as, say, a bunker with a steel-reinforced roof. These several thousand Westerners, Saddam decided, would become his living coat of armor, his human shields.

THE Brits were funny. Even in bad times, they always had a droll comment. Here were all these people, taken from their homes, packed on buses, driven into the desert in hundred-degree heat, babies crying, everybody thirsty and frightened. Lorin and Jean Hubbard had one of the few bottles of water on the bus, and they were passing it around to people. And they offered it to this one Brit and he looked at it, sniffed and said:

"Is it cold?"

Everybody had a good laugh. Nothing was cold here. Lorin and Jean had lived in Kuwait for five years. It wasn't exactly Seattle. They weren't crazy about it, but it was his job. He worked for Boeing, in technical services. If Kuwaiti Airlines had a mechanical or operational problem, he was the guy they came to. The couple lived in a huge apartment in a luxury high-rise south of Kuwait City. It was called Al Fintis Towers, two nineteen-story buildings connected by a lobby. They hung around mostly with other Americans, and the British. The place could be grim, what with the heat and the restrictions on women.

And the political problems, of course. Everybody had followed the dispute between Iraq and Kuwait. Everybody had known that Iraq had moved troops to the border. And everybody pretty much had been relieved when the papers announced in bold type that the dispute had been resolved. And everybody had been stunned the next day, when Iraqi tanks rolled through the streets.

Lorin found out in a phone call from a friend of his, an Australian who worked for Kuwaiti Airlines. The Iraqis had invaded. He put down the phone and he and Jean could hear the gunfire coming from the city. From their apartment window they could see the tanks and the troops, not many of them initially, deployed on the shore of the Persian Gulf. A member of the royal family had a palace right across the street, and Jean and Lorin saw him and his family pile into limousines and get the hell out. Then they saw the Iraqi troops go into the place and start tearing it up, looking for money or gold.

All the cops disappeared; either they were killed or just ran away. The Filipinos, the poorest group in Kuwait, were stealing cars to get out of the country, since Saddam Hussein was letting Asian domestics like them leave. The people in Lorin's building, most of them Westerners, set up round-the-clock watches. The men would gather in groups and go to the grocery stores to buy supplies. The Iraqi soldiers weren't molesting the Westerners in the first couple days. But they would eyeball them on the street and at the checkpoints, their automatic rifles hanging from their shoulders at hip level. The soldiers would casually point their barrels at Lorin and the others as they drove or walked by, the big guns and baleful glares the very image of latent violence. It was spooky. Then the Iraqis began recruiting Palestinians into a kind of local security force, giving them old-looking uniforms and AK-47s. Some of them were kids, old men. These guys are really scary, Lorin thought. And every night, Lorin and Jean would hear shooting.

Nobody was sure what to do. Lorin talked to a colleague who talked to someone who worked at the U.S. consulate, and the word was: Just keep a low profile. Don't try to run, don't draw attention to yourself. Just stay home. This advice turned out to be a joke.

About the fourth or fifth night of the occupation, Lorin was working the watch on the ground floor of the towers when he heard a clatter. Then another clatter. Pieces of concrete and glass were falling from the sky. Somebody was shooting at the building. Lorin ran up eleven flights — the last thing he wanted was to get stuck in the elevator — and found Jean on the floor, taking cover. An Iraqi officer claimed the next day that some-body had been shooting at Iraqi positions from the building.

Almost every night after that, the Iraqis would take potshots at somebody's window.

Nobody could take it anymore. Some of the Westerners heard from somebody, it might have been a woman at the British consulate, that the border was open and that anybody who wanted to leave could drive to Saudi Arabia. So hundreds of expatriates in the area all gathered by their cars and trucks to make a mad dash to the border. It wasn't very organized. This one Lebanese guy was skeptical. All of them were going to make a run for the border — based on some hearsay?

"This is not going to work," he kept saying. "If this is true, then we would have an escort."

He went along anyway, drawn by the collective will of a large group of people with an irresistible urge to take their chances on the road. It was like the Oklahoma land rush. Hundreds of vehicles barreling down the highway, clouds of desert dust swirling skyward. This crazy convoy blew past burned-out Kuwaiti tanks, all sorts of debris. And then, sitting like a monstrous toad in the center of the road was an Iraqi tank, pointing its barrel right at them. An Iraqi officer strolled up to the fleet of cars, idling en masse, like a red light at rush hour.

"You can't go this way," he said.

Lorin and a couple of the guys got out to talk to him. His English was pretty decent. Sorry, he explained, but nobody was allowed to transit into Saudi Arabia. The border was closed. You can only return to the nineteenth province of Iraq. Or anywhere else in Iraq, for that matter.

"Anybody who wants to go to Iraq can turn around and go to Iraq," he offered, a bit sardonically. "Nobody will stop you."

Everybody drove back to Kuwait, of course. The place was sliding into hell. Bands of different nationalities were roaming around. Cash was running low, food was really scarce. Many of the Westerners hung together, pooling their supplies and keeping in touch, though others hoarded what they had and, in some instances, collaborated with the Iraqis by pointing out which nationalities lived in which apartments, so the Iraqis would make sure they were taking potshots in the right places. It was pretty sobering to Lorin and Jean to see how some people acted when things got rough.

Two weeks into the invasion, they got a knock on their door while dinner was cooking. Lorin opened the door and was confronted by ten, maybe fifteen Iraqi soldiers. One of them wanted to know if the Hubbards were British.

"No, we're Americans," Lorin said.

"You have five minutes to pack," the soldier said. "Then we're taking you to Baghdad."

Lorin would talk about this moment with the others long afterward. They'd talk about the sensation that many of them had when the Iraqis finally took them into custody. Every day they had been worried about getting food, getting water, getting hurt, getting home. Every day had been maddening in its uncertainty. It was hard to explain, this constant queasiness, this fear of fluidity. Now, at least, they knew what was in store for them. It was hard to explain. But Lorin felt almost a sense of relief when they were seized.

Jean was worried about getting enough things together.

"Five minutes isn't time enough to pack," Jean told the Iraqi soldier who did the talking.

"You can have ten," he said.

"Well, that's not enough, either."

"Please ma'am. Get ready."

So they packed. Like an airport shuttle, a bus took all of these people away, stopping at different hotels and apartment complexes to pick up more Westerners. The bus ran out of room, so some people got to drive their own cars. This motley caravan kept stopping at different police stations, and Iraqi officers would disappear for hours, apparently for some sort of hostage paperwork. Then it got late, too late to go to Baghdad, so the soldiers took everyone home and let them finish the dinners that had been left sitting on dozens of stoves. The Iraqis picked everybody up the next day, made the rounds of the police departments again, then finally, in the hundred-degree heat and with the babies and even some of the adults crying, took off on the eleven-hour trip across the desert, down the highway to Baghdad.

As they left Kuwait City, Lorin and Jean saw the emir's fabulous palace, blasted with rocket holes. And there were cars jacked up on blocks all over. The Iraqis seemed to be stealing as many wheels as they could. Lorin and Jean passed around their bottle of water, laughed when the Brit made the funny comment, gazed out the windows as the road connected dusty little towns like dots on the desert. Then, gleaming in the distance, they stared at the approaching skyline of Baghdad.

The soldiers took everybody to a hotel downtown. They stayed there for two nights. Then, some Iraqi security people announced during one of the mealtimes that Saddam Hussein had decided to let all the women and children go home, if they wanted to go. The men, however, would have to remain in Iraq. They would be sent to various "strategic points of interest."

This news was stunning. Couples and families began quiet and queasy discussions about whether it was better to split up or ride this thing out together. Maybe the Iraqis were lying, maybe the women and children really wouldn't be released. One by one the people returned to their rooms to ruminate and wait.

"I don't want to go off and leave you," Jean told Lorin.

But Lorin told her that it was better if she left, that somebody had to get back home and take care of the couple's personal affairs.

Jean was unconvinced.

"Look," Lorin told her. "Your being here puts an additional burden on me. If I only had myself to worry about, it'd make it easier for me to make . . . decisions."

Jean knew Lorin meant decisions about, perhaps, taking a risk he wouldn't otherwise take, maybe even trying to escape. She knew that as long as she was around, Lorin would play it safe. Eventually, Lorin convinced her that it was better if she went back to Seattle. Most of the other wives would make the same decision, though some insisted on staying with their husbands. A couple of these husbands came up to Jean and said, "Talk to my wife, would you, please? Tell her she's gotta go home." Jean did her best, but some of these women were just determined to face whatever it was Saddam had planned for their men.

Lorin was getting nervous. He desperately wanted to see his wife get on a plane before the Iraqis shipped him off to one of those "strategic points of interest."

"Will I be able to stay here long enough to make sure my wife gets to go?" he asked one of the Iraqi guards.

"Of course," he said.

Of course, the Iraqi soldiers never did what they said they were going to do. A few minutes later, the guards came by the Hubbards' hotel room and told Lorin that he had fifteen minutes to get ready. He and Jean scrambled with their bags to make sure he would have whatever toiletries and supplies he might need. They both had that nervous feeling in their stomachs. And then the guards came by and led Lorin away.

Jean peered out the window and saw him get in a bus that was sitting in front of the hotel. It sat there for a long time. Finally, she and another woman went up to one of the guards and said: "Look, if that bus is just going to sit there for a while, can we at least go downstairs and sit with our husbands until it's time to go?"

He said OK.

So Jean went down to the bus and sat with Lorin while the Iraqis, who always seemed so horribly disorganized, dealt with whatever human shield bureaucracy they had to deal with. They sat there together and said their good-byes all over again. They sat there for a couple of hours, until they ran out of things to say, until the conversation they figured just might be their last became stilted and strained, until they both actually felt relieved when the Iraqis started the bus and took Lorin away.

As it turned out, Jean and the other women who had stayed behind would be back home in the States in less than a week. Not Lorin and the rest, though. They were divided into groups, with the various nationalities all evenly distributed. Lorin's group had two Germans, two French, two Americans, two

Japanese, and four Brits. They were taken to a big industrial complex outside town, winding up in the offices of a plant that made these little five-inch shells that Lorin guessed were tank rounds. The dozen guys in Lorin's group were given cots to sleep on. They listened to the BBC and Voice of America on their shortwave radios. They watched Saddam on Iraqi television. The Iraqis kept referring to them as guests, but they knew from the news exactly what they were.

Being a human shield was an extremely boring job. The hostages were irritable. Some of the guards were arrogant and surly jerks, and others were plainly embarrassed by what their crazy ruler had done. There was a certain tension.

"You don't love us, do you?" one of the less lovable guards suddenly said to Lorin one day.

"Let me ask you something," Lorin said. "You got a family? You go stay with your family?"

"Yes. I go home every few nights and see my family."

"Well," Lorin told the guy, "I can't do that."

But, the guard seemed to say, Lorin had a job, a purpose, a role to play.

"You're here to protect us," the guard told him.

So they sat there, waiting, while a troubled Mikhail Gorbachev took time out from the fissures forming in his wobbly empire, trying frantically to mediate a settlement between an occupying Iraq and a mobilizing United States. It didn't work. Gorbachev just wasn't operating from a position of strength these days. Russia and the other republics were too busy busting the membranes of the Soviet Union.

So they sat there, waiting, while Bush kept beefing up troops, enlisting other nations, building a massive coalition that defied the old ideological divisions. He got Soviet approval at a summit in Helsinki and then went on television and proclaimed a "new world order" in which the two old nemeses would fight the forces of instability together. On November 29 the UN Security Council — now just a handy appliance of the paramount superpower — gave Iraq six weeks to get out of Kuwait. Or else.

And all of this time Lorin Hubbard sat there, waiting, while the months dragged by, while everybody tried to come up with some solution to avert what seemed inevitable. He'd lie in bed at night and get that same disembodied feeling he'd had back in World War II, on the aircraft carrier, in the South Pacific, under attack.

"I'm not really here," he'd think. "This isn't really happening."

Lorin's company, meanwhile, put Jean up in a nice condo outside Seattle and paid her bills while she floated in a state akin to a trance, unconscious of time or place or events outside her world. That world was peopled by voices on the telephone, voices belonging to the relatives of other human shields, voices of people whose sole goal was to keep one another from tumbling into utter despair. The State Department had some people working on the crisis who had promised to keep in touch with the family members, but they barely did. It was those voices on the phone that pulled Jean through.

With the holidays approaching and the deadline for war not far behind, a breakthrough came out of nowhere. Maybe Saddam was trying to buy some time by making a strategic gesture of goodwill. Maybe he figured his bluff wouldn't work. Maybe he realized that sacrificing thousands of innocent lives would put the ruthless glint of vengeance in his adversaries' eyes. Who knew? In any case, in December, right on Pearl Harbor Day, Saddam said he was going to let everybody go, every one of the thousands of Westerners he had been employing as human shields.

Jean heard the news and thought: What's the catch?

A couple days later, however, some of the security men came into the office where Lorin slept and said: Time to go to the airport. All the hostages were put on Iraqi airliners and flown to Frankfurt, where they could all catch flights to their respective homes. They got off, some of them forty pounds lighter, and walked down a corridor lined with police barricades, on the other side of which were reporters who were desperate to have a word with these human shields who'd been plucked from their homes and converted to currency.

Lorin Hubbard, tired and irritated, came over and talked about how he had hoped this human shield business would have backfired on the Iraqis, how he and the others had wished that the great coalition of disparate nations dedicated to the preservation of existing oil agreements would have unloaded whatever arsenal was available on top of that munitions plant where he sat. He would have taken his chances.

"We were hoping they would blow it up!" Lorin Hubbard said, flashing a ferocity that belied just how weary he was. "I want to see them make a hole in the ground at that place!"

And then he ambled away, down the corridor, off to a hotel and then on to the next flight, off to Seattle, where Jean had sat for more than three months hoping that no bombs would land on Lorin.

One by one, the people once known as human shields stumbled down the airport corridor, gaunt and raggedy. Most had been hostages but a handful of them were escapees who had slipped deep into the underground, emerging only when Saddam had said everybody could go. They had been aided by the Kuwaiti resistance, and they came out of nowhere with tales of violent repression and merciless retribution.

The fact that these displaced Westerners were transiting Germany was oddly fitting. The Americans were busy marshaling a great army. They were shaking down the wealthy nations for contributions to a multibillion-dollar effort. Newly united Germany, which just a couple of months earlier had envisioned itself as an ascendant superpower deserving of a permanent seat on the UN Security Council, had collapsed into an internal debate over whether it should take part in the anti-Iraq coalition. West Germany's postwar constitution, the law of the combined land, prohibited it from dispatching troops beyond the territory of NATO. Helmut Kohl had floated the idea about altering the constitution, but the opposition was insurmountable. The Germans weren't ready for a foreign war. There were demonstrations in the street. The newly coalescing nation turned inward while the rest of the world reconfigured around it.

Germany had reunited in a burst of fireworks in October, nearly three months into the crisis in Kuwait. Nobody noticed. Sudden and seemingly inexplicable new wars uprooted millions in Liberia and Somalia, places that mattered in the days when superpowers stockpiled satellites. These were ignored. Saddam Hussein, stock Noriega or latter-day Saladin, had until January 15 to get out of Kuwait. He had an entire region in play, hundreds of thousands of people on the run, the global economy in flux. Nothing else mattered. The calendar was just too compelling.

4 bombing babylonia

WHERE is he taking us? He must have something clever planned. He can't be serious about waging war against the Americans, the French, the British, the . . . Hondurans? The Bangladeshis? The world! The men in Ali's unit talked about it constantly. No way we can win this war. No way. Saddam must be bluffing. He has to be. Where is he taking us?

When the deadline finally came, Ali and his men expected an extension, a strategic concession, a card to be played. The last thing they expected was a swarm of fifty enemy aircraft, blowing them to bits. The attack was so quick, so big, so furious, Ali and his men thought: They aren't kidding.

Ali commanded an anti-aircraft artillery unit at Umm Qasr, Iraq's only port. This was where Saddam kept many of his Silkworm missiles. It was the country's only naval base. It was almost a stroll away from the Kuwaiti border. Now, it was getting bombed. Ali and his men didn't have a chance to think about defending the place. All they could think about was survival. Laser-guided bombs entered bunkers like burglars. Trenches collapsed, burying hundreds of men. Factories burst into flames and oil refineries exploded. Supply lines were destroyed. Food and water became scarce.

First, there had been the war with Iran. Eight years of fighting for control of a river formed by the confluence of the Tigris and the Euphrates, not far from where the Garden of Eden supposedly grew. And then two years of cracking down on the Kurds up north. And now this, a war waged against the entire world. The soldiers had no fight left in them. The allies dropped thousands of little leaflets, urging the Iraqis to desert. Hundreds did, every day, either heading back to their hometowns or south, toward Saudi Arabia, to surrender while they still could. Soon, Saddam's loyal officers began laying mines behind the lines to keep people from leaving.

The air war against Iraq triggered a new flood of refugees throughout the Middle East. Many of them were foreign workers who had stayed behind in Kuwait or Iraq. Many others figured that the war would explode into a regional conflict, particularly after Saddam began firing Scud missiles at Saudi Arabia and Israel. Even some Jews who had fled the unstable Soviet Union for asylum in Israel jumped back on the plane and moved on to Germany, of all places.

And then there were the Iraqis themselves. Roughly a quarter of the country's 17 million people fled into the countryside to escape the bombing of the cities. Power stations were ruined, water and sewerage systems stopped functioning. The decimation of the refineries created fuel shortages, and what gas did get distributed was impure, creating a nation of stalled cars. Stealthy jets riddled countless buildings with high-tech holes.

Punctured bridges sagged and corkscrewed over the Tigris and Euphrates rivers, over the basin that once coaxed a civilization from ancient nomads, and which now scarcely nourished parched villages laid waste by war.

If the air war was hard for the noncombatants, it was murder on the military. Much had been made of the battle-tested toughness of the Iraqi army. American military leaders, as they tried to woo nations to send guns, troops and money, spoke in awe of these half a million fierce and rugged fighting machines. Many people had hoped that the air assault would be enough to drive Saddam from Kuwait so American boys wouldn't have to engage these desert warriors on the ground. If they could have seen the scrawny young men like Ali cowering amid the carnage, wolfing down meager rations of rice, they might not have been so worried.

Five weeks into the air assault, the allied forces launched their land invasion, driving through southern Iraq and outflanking the enemy. A terrible army of unfathomable capabilities rolled north in long sweeping arcs. Grinding waves of armor and mobile artillery spanned the four horizons, canopies of attack helicopters buzzing overhead like lines of incensed hornets.

Exotic new weaponry was employed alongside old-fashioned armaments. Shrieking comets packed with hundreds of tiny bomblets mingled with the flash and boom of howitzer rounds. Planes dropped computerized explosives and unfashionable yet effective napalm. Stealth Fighters shared air space with B-52s. Allied gunners with thermal sites picked up infrared images of Iraqis sitting in old Soviet tanks. They would realize they were dying before they knew they were hit.

Saddam began pulling his troops out of Kuwait. The soldiers stole what they could carry and wrecked what they couldn't.

63

They set fire to seven hundred oil wells, paralyzing their enemy's sole source of wealth. They loaded their loot onto anything on wheels and staged the mother of all getaways. But they didn't get far. Allied war planes spotted the convoy west of Kuwait City, a three-mile line of ants leaving a large picnic. It crawled along a long stretch of road that linked two slowly rising hills. It was flanked by fields filled with land mines that the Iraqis themselves had planted. This gentle valley was not unlike the killing pocket at Gettysburg. This was war at its most one-sided. The enemy was contained and concentrated and incapable of putting up much of a fight. And the pilots could get close enough to see each little getaway car go boom.

When it was over, it looked like the last traffic jam of the apocalypse. Fuel trucks, fire trucks, troop trucks, dump trucks, a Czech welding truck, Soviet tanks, British rocket launchers, white Oldsmobiles, dozens of school buses and a handful of looted motorcycles all lay scattered on their sides, flipped upside down, tossed off the road and seared to a metallic crisp. Three thousand vehicles, hundreds of bodies. The booty was everywhere, mortars and silver slippers, a jewel box filled with plastic pearls, perfume by Dior, gas masks and dinnerware and crates of ammo from superpowers who once courted a country that both now agreed must be crushed.

Ali and another officer abandoned their units and headed north, toward Basra, as far away from Kuwait as they could get. Halfway there, they heard on their radio that a cease-fire was imminent, that Saddam would surrender and therefore cling to power. They decided that perhaps they had better scurry back to their units. They turned around and began walking back toward Kuwait. But the army was scattered, dismantled by deaths and desertions and wild retreats.

Ali walked down the highway through southern Iraq, through scorched wreckage and splattered soldiers, past dogs chewing on dying men. He turned around again and headed north. Maybe, he decided, it would be better to just go the hell home and see his mother.

THE major stuck his bayonet in the sand and drew a little square. Marsh stared at it in disbelief. That was it? That was the floor plan, the blueprint? Marsh had spent weeks collaring any officer he could, asking, "What's my job? Whaddya want me to do?" in that brogue of his native Boston. The brass was so disorganized that nobody could ever tell him anything. Now, he knew. Build a camp, based on this sophisticated design, on two square kilometers of Saudi desert south of Iraq.

It wasn't just any camp. It was an EPW/CI — Enemy Prisoners of War/Civilian Internees. The next morning, Marsh paced it off in his truck. He and his four-man crew were just getting ready to get started when one of these officers said: Never mind. Build a camp for the MPs first. The MPs would have to guard the prisoners, right? Better build their camp first. Naturally, that turned out to be another bonehead decision. Because as soon as the ground war started, troop trucks rolled in with hundreds of Iraqis, either captured soldiers or willing deserters or civilians just running from the war.

These prisoners mostly were being delivered by British and French troops, who basically just tossed them off the trucks and said: We heard there was a prison camp here. So here's some POWs.

Except there wasn't a camp. Marsh, exasperated, borrowed some bulldozers from the Nigerians and started moving sand around while the Iraqis sat there, watching. He pushed the sand into four big berms shaped like a square. The Iraqis were herded inside and given some blankets and some food and told: This is it. For now, this is home.

The next day, he started getting some supplies, toilets and showers and wiring and two monstrous generators. The engineers started digging some ditches. And trucks kept rolling in, bringing more and more Iraqis.

Marsh was a construction contractor back home in New Hampshire. But here, he was an engineer in the active Army Reserve. He knew how to put together a camp and run it. But he needed some bodies. He needed to organize some labor gangs to dig some ditches and lay some line. He'd have to use some of these Iraqis. Even though the Americans had been told that these assholes had committed some pretty terrible atrocities, even though they'd heard that the Iraqis had ripped Kuwaiti babies from their incubators and tossed them around like footballs, even though they had heard these Iraqis were tough and remorseless killers, Marsh didn't buy it. They were so timid. And so little.

"We were looking for warriors," he thought. "Here we got these wimps."

The camp took shape in a matter of days. POWs in one section, civilian refugees in another, and Iraqi army deserters in yet another. Everybody got sprayed with the same delousing chemical. The brass set up tents to process and interrogate the inmates, who usually stuck around for a couple of weeks before they'd be sent off to a camp somewhere else. Each would be asked: Do you want to go back to Iraq? Or do you want to declare yourself a refugee and go live somewhere else?

Marsh got into a little routine, usually rounding up the fifteen or twenty laborers a day from the deserters' section to help his people fix fences, put in lights, build towers, load and unload supplies. When one of the crew got shipped off, Marsh or one of his staff would go recruit a replacement. He got to know the POWs pretty well. Some of these Iraqis turned out to be pretty good guys. He even started giving some of them his address back in the States.

ALI came home to his city in southern Iraq and immediately regretted it. He had left a war and wound up in the middle of a rebellion. It began with men standing on street corners, in large groups, grumbling about Saddam Hussein and the misery he had wrought. Some of them were deserters. These soldiers were among the most vocal advocates of revolt. The economy was in shambles, the army scattered and demoralized. Now was the time. In days, rebel armies were quickly raised in cities all across southern Iraq. They stormed police stations, blew away the cops and freed all the prisoners. They shot city officials and declared themselves in charge.

This uprising broke out in the southern Iraqi cities where opposition to Saddam ran deepest, in the region where the Shiite sect of Islam was born. Shiites, in terms of philosophy, were stricter Muslims than the more mainstream Sunnis. Among other things, the Shiites considered their religious leaders to be infallible.

Saddam was a Sunni, though his brand of secular Islam recognized nobody's infallibility but his own. When he had begun his rise to power, he made it a point to kill as many Shiite clerics as possible, since they posed a threat to his autocracy. He destroyed many of their religious shrines all across the Shiite heartland of southern Iraq. Even though the Shiites were a slight majority in Iraq — hence their principal demand for democratic rule — and even though they were supported by the Shiite-dominated government in neighboring Iran, Saddam was extremely successful in marginalizing them. Not many people could match his remorseless brutality.

The Shiites weren't the only enemies of Saddam. He was periodically threatened by the Kurds in the north. These ancient nomads and the tramping grounds they called Kurdistan were conquered by the Arabs in the seventh century and the Turks a few centuries later. They had been trying to get pieces of their homeland back from a succession of conquerors ever since. Some of it had wound up in Syria and some in the Soviet Union, but most of it was spread over Turkey and Iran and Iraq. After the Western world reneged on a post–World War I promise to give the Kurds a home in 1925, they spent the succeeding generations waging sundry wars on the countries that sat atop Kurdistan.

When Iraq lost the Persian Gulf War, both the Kurds in the north and the Shiites in the south had an opportunity of a millenium. Encouraged by the United States and its allies, they each launched a rebellion. The timing had seemed perfect. But Saddam rallied his army, almost miraculously, like a conjurer rejoining pieces of a severed sand viper.

Ali was a Shiite, but he didn't get involved in this rebellion. It started to crumble just days after it began. The string of cities that the rebels had so jubilantly claimed were quickly surrounded by loyalist elements of Saddam's army. Ali thought: Where are the Americans now? They instigated this thing. Now that it was falling horribly apart, they were nowhere to be found.

The army attacked Ali's town just days after he returned home. They fired rockets and artillery shells at the mosques where the rebels had holed up. Ali's mother was worried. Ali's little brother, Mohammed, had taken part in the uprising. When the army asserted its control over the town, it began rounding up and killing young men presumed to have supported the rebellion.

Ali's mother had already lost two sons in Saddam's previous Shiite purges. She thought little Mohammed would be next. She urged Ali to help him.

Ali went to his sister's house, where Mohammed was hiding, and told him they were going to leave Iraq. They got in the car and began driving south, in the direction of Kuwait. There must have been a thousand checkpoints. Because Ali was a lieutenant, nobody questioned him. If anybody did, he would simply tell them that he was trying to find his brother's army unit. It was a good excuse; a lot of soldiers were trying to find their units in these days.

The brothers went to Ali's unit in southern Iraq. It turned out to be just a few hundred yards from the American frontier. When night fell, Ali and Mohammed stepped over a wooden fence and walked toward the American checkpoint. Two American soldiers raised their rifles and ordered them to halt.

"He's wanted by the government," Ali said, gesturing to his brother.

The soldiers thought for a moment.

"Well, you're safe now," one of them said.

The two brothers were taken to a camp filled with thousands of other Iraqi refugees. Because Ali was an officer and Mohammed was a civilian, however, they were separated right away. A Kuwaiti army officer interrogated Ali, kept asking him whether the Iraqis had used chemical weapons, where Saddam was hiding his missiles. Then they moved him into a camp inside the Kuwaiti border. This camp was filled with many Palestinians and other third-country nationals, such as Asians, whom the Kuwaitis didn't want back in their country because the Kuwaitis figured they had collaborated with the Iraqis.

From this camp, Ali got his first good look at the oil wells that the departing Iraqi soldiers had ignited. As far as he could see, pillars of fire burst from the ground with a volcanic roar, like a bellowing forest of giant blowtorches. They formed a single black cloud so thick it looked as solid as slate. It hung low and flat and covered the sky. Only at the horizon, where the atmosphere curved with the world, was there an unsettling glimpse of something resembling daylight, a band of brightness between black heaven and burned earth. The normally dry air was humid with vaporized oil.

Ali was afraid. It was too late to go back to Iraq, and he didn't know what was going to happen next. He spent three days in the camp and then was put on a bus and taken to yet another camp, this one in Saudi Arabia. It was run by Americans. They put him in a section with other Iraqi officers who had deserted.

One morning, a strawberry blond sergeant dressed in chocolate-chip camouflage strode into Ali's compound of tents and said she was looking for a few good men to join a labor crew. This dazzling American woman in chic desert battle dress looked like a daydream. The head of every Iraqi deserter in the camp swiveled with the sort of synchronized precision that the Iraqi air defense system could have used during the war. Ali instantly volunteered for this labor crew.

The British and French treated the Iraqis like animals. But these Americans, the first Ali had ever met, were pretty decent. Convivial. Always willing to chat, share a smoke, rip open a ration. Ali became a regular part of the labor crew, which was run by the senior enlisted engineer, Master Sergeant Eric Marsh. Marsh would say, "C'mon, let's take a break," and then he'd cook something up for the Iraqis on his little stove. They'd sit around in his tent, where Marsh had built a picnic table, and they'd smoke cigarettes, drink tea, thumb through girlie magazines. A Saudi liaison soldier assigned to the camp would hang around, too, and translate. Some of the discussions got pretty deep. Marsh and the Iraqis talked about religion, politics, history, you name it.

Marsh liked Ali, though he sometimes figured that the Iraqi was a tad too cocky for his own good. Ali had that infuriating officer's mentality, always figuring that he knew best, while Marsh had a healthy disregard for people who equated rank with competence. Marsh also thought that Ali didn't like to work especially hard. His favorite thing, as near as Marsh could tell, was thumbing through the skin magazines.

Still, they were friendly. Ali told Marsh about how he dreamed of going to Sweden — for the women, Marsh assumed.

Ali had applied for refugee status, and there was a chance he might actually wind up there. Marsh traveled to Europe now and then, and he gave Ali his address in New Hampshire.

"Send me a letter when you get resettled, lemme know how you're doing," Marsh told him. "Maybe I'll look you up when I'm in Europe."

Soon afterward, Ali got shipped off to another camp run by the Saudis near the Jordanian border. It was a regular barracks, not a collection of tents, and the food was pretty good. He was lucky. His surroundings took on a certain solidity that many others could only dream about.

Like the Kurds. After blunting the uprising by the Shiites in the south, Saddam turned his attention to the rebels in the north. He bombed and burned their cities with pitiless resolve. Nearly a million and a half refugees escaped into Iran, which let them inside. Another half a million Kurds tried to get into Turkey, which bolted its doors. Turkey was already waging a low-intensity war of sorts with its own Kurdish minority; it was not about to increase their number. And the United States was not about to pressure its strategically important ally to open its borders to the refugees. So the refugees huddled on the hillsides in the borderlands and began to die.

There was only one solution. The fall of the Berlin Wall and the stunning success of the Persian Gulf War had proved one thing: There was only one superpower left standing. One empire with the raw strength to bend the world to its will.

On April 5, 1991, the UN Security Council did something it had never done before: It criticized a nation's handling of its internal affairs. It condemned Iraq's repression and demanded an end to the government's air and artillery attacks on the Kurds in the north. The measure had been sponsored by the United States, Belgium and France. It was a testament to the superpower's paramount place in the world that the Soviets also supported the measure and the Chinese only abstained rather than opposed it.

A few weeks after winning a war it had organized, the United States formally altered what had been core precepts of international law. It forced the United Nations to tacitly change the definition of a refugee and to overrule the sanctity of a nation's sovereignty. Refugees no longer had to be people who fled from one nation to another; they could be people displaced within their own borders. And a nation's sovereignty was discounted in a world where borders were increasingly fluid, random and contested. The Americans sold this resolution by arguing convincingly that this particular refugee catastrophe was a threat to regional stability, to world peace.

A precedent was set. The United States had bought itself a UN–certified pass to enter a foreign nation and stop a government from attacking its own people. It had used its new supremacy to establish acceptable criteria for foreign intervention in a nation's domestic affairs. This acceptance of intervention reflected, more by accident than by design, the fact that wars of the post–Cold War era were more likely to be internal affairs, the result of battles between people struggling to fill a power vacuum. Superpower proxy wars were passé. Destroying nations from within to create small, overlapping and incompatible new places was the thing to do. Displacing entire populations wasn't just the side effect of such struggles. It was the whole point. Only one entity on earth could stop it.

After the UN rubber-stamped his resolution, President Bush sent troops to protect the Kurds. The mission was called Operation Provide Comfort. The Americans dropped thousands of boxes of rations on camps of refugees stranded atop the mountains of Turkey, caught between two countries. They dispatched convoys of supplies. They dug latrines, delivered food and shook hands with grateful refugees who were overwhelmed with gratitude.

Then the U.S. force and its allies moved into northern Iraq and carved out a security zone, warned Saddam not to come near it. They set up electricity and water and hospital tents while U.S. Marines manned mortar positions on the perimeter, while U.S. fighter craft built a protective shield around what would become a de facto Kurdish homeland. They spread word to the camps on the Turkish border that it was safe to come home now, that there was food and shelter and protection against the Iraqi army.

The Americans escorted the Kurds through a mountain pass back to their homeland, gently lifted babies onto trucks and accepted invitation after invitation from the Kurds to come to their homes for dinner. Their homes, in northern Iraq, in Kurdistan, not in some refugee camp in Turkey.

Weeks after the war, news clips of brainy bombs finding the doorways to bunkers were replaced by images of American soldiers bonding with weak and hungry and tremendously grateful refugees in exotic locales. It was a happy humanitarian coda to a clean and quick war. The United Nations had predicted that the operation to repatriate the Kurds would take seven months. The Americans and their allies had made it happen in seven weeks. The mission was proof of the last superpower's capacity to halt catastrophe when it summoned the sufficient courage. The Soviet empire had crumbled and communism was dead. At no time in history had one ideology and one nation been given such a clear path to influencing the flow of events, to halting evil of historic scale.

But the Shiites in the south were another matter. Asked about their plight, U.S. Army Brigadier General Richard I. Neal told reporters that it was "an internal problem and one I assume the government and the military will eventually resolve."

He was referring to the Iraqi government and the Iraqi military, and resolve it they did. Saddam's army massacred tens of thousands of Shiites in the south. More than a million fled into Iran, or into the swamps that separated the two countries. Saddam began draining the marshlands in the summer of 1991, aiming to eliminate this threat once and for all. While the United Nations ordered Iraq not to fly a warplane anywhere near its northern skies, Saddam dispatched his helicopters and planes to bomb and strafe the Shiites in the south. He built death camps and dug mass graves. Some refugees said he sprayed villages with mustard gas. Reports of starvation and brutality trickled out right away, but they were overwhelmed by the big effort to help the Kurds. It was much easier to focus on rugged Marines ripping open rations and feeding the hungry, on a mission that was, in many ways, the greatest humanitarian success of all time.

In May, the United States pulled its troops out of the part of southern Iraq it had been occupying near the Kuwaiti border. The United Nations then told Saddam that he could exercise civil control over the area where the Americans had been. The world body sent a token contingent of observers down there to keep an eye on things, and declared the borderlands with Kuwait a demilitarized zone. But it wasn't enough. Saddam was back in full control of his southern frontier. He was allowed to seal an escape hatch left ajar by the war. Even as the world changed the rules of intervention in one place, it forfeited responsibility in another. While the refugees in the north had a heavily protected place to hide, the refugees in the south had nowhere left to run.

Ali sat in his camp in Saudi Arabia, hearing word from the new arrivals about Saddam's rampage through the south. It unsettled his stomach to think about the man, once again exercising his lethal rule, in the heart of Ali's homeland. He knew why the Americans and the Brits were helping the Kurds: Their lands had oil. Ali felt adrift.

One group of refugees, however, fared much better than either the Kurds or the Shiites. They had the means to simply convert their forced exile into extended vacations. Despite the exhortations of the newly reinstalled government to return home and rebuild, most of the Kuwaiti refugees stayed away from the mess left by the Iraqi army. Some came back only to find their homes emptied of valuables and filled with garbage and rats, with no running water or working air-conditioning. They had the money to spend a hellish summer somewhere else, so many turned around and left. And many of the 200,000 who had remained through the occupation themselves took a badly needed vacation. The number of Kuwaitis in Kuwait actually decreased when the war ended.

Meanwhile, the Army Corps of Engineers and a phalanx of well-paid Western contractors — selected from the nations in pretty much the order in which they had helped liberate the country — were hired to make the place livable again. The Army in particular did everything from restore phone service to reopen the airport to feed monkeys at the zoo to oversee repairs on the gold-plated bathroom fixtures at the emir's palace.

At the same time, the Kuwaiti government decided to keep out many of the Third World foreigners who had staffed the service industry, and who had kept the country clean and running. The largest group denied re-entry was the Palestinians, who were viewed as the enemy because the PLO had supported Saddam. But many Palestinians had been born in Kuwait and had, in fact, fled the Iraqi occupation. Many were the children of refugees from the 1948 Arab-Israeli war. Many were professional people who had been woven deeply into the society and the economy. More than 200,000 of them were stranded in Jordan, unable to return even to withdraw their life savings.

Likewise, the Kuwaitis sealed the country to an almost equally large population of the traditionally stateless Arabs who had spent centuries wandering the desert, oblivious to borders. Ethnic Iraqis, of course, were also unwelcome. Many were expelled or prevented from returning. Some were beaten, some executed by roving bands of vigilantes. The government was determined to make Kuwaitis the majority.

Because Kuwait was adamant about keeping Iraqis out, the West pressured Saudi Arabia to grant asylum to people like Ali, who were afraid to go home. But the Saudis would not allow the refugees to resettle permanently. In fact, it got sick of housing them pretty quickly. The government began consolidating them into bigger and more crudely run camps. And it even began to forcibly return thousands of refugees to Iraq, where many faced death.

Ali was sent to one of the new camps and the treatment was harsh. The guards beat people, sometimes killed them, and raped the women. The refugees responded with riots. One of Ali's friends told him: "You still got that address of that American? Maybe you should write him."

What did he have to lose? Ali wrote a letter and gave it to the Red Cross. Less than a month later, he got a reply.

"I will do all I can to get you over here," Marsh wrote in the letter. "We will sit together once again and drink tea."

Ali stared at the letter. "This guy is dreaming," he thought. "If he can get me from the desert to the United States, it would be a miracle."

Marsh went to work. He contacted the refugee coordinator for the state of New Hampshire. He went to the local newspapers with the obvious angle: GULF VET INVITES OLD ENEMY TO NEW HAMPSHIRE. He got some nasty phone calls, but he was undeterred.

The UN High Commissioner for Refugees, meanwhile, got Saudi Arabia to stop forcibly repatriating Iraqis. It leaned on some third-party countries to resettle them. The United States, Iran, Australia and Sweden — strange bedfellows indeed — cooperated the most fully. Marsh heard about this program, begun very quietly by the Bush administration, and made a pitch for Ali. Both men had to go through interviews by U.S. immigration people on both sides of the world. Ali had to get an AIDS test, answer questions, fill out forms.

Then, just like that, he got a departure date. He was going to America.

But while he waited, word of this resettlement program got around. Some conservative U.S. congressmen were upset that Arab enemies once dedicated to American deaths were coming to America. More thoughtful critics, typically refugee advocates, were angry that Iraqis, many of them soldiers, were getting special treatment purely to placate an oil-rich ally like Saudi Arabia. Why not host hungry children from Liberia?

Senator Jesse Helms began a campaign that ultimately would derail the resettlement program, but not before a couple thousand Iraqis would make it to American soil. Hundreds were on a commercial jet one evening as it approached Kennedy Airport in New York. Ali peered out the window at the skyline of lights. The city was huge. It was gorgeous. The mood on the plane was electric with anticipation.

Immigration and Naturalization Service people were waiting in the terminal to process the new arrivals.

"Well," said an INS man, "it looks like you're the only one going to New Hampshire."

He led Ali to another gate. Ali boarded a much smaller airplane. An hour later he was touching down in a city called Manchester, his new home, his New Hampshire.

Eric Marsh was there, along with the local news media. The two men hugged, even cried a little. Somebody at the airport gave Ali a shirt with the state's motto: LIVE FREE OR DIE. Ali was moved. Marsh and his wife even had a room waiting for him in their home.

Of course, it would take time to get acclimated. Time to find the right job, time to find the right woman, time to get his

English pretty close to perfect. Time to travel around the country and realize that this little city in New Hampshire was a pretty good place to live after all. Time to find out that he and Marsh just could not stand each other. Time to move into his own place. Time to arrange for Mohammed and another brother to come here and live, too. Time to learn how to square dance. All of this would take time — a year, maybe — before he would fully grasp the distance he'd traveled.

5 backlash

THE Persian Gulf War and the two rebellions that followed uprooted 3 million people in great swirling cur-
rents of communal flight. It hurtled Kurds as far as
Oklahama and Shiites to Sydney. It caged thousands in camps
for many years and forced thousands to go back to the places
they fled. It compelled a newly crowded country called Yemen
to evict people who seemed to be fleeing some incomprehensible calamity in Somalia.

It trapped a multitude in a paradoxical state of statelessness
that seemed part perpetual motion and part suspended anima-
tion. It planted thousands of time bombs in future generations,
creating a new race of children who would be raised with dark
dreams of vengeance and a passion to recapture what would
become a mythic homeland.

Semir Khemmas tried to return to Kuwait when the war
ended, but the Kuwaitis wouldn't let him come home. He was,
after all, an Iraqi. This presented a problem, because as soon as
his studies were finished, he would have to leave Germany. The

only country that he could get into was Iraq, the last place he wanted to be.

Semir tried to get a German passport so he could then emigrate to Kuwait as a German, but he was turned down. He tried to get a Kuwaiti tourist visa so he could at least visit his country. This also was denied. He applied for a German residence permit so he could at least stay in Germany and avoid getting sent to Iraq. But a lawyer told him that foreign students rarely get permanent residency. He would have a better chance if he declared himself a refugee and requested asylum. So he did.

He was now just like those Gypsies and Yugos who tumbled out of the train stations. All he could do was wait while his application wound through a bureaucracy buried under the weight of countless asylum requests. Surely someone would see the validity of his case.

His family was fractured and couldn't come together. Semir's sister Yusra found herself in an even worse situation in Yugoslavia, or what used to be Yugoslavia. She, too, was denied permission to return to Kuwait. And then the ethnic Serbs in the town where she was studying, Banja Luka, began pressuring the "foreigners" to leave. The Serbs were the majority in that city, even though it was in a republic, Bosnia-Herzegovina, that was dominated by Muslim Slavs.

Semir's sister fled to the Yugoslav republic of Croatia. She had to begin her studies all over again, because the university there would not recognize the credits she'd earned in Banja Luka. It was, they insisted, in a different country. And then the Serbs bombed Croatia. She fled again, this time to the Serb town of Nis, where things seemed quieter, because it was nothing but

Serbs. Like Semir, she continued her studies, hoping something would change.

Semir's student visa was now his only alternative to Iraq. He had maybe two years before he faced expulsion, perhaps enough time to find a solution while he finished his degree. Even with deportation hanging over his head, even with the German economy taking a beating because of the costs of unification, even with hostility toward foreigners rising seemingly by the day, Semir began a little streak of pleasant experiences.

It began when he got a new job as a night nurse in a Berlin hospital. This was much better than the factory job. Not long after he started, a German woman who also worked as a nurse suddenly took an interest in him. She kept asking him questions about Islam, about the Koran. Semir was shy, but the woman was not. She asked him how a Muslim woman should dress, and Semir said she should not wear short skirts or slacks. When she came to work the next day, she told him she had thrown away all her suggestive clothing, a big deal in a town where tight pants and tiny dresses seemed more popular than underwear.

All this took place in a matter of days, and Semir was flustered by the woman's interest. Then, one night, the woman came over to Semir's house, and it just happened. It was the first time for him. He was, needless to say, very moved by the experience. He asked this woman to marry him. She agreed to a religious ceremony in a mosque, on the third day of Ramadan.

They moved in together. After a time, it seemed as though his wife began to lose interest not just in Islam, but in him as well. She didn't want to go shopping with him or see a movie or take a walk or stop at a café. Or have sex. She always had an excuse. And she had her German friends over, and sometimes she'd ignore the fact that she had converted to Islam and would drink alcohol with them. He had a separate set of glasses in which alcohol was not to be served, but sometimes she'd make drinks in those glasses anyway, even though she knew it bothered him.

He tried to please her. One time, he came home from his late shift and painted the apartment — just painted the whole place because he wanted to surprise her. It was a spontaneous gesture of his affection. And the place needed painting.

"Are you crazy?" she said, walking through the door. "Why are you doing that? You just got home from your night shift!"

No appreciation. No understanding. No respect. Not like in Kuwait.

Semir always talked about having children. He was very family-oriented. But one day his wife said she couldn't have kids. "Well, then," Semir told her, "when we get to Kuwait, I'll have to take a second wife."

She said she wasn't sure if she could accept such an arrangement. So Semir did what he had to do: He renounced their marriage. And she moved out of his life as quickly as she had moved into it. Because the marriage hadn't been binding under German law, he hadn't even gotten a visa out of the relationship.

Semir became depressed again. He hated Germany more and more. Thugs attacked foreigners almost every day. The frequency and ferocity seemed to grow in proportion to the numbers of asylum-seekers who poured into the country. Semir pretty much stayed in western Berlin, which was safer than the places in the east. Even the police warned foreigners to stay out of certain parts of the former East Germany, particularly rough neighborhoods like Lichtenberg, where gangs of skin-heads roamed the alleys and loitered in the train station, beating up Gypsies and Yugos.

A couple of times, Semir took a field trip with other students to visit the east German city of Potsdam, just outside Berlin, and tour such landmarks as the fabulous old palace of Frederick the Great. This made him long to see some of the other cultural treasures buried deeper in the eastern part of the country. Leipzig, for example, where Goethe and Bach had studied, where Wagner was born. Or Dresden, a town with remnants of the complex beauty it epitomized before it was destroyed during World War II.

He would have liked to have studied these things in person as a student, but he was, let's face it, a refugee. And places like Leipzig and Dresden were teeming with angry young east Germans who blamed the refugees for their own dreary prospects in this suddenly unified land. Refugees like Semir were better off not even setting foot in places like Dresden.

SHE was lean yet large, as broad-shouldered as a boy, but as felinely supple as the most graceful of girls. She had blue eyes and black jeans and a black denim jacket that looked too tight to button. She had a faint sprinkle of cinnamon freckles around her nose. Her skin was so pale, her hair so black and symmetrically shaped, she looked like a punk Cleopatra rendered in porcelain. Her name was Simone Kisza, but her friends called her Sims.

She was with a boy who had an even paler complexion, though his pallor seemed more a product of poor health than sullen fashion sense. His small eyes were sunken and set close.

85

Next to his arrestingly assembled companion, he looked bony and small. His long, scrawny neck arced forward like a vulture's. He seemed swallowed up by his oversized clothes: army fatigue pants tucked into combat boots, a camouflage jacket thrown over a white shirt emblazoned with the stylized eagle from the old Prussian flag. To top off this carefully constructed look, every hair had been shaved from his surprisingly spherical head.

The boy and the girl were sitting alone on a huge, high-backed bench in the center of the train station, swigging tall cans of beer and staring at people with places to go. The girl was animated and grinned hugely and talked loudly and continuously, big shoulders bouncing and arms flying as she made whatever point she was making. Lower lip drooping, eyes a bit glassy, the boy's face showed neither mirth nor malevolence, only the empty gaze of the newly departed. He had a fresh cut over his left eye. His name was Maik Jacob, but his friends called him *Leiche,* the German word for *corpse.*

Maik was fresh from his first real stint in juvenile jail, where he'd spent six months honing his survival skills. His crime was *Schwere Körper Verletzung:* severe bodily injury. He and his friends had chased a Vietnamese man until they caught him and kicked him into a bloody little ball. He had regrets, of course; he never should have got caught. Once he got out, he returned to the routine. Waking up at noon and going to bed at 4 A.M., spending most of his day in the drafty and cathedral train station in the decomposing city of Dresden, drinking beer and harassing people with swarthy skin. Getting drunk, scraping money together for a movie, exchanging secret handshakes with his friends. Spouting fascist slogans from wrinkled pamphlets.

The girl was sixteen years old, just like Maik. Her mother had died of cancer when she was seven and her father had just lost his job as an engineer at Robotron, the former East German computer monopoly that was being eviscerated by slicker systems borne in from abroad by the free market. She and the boy were, needless to say, an odd pair. She looked like she could crush him, yet she was more or less content with the rhetoric and rallies and skinhead social swirl, while he needed the action, the kicks, the clubs to the temple. It was the only way that anybody would notice that young people like him had been dealt a bad hand, man.

When he listened to music, he liked to crank up a certain kind of thuddingly anthemic punk — rock for boys who liked to hurl one at a foreigner. Music with a stance you could beat to. Outlawed songs by such hot new groups as Störkraft, which glorified boot-swinging assaults. Or the veteran Brit band Skrewdriver, some of whose members celebrated the first anniversary of German unity by stabbing a German leftist to death. Or the Bösen Onkles — the Evil Uncles — who spun racist rants so rousing that they inspired about seventy youths at an east German disco to go hunting for African guest workers. They found an Angolan man and pounded him into pulp with baseball bats bought specifically for such sightings. He died two weeks later. Every country had fascist rock bands that supplied the sound tracks to menacing teens like Maik Jacob, a social mutant spawned by an unparalleled period of chaotic world migration.

The naturally bohemian Sims, on the other hand, dug the moody art rock of Depeche Mode and the threnodial descants of The Cure. She liked to look at magazines with pictures of other places, of hip young people dressed in cool clothes on the streets of, say, New York City. She wanted to travel and dance; he wanted to hit and run. To her, life was a party; to him, a riot.

What they shared was a circle of friends that formed a single cell of a local subculture. It was a club, a clan, a sort-of-secret society that filled the weird void left by the Free German Youth, the old Stalinist youth group that had been woven into every aspect of childhood and young adulthood. It had gone with *die Wende*, "the change," as the revolution was known. While the old club had stressed discipline and order, the new one fed on chaos. Skinhead antics ranged from arson to assault to the occasional killing. One spring evening in 1991, ten Dresden skinheads were riding on a streetcar when they spotted an unfortunate Mozambican, a guest worker named Jorge Gomondai. They moved on him, and he darted to the back of the car, near the exit. They kept coming, and he jumped, landing in a jumble on the cobblestones and cracking his skull in the process. He died in a hospital six days later. Gomondai's funeral became a political event, drawing liberals and leftists and activists from around the country. Three thousand of them were marching in a funeral procession when hundreds of local skinheads descended on them. Fights broke out and a few skinheads clobbered a few mourners with baseball bats before the cops broke it up.

Then there was the big funeral for Rainer Sonntag, the neo-Nazi leader who had decided to target a Thai brothel but took on a bit more than he could handle: crabby pimps. He was shot dead from a passing Mercedes, a symbol of the new world. Sonntag's supporters actually got a parade permit to march in mourning. A few hundred showed up. They sang a forbidden verse from "Deutschland Über Alles," flashed the outlawed stiff-armed salute and pretty much enjoyed themselves. Thousands of locals lined the parade route, some curious, some outraged, some silently supportive.

For Maik and Sims, such moments were absolute ecstasy, a return on the investment of countless nights like tonight, when there was nothing to do but sit and drink and stare, sharing space and time in the encompassing void.

A reporter, an American, had been watching them both from a bench nearby when he realized it was probably time to make a move or go home. He was trying to make a personal connection with the nation of young neo-Nazis that had emerged, seemingly overnight, in the newly united Germany, and in fact in much of Europe in general. The violence was escalating almost daily, paralleling in frequency and intensity the numbers of refugees entering the country and fanning out across the continent, the world.

In Germany, there was something resembling an organizational core of radical neo-Nazis who kept in loose contact and maintained some consistent aspects of a cockeyed ideology. Many had been around for years. In Berlin, such professional skinheads had already begun to charge money for interviews, to set prices for poses whenever a news photographer wanted to capture a stiff-armed salute.

But the elusive legions that gave this ascendant movement its strength were the disenfranchised east German kids like Maik, the penniless offspring of jobless parents living in tiny apartments in suffocating, socialist-era housing projects. They were the shock troops, the *numbers,* and they listened to the self-styled leaders only when they felt like it. Violent mobs of these youths, often joined by seemingly typical members of the local citizenry, were staging almost daily attacks on refugee homes housing foreigners seeking asylum. The majority of attacks took place in former East Germany, in obsolete industrial towns, where the collapse of the economy had spawned widespread pessimism while the demise of communism had left an ideological vacuum.

So, in search of some skinheads still somewhat untouched by what had become enormous media scrutiny, this reporter from America had driven down to the surreal city of Dresden, the old Saxony capital famed for its beautiful porcelain and intricate architecture before it was bombed into oblivion by the Allies. It wound up in what was to become East Germany, and the Communists erected poisonous factories and hideous high-rises around the crumbling pieces of a prettier place from the past. After unification, the Western investors moved in, with their pricey restaurants of brass and glass and their blueprints to remake Dresden into something that blended the united Germanys of the imperial past and the profitable future, but skipped the unchic socialist interlude just concluded.

The reporter sat down next to the girl and launched into a comic impression of an American blurting bad German, a technique that rarely failed to elicit a smile of superiority from the targeted Teuton. The girl uncorked a broad grin and even the boy smiled shyly as this American tortured the mother tongue, nuking genders and jettisoning articles and gargling with umlauts as he slammed around his central point, which was that he was an American journalist who wanted to know what young people like them thought about things, strategically not implying that young people like them were monsters.

There was no pretense here, not like among the cagey professional skinheads up in Berlin. They were unabashedly delighted to be singled out. Maik was wearing the full regalia, and the striking Simone was wearing Maik like a neo-Nazi accessory. Their particular pose was to intimidate and threaten, to attract attention and thereby establish an identity in a shifting cultural tide that had left many east Germans feeling dislocated without leaving home. Without this fearsome coloring, they were just badly educated kids destined for second-class citizenship in a reconfigured country that, if they were lucky, would provide them with dead-end jobs in dying towns. And they knew it. This reporter may have been a foreigner speaking bad German, a member of the hated class of *Ausländer,* but he was an American *Ausländer,* an emissary from the culture they, like the foreigners they hated, now coveted pretty badly. Their intimidating defenses crumbled to their curiosity.

Sims peppered the American with questions about New York, about the clubs and the music and the clothes. She was wearing imitation Converse All Stars, black with white trim. "Can you send pictures?" she implored. "I want to see how the young people live."

Maik the Corpse, on the other hand, expounded on the political nature of skinhead violence. Riots and firebombings were strategic necessities, the only way to get the government's attention. He noted quite correctly that the more firebombings there were, the more the politicians screamed for the nation to repeal its liberal Cold War–era asylum law, which was born in a time when refugees from behind the Iron Curtain were ideological currency.

"It's the only way Bonn will listen," he said. "Television isn't interested in peaceful demonstrations."

An obviously drunken youth weaved into their vicinity, and Maik shouted to him. Eighteen-year-old Markus Lieske struggled to maintain a controlled careen as he veered over to their bench. He regarded the American with tipsy suspicion. He looked rather normal for a plastered teen, except for the patch on his black vinyl bomber jacket that read BLESSED BE OUR FATHERLAND.

Neofascist organizations had existed for years in West Germany, and there was modest evidence that small cadres of Nazi revivalists even managed to operate in the authoritarian East. Lieske offered proof, parting his short but conventional head of black hair to expose a half-moon scar on the crown of his head, the legacy of a policeman's truncheon. It came when he was fourteen, he said with drunken pride, when he participated in a neo-Nazi riot in Communist times, and was beaten and detained because of it.

"I had to stand against a wall all night with my hands behind my head," he said.

Since then, he had become casually lawless. He quit school before he was of age and moved in with his grandmother without bothering to register with the local police, both minor crimes in Germany. He had an early start on a long career as a failure.

"Do you know why I'm drinking? Do you? Do you?" he shouted, waving his beer can and drawing worried stares from the train travelers hurrying through the dank station. "I don't do anything! I have no job, no hope. The foreigners are cheap labor.

"These are the only pants I have," he cried, pulling at his faded brown overalls. He spoke frantically and seemed a step away from a sob. "The hate grows stronger and stronger. Unemployment. Suicide. Alcoholism."

He mumbled: "I myself am almost an alcoholic."

The night went on and the beer went down and soon there were half a dozen members of this little clique of train station kids gathered around, a couple cross-legged on the floor and the rest leaning against the benches.

The youngsters took turns telling their stories. Michael Petermann hadn't found a job since he left trade school the previous year, and he knew whom to blame.

"I hate niggers and Turks and Vietnamese," said Petermann. He was tall and wiry and hyper with rage. His nickname was Skorpy, as in *scorpion*. He dripped venom.

"The niggers are swine. I hate when a German woman is with a nigger. They have mixed children. Aaaggh! They sell drugs. The attacks on foreigners are justified because they are niggers and Asians."

He took a gulp of beer. "I hate blacks working when I'm not. I hate all colors other than white. White power!"

Petermann said he liked to run through the train station at full gallop and look for the knots of nonwhites walking the corridors of the arrival gates. "You run up and do this — *boosh!*" he said, faking a punch to Lieske's startled face.

Like most people obsessed with their spot in the social strata of their environment, they hated those ahead of them almost as much as those nipping at their heels. They disliked their new brethren, the wealthy *Wessis*. The bonhomie of the Berlin Wall's removal had given way to distrust and class hostility. East

Germans and West Germans who had hugged at the broken wall were soon checking to see if they still had their wallets. The westerners were paying higher taxes for the huge subsidies and social benefits being poured into the pockets of the easterners, who in turn had their economy destroyed by the uncontrolled competition from the West. Some westerners saw the *Ossis* as crude and godless former Communists who would spy on their own spouses for the secret police. Some easterners saw the *Wessis* as aloof and arrogant, a galling behavior for a people who had the dumb luck to be conquered by the Americans, who offered the Marshall Plan, rather than the Soviets, who demanded reparations.

"They treat us like pigs, like we were Turks," Markus Lieske said.

Soon, a young man named Udo Ahrend was expounding on the nuances of building a proper firebomb. You began with a Trabant, the comically square and undersized East German auto with a two-cycle engine. The gasoline caps did not have locks.

Ahrend was willing to travel any distance across the country to participate in an assault on a refugee home. Unlike Maik, Udo Ahrend paid no lip service to the politics of it all. He was just a happy hoodlum, a smiling sociopath. He was short and stocky and so self-assured that he exuded amiability. He grinned easily and spoke casually and made no attempt to strike a pose or spew out a badly recycled philosophy. He was what he was, which was just a fun-loving thug who liked nothing better than inflicting damage on property and people.

He was imprisoned three years ago for car theft. He had moved to Dresden a couple of months earlier, after his family had kicked him out of the house in the little village of Hinterhermsdorf. He was laid off from his job as a house painter and said he made ends meet by stealing cars and tape decks and sell-ing them in Czechoslovakia and Poland, where the coveted toys of Western affluence were a bit harder to come by.

His nickname was *Kreute,* which means *club.* "Like baseball," he said with a sly smile, swinging an imaginary Louisville Slug-ger at what, presumably, was not an imaginary breaking ball. While some of the other skinheads carried neo-Nazi business cards with their nicknames and favorite slogans, Ahrend's call-ing cards were the similar-sized printed messages that were sup-posed to be positioned on dashboards and windows to warn would-be thieves that a cassette deck in the car was registered with the police. Udo snatched these cards when he stole a tape deck.

"Here, this is from an Opel." He laughed, handing the Amer-ican a yellow card with a serial number.

Ahrend, who sported a buzz cut, said he sometimes won-dered what life would have been like if his parents, astound-ingly, hadn't moved from the West German city of Hanover to Communist East Germany in 1968. He said his mother wanted to be closer to her mother. So Ahrend, born five years later, grew up an *Ossi.* An *Ossi* with a *Wessi* background, which put him at a disadvantage right away, because the Communists figured his mom could be a mole. So there were no perks. He hadn't been able, for example, to get into East Germany's famed sports schools, which were privileged places for young children who exhibited early athletic ability.

"I was a good soccer player," he said. "I could have gone, if they had let me."

It was close to midnight and twenty young people had slowly coalesced into a boisterous discussion group. A tense policeman posted himself on the periphery. Travelers glanced over and hurried along.

The kids in the train station were all pretty much drunk. In the old days, before the open borders, when society was rigidly structured, a kid's livelihood was essentially determined by age twelve. Now, there was no plan, other than a loose affiliation with a neo-Nazi organization called Viking Youth, which told them where to gather, what to believe. Even the inherently hip Sims, who seemed to instinctively seek entrée to a different world entirely, stumbled blindly into the dark alleys of unreasoning hatred that riddled her current locale.

They struggled to explain the things that bound them together.

"National socialism," said Maik Jacob, alias *Leiche,* alias the Corpse.

Lieske pointed out that national socialism is not the same as, ahem, Nazism.

"It is!" Sims corrected him. "That's what *Nazi* means."

Lieske looked embarrassed and gulped his beer.

Dresden was a graveyard of two eras on which the west Germans intended to begin a third. Prices and rents were skyrocketing. The new stores were different, almost intimidating. Beneath the fury over foreigners and the twisted logic of hate, the kids in the train station sensed they were being left behind. The next morning, the American took four of these young toughs out to breakfast. They had to be coaxed through the doors of one of the new restaurants, into a frightening new world of threatening unfamiliarity. They fidgeted with the menu and its bewildering array of mysterious dishes, things like grilled turkey breast and tomatoes stuffed with tuna salad, stuff far more complex than the chunks of pork and boiled potatoes they got at home. They needed help ordering. Only Lieske saw right away what he wanted, finding quick comfort when the waitress delivered to him his morning beer, the cool and familiar start of a brand-new day.

6 the point of origin

WHAT began as violence against refugees committed by shiftless gangs of remorseless neo-Nazis soon became something much broader: a culture war between those on the move to someplace better and the stationary folk they met along the way. It demonstrated a basic principle of human migration, in a way. The more pilgrims migrated to the promised land, the less promising it became. The earlier inhabitants typically responded by allying themselves against the newcomers, beginning with the most recent arrivals and working as far back as necessary.

Pedro Montanau discovered this pilgrim principle one day. He was a coal miner who worked a thirty-minute train ride from Dresden, in a town called Hoyerswerda. Historic Hoyerswerda was a small gingerbread village of turn-of-the-century buildings. The Communists built a new town around it in the 1960s purely to house workers brought in to mine the vast deposits of brown coal that provided most of the power to the nation. More than seventy thousand people were crammed into what was called the "new city," a staggering forest of slablike apartment buildings. There was more work than workers, though, so the Communists imported thousands of foreigners like Pedro to help out.

Pedro was a Marxist from Mozambique who had been dispatched by his country to work in what was considered the showcase socialist society. He was a *Gastarbeiter*, a guest worker, one of the more than 100,000 people from Third World countries who had been offered the chance to live and learn in the pride of the Soviet trade bloc. They sent home money and then, after their three-year contracts expired, took back expertise. They were currency used to help keep little and poor countries in the ideological fold.

During his years in Hoyerswerda, Pedro drank an occasional beer in the local taverns, took in the local soccer matches and routinely said hello to strangers on the street. Then communism fell, a tumble that once seemed as unlikely as the sky's. When Germany reunited and former East Germany began to feel the pain of unemployment combined with higher living costs, these guest workers — once comrades — were seen as parasites. Factories tried to lay them off, the government kept trying to send them back. But they fought hard to stay, even invited their friends and families to join them. They had caught the spirit of evangelical capitalism that spread around the world.

The number of Vietnamese in Germany, for example, went from 60,000 before the wall fell to 100,000 afterward. Africans fleeing the chaos of their continent's own wrenching experiments with democracy surged northward through Spain and France. Kurds poured in from the Persian Gulf. Many tried to make a living, honest and otherwise. Gangs emerged, rivalries broke out. Vietnamese, both guest workers and asylum-seekers, built an industry on black-market cigarette sales. They sold them in every city, tax-free, and waged turf wars among themselves. They became conspicuous examples of crime and competition, especially in ill-tempered towns like Hoyerswerda.

After reunification, the mining operations were no longer considered very efficient, and brown coal was deemed an old-fashioned and environmentally hazardous energy source. The coalworks would have to be scaled down. By the summer of 1991, everybody had been put on half shifts at half pay to minimize the layoffs.

But what rankled people in the town, who suddenly saw prices for food and milk double in the newly capitalist supermarkets even as their paychecks shrank, was the fact that so many of these guest workers were still around, joined by these armies of so-called asylum-seekers. And whether it was worker or refugee or street hustler, foreigners suddenly seemed central to the town's problems. So when a couple of skinheads decided to beat up a couple of Vietnamese men selling smokes on the street one day, the whole town went over the edge.

The skinheads chased the Vietnamese all the way back to the blocky apartment house where Pedro and the rest of the 130 guest workers lived. The Vietnamese men ran inside, but the skinheads didn't give up. They threw rocks, bottles, then bottles filled with gasoline. When a stone sailed into Pedro Montanau's fourth-floor room, he looked outside and saw the people, their faces red and twisted.

The next night, an even larger group of locals went to another apartment building across town, where Saxony state officials had begun housing a couple hundred Asians, Africans and East Europeans who were seeking asylum.

"Germany for the Germans!" the mob screamed. They hurled firebombs.

The following night, mobs showed up at both apartment houses. It went on and on, every evening, for eight days. The police couldn't control the mobs, didn't really seem to have their hearts in it. A group of leftists came down from Berlin to show solidarity with the foreigners by engaging in some bloody street brawls with the locals. More skinheads poured in, from Dresden and places even farther away. Copycat attacks spread to several other eastern German cities and even affluent west Germany, where a fire ripped through a refugee home and killed a young Ghanaian.

The fires burned every evening in Hoyerswerda, but every morning was deceptively quiet. The sun and the silence brought a beguiling promise of peace. The refugees on one side of town and the guest workers on the other would be hungry and thirsty, and every now and then some would venture out to look for food.

Pedro took a chance. He went into town and headed for one of the stores. He saw some young people across the street, saw one of them pointing at him, and then suddenly he heard a pop. Somebody had singled him out. Somebody had put a small-caliber bullet just below his belt line, something just strong enough to put a hole in him. He went to a hospital, got the wound cleaned and dressed. Then he went back to his apartment building and began knocking on doors of the other guest workers, peeling back the top of his trousers and showing them with utter incredulity the purple mess of mangled flesh he got in town.

"I got shot today," he told them.

By then, the nightly riots in Hoyerswerda had become news around the world, an easy symbol of the dark side of German unification. The government blamed the violence on the hordes of foreigners trying to get into Germany. Chancellor Helmut Kohl and other conservatives agitated for tougher asylum laws. They pointed to Hoyerswerda as an example of what the country was coming to.

In the city itself, officials struggled for a solution. This was a popular uprising. It could not be halted. State and local officials finally settled on what they said was the only answer: They would throw out all the foreigners, both refugees and workers. All of them, guest and gate crasher, would be shipped off to a more secure place. There was a logic to the solution but the idea of it, the symbolism of it, the way it echoed a fairly recent past, was astonishing. German authorities had decided to ethnically cleanse a German city.

Hundreds of local people lined the police barricades as the foreigners boarded the buses that waited to take them away. Some of the onlookers chanted, some chortled and some exchanged satisfied handshakes as the newcomers from the exploding Yugoslavia and the imploding Soviet Union and Nigeria and Bangladesh and a dozen other rather unstable places lugged their bags up the bus steps.

The local officials had washed their hands of the matter. It was bigger than them, something caused by forces beyond their control. "This isn't a police matter," Mayor Armin Ahrndt told reporters. "It is a social and political issue."

Standing among the crowd of onlookers was a man who looked more troubled than triumphant. He was a preacher, the

Reverend Frederick Vogel, the superintendent of the local Lutheran church. Even the clergy was endorsing the removal of the foreigners.

"This is a victory for the radicals, of course. But there is no other way," he told a reporter, an American. He gestured to the delighted youngsters in the crowd. "We have to learn to live with others. We must learn tolerance. The young people here, they never learned that."

One by one the buses pulled away from the curb. The people of Hoyerswerda bade the foreigners farewell with a fusillade of rocks.

THE bus was coming up the hill, chugging along the twisting road that rose through forest and field. It was the only moving object in a perfect picture of mountain vista. The people of Breitenheerda came out of their homes and chattered anxiously. Today was the day. The foreigners were coming. They were Slavs and Asians and Africans and they were coming to live here, on the old army base.

The village had had big plans for that old base, where the East German army once waited to fire missiles at the American bombers that never came. The village needed that four-story barracks built of sturdy white brick. The farm economy had pretty much collapsed. That old garrison represented economic salvation, maybe. And now it was being snatched away by dirt-poor Slavs and Asians and Africans.

A group of people stood near the road and watched the bus creep up the hill. Wolfgang Kretschmer, a dairyman and deputy mayor, could not believe they were sending, among others, Africans. The authorities originally had said they would send ethnic Germans from the Soviet Union. That would have been much more tolerable.

He figured that the government was putting refugees in rural areas because there were fewer voters in the boondocks. But what rankled him most was the proportion: five hundred refugees in a town of three hundred people. "That is not normal," he thought. He believed little Breitenheerda was a prototype for what Germany itself might become.

Kretschmer was a working man of thirty-three with wavy brown hair and brawny arms who had grown up on a farm in a tiny village in an isolated corner of a suffocating and scary Stalinist state, just like everybody else here. They had worked on cooperatives that were run like factories, with this person in charge of mixing feed and that one in charge of baling hay, all of them working shifts that ended on time, or earlier. The food and the rent had been cheap and the production quotas reachable without too much sweat. There always had been someone to deliver what you grew or raised, someone to sell it for you and someone to buy it. That disappeared with unification, along with the National People's Army brigade down the road.

But then something good had happened, a sliver of hope. Maybe the transition wouldn't be too traumatic after all. A tent manufacturer had wanted to lease the barracks. That meant jobs, that meant taxes, that meant spin-off benefits. Everything had been all set up. And then the government said it needed those barracks for refugees.

"Refugees? Hah. These people were here for the D-mark," Kretschmer thought.

The village council had tried everything. They pleaded with the state: This is a German city. Do you realize you plan to send more foreigners than there are Germans in Breitenheerda? They pleaded with the federal government: Can't you find someplace else? They even polled themselves. Only 7 of the 141 voters were in favor of these refugees. The state said sorry, this is not a voting issue. The foreigners had to live somewhere, and Breitenheerda was located far from the hostile urban areas where gangs of working-class skinheads spent their idle evenings and empty weekends whipping bottles of gasoline at refugee homes. Breitenheerda was in the middle of nowhere, the perfect place to put these Slavs and Asians and Africans.

So, on the sunny spring morning the bus was supposed to arrive in Breitenheerda, Kretschmer and the rest of the village council gathered by the front gate of the old East German army barracks. The backwoods burghers had one final action to take, one last motion to pass. As the bus swung around to pull into the drive, the men and women of the village government of Breitenheerda sprawled on the ground and blocked the entrance to the barracks with their bodies, daring the bus to drive over them.

Well, that didn't work either. The people from the state said: Move along, now. This is not the way to do things. Besides, the ground was dirty. There was shouting all around, fist shaking and foot stomping, but the mayor and deputy mayor and council members of Breitenheerda nevertheless got up, dusted themselves off and then resigned en masse from their respective offices. That evening, the townsfolk turned off their lights. They locked their doors. They ordered their children to stay inside.

Such hostility never failed to amaze Robert Mukisa, who was moving into his third refugee home in twice as many months. Some Germans just assumed you were less than worthless if you were a penniless foreigner, particularly a dark one, pleading for asylum. Just look at them, splayed out in the driveway like idiots. He wasn't crazy about coming here, either, but this was the chance he took when he decided to leave Uganda and come to Germany. He spoke four languages, had a university degree. He was a writer. How many people here could say that?

He wasn't going to be a prisoner of this shabby barracks behind a high wire fence on a gravel field. Most of the other refugees were afraid to stroll beyond the base perimeter, but not Robert. He went for a walk down the winding country road out front. His first time out, an old man rode by in a tiny car, honking his horn. Robert looked up, then realized: The old man was giving him the finger. He took another walk and two boys on a motorbike passed by, staring at him. Then the motorbike stopped and the boy on the back jumped off, picked up a stick and chased Robert all the way back to the barracks.

After a while, he stopped taking walks. In fact, all the refugees stepped outside as little as possible, even for a smoke, since the kids in town had begun shooting BB guns at the barracks as they rode by on their bicycles. So Mukisa began work on his pet project: a book about racism in Germany.

As far as refugees go, Mukisa did not have the strongest case. He told the authorities that he'd had to leave Uganda because he was being persecuted for his membership in an opposition political group. His life was in danger if he returned, he said, a claim that by necessity was routinely made by asylum-seekers.

Yet, after decades of tyranny and slaughter, Uganda was experiencing a rare period of stability under the reformist government of Yoweri Museveni, a man some people considered a visionary. Museveni had demonstrated a talent for submerging the ethnic distinctions that previous rulers had fiendishly exploited. His most controversial and seemingly undemocratic move had been to ban political parties, which he'd convincingly argued were merely camouflaged ethnic groups. Museveni insisted that Western-style democracy couldn't be transplanted to African nations polarized by tribal divisions. Yet he did hold an honest and contested election that he won fairly easily, restored civil order and stabilized the economy. He tolerated open political debate. He had long been a pro-Soviet leftist during the Cold War, but now that he was in power, he was a convincing proponent of the prevailing free-market theology. Like everybody else.

Robert was a member of one of the political parties that Museveni had banned. He was, he said, persecuted because of it. Yet the most serious oppression he had faced in Uganda was the lack of opportunity. He was clearly an economic refugee, somebody with an education who figured he could make himself a success faster in the West than in Uganda, which remained one of the poorest places on the planet. He'd left his wife and daughter at home, walked to Kenya and bought a plane ticket to Frankfurt. He'd declared asylum at the airport.

And he'd pretty much hated every second of his sanctuary. They all did. The barracks was a Babel of complaints by people who were unhappy with their hosts. Robert had to get tested for syphilis, for AIDS, and some refugee workers actually had the temerity to try to teach him to use a toilet, just assuming that he didn't know how.

A family of ethnic Albanians who had fled persecution in the Serb province of Kosovo were legitimate refugees, but they complained endlessly about the food and the water and the fact that their seven children — the youngest had been born in Germany — were always ill.

"I don't like what I'm eating," griped a Ghanaian man as he forced down a liverwurst sandwich.

Ilya Serednitsky had come to Germany from Moscow to start up an export-import business. He declared himself a refugee, figuring that, as a Soviet Jew, he'd have a pretty good chance of getting asylum. Once he got legal residency and his business underway, he'd planned on sending for his wife and seven-month-old daughter.

It had seemed like a good plan. But then the government decided to start moving refugees to military bases out in the countryside. Serednitsky was stunned. He had university degrees in economics and management. He figured he could have made some money in Berlin. Now, he was stuck in the wilderness.

The griping was endless, which raised the question: So why come here? Didn't the newly united Germany have a global reputation yet? Hadn't the daily assaults on refugees and their residences made it into every paper in the world by now? The country was tinkering with every regulation imaginable to tighten its asylum law, speed deportations and streamline the bureaucracies that processed refugee applications. The message? *Get out!* Kohl and other conservatives complained constantly that the country was being dragged down by freeloading foreigners. They made it seem almost patriotic to take a poke at one.

Germany wasn't the only nation reacting badly to this unforeseen burst of global migration. The United States and every country in Europe were almost reflexively looking to seal the new cracks in the world. Every nation had its violent anti-immigrant fringe. But Germany was the worst. It bore the brunt of the onslaught because it was the easiest to enter, it was perfectly positioned between north and south, east and west. The biggest rips in the old world were on its borders. It was the only unimpeded portal, the only clear shot at happiness through market theory, peace through prosperity. Germany became a tidal pool, a catch basin for people hurled from their countries by post–Cold War turbulence. It was a confluence of several rivers of migration, from the Middle East and Eastern Europe and all across Africa.

The skinheads like the Corpse and the Club didn't care anymore whether they clobbered a Uruguayan or an Iraqi or a Pole. They merely posted themselves on their side of the portal and punched whatever head popped through. After a while, these young German xenophobes even began setting fire to refugee homes rapidly filling up with a particularly large ethnic group that was fleeing the increasingly unstable USSR. This ethnic group had gone to Russia to farm and then found itself trapped there when the Communists toppled the czar. This ethnic group had spent generations yearning to return to its ancestral homeland, which just happened to be Germany.

*   *   *

THEY came into his office every day, asking for advice, demanding applications. They wanted tips on what to say, how to prove it, where to send it. And every day Viktor Schulz would say the same thing, only every day he would say it more frequently: Fill this out. Bring it back. I'll send it off.

He could barely keep up with the paperwork. The volume was incredible. And it bothered him that so many of these people who wanted to go to Germany, who claimed to be German, who had German names and German ancestors and a German lineage they could trace back to the time of the Russian empress Catherine the Great (born a German, by the way), could not speak one word of the language.

Not that Viktor Schulz's German was that good. He spoke it with a Russian accent as thick as porridge. His vocabulary and grammar were pretty poor, he knew, and talking German with other Soviet Germans wasn't the fastest way to fluency. Still, he was a German. He felt it, even though he didn't really see himself living in Germany. Working in Russia was, after all, a very German thing to do. His family had done it for generations.

Catherine the Great began inviting German farmers and craftsmen to come to Russia in the eighteenth century, to help modernize a country she sought to make more Western European than Slavic. Millions came. After the Communists took over, all the Germans were herded into their own republic on the lower Volga River. This lasted only until World War II, when Josef Stalin broke up what he considered a Nazi threat in his own backyard. He imprisoned many Germans and scattered most of the rest across Siberia and the bleak Central Asian republics in the south. Thousands died during the forced marches.

Schulz's father was sent to a labor camp and his mother had to travel alone with her small children to Kazakhstan, of all places. They had to give up their farm in the Volga River basin. They were allowed to take only what they could carry. The Soviets then proceeded to lose more than 20 million people fighting the Great Patriotic War against Nazi Germany, and relations between the two tribes were never the same again. Schulz's family was eventually moved to Sverdlovsk, a city in the mineral-rich Ural Mountains. This was where the Bolsheviks murdered the last Russian czar, Nicholas II, and his family. It used to be named Yekaterinburg, after Catherine. But when the Communists took over it was named after the official who orchestrated the executions of the last of her line.

A lot of the relocated Germans worked in the big factories and refineries that processed the platinum and copper and iron that was mined in the region. This was hard work in a grim town, and the Germans did not even have the same meager opportunities as the Russians. They got the worst jobs and were routinely denied any chance to better themselves. Schulz, for example, tried to enroll in engineering school in 1985. He certainly had the brains. But his application was denied.

"We will not allow a German in a Russian school during the fortieth anniversary of the Great Patriotic victory," one of his high school teachers told him.

Because of this sort of treatment, the Germans formed tightly knit communities. They were a unique hybrid, distinctly German yet more at home in the Urals than in the land of their ancestors. Schulz was elected head of the German community in Sverdlovsk, and one of his duties was to process the applications of the Germans who actually wanted to go to West Germany.

West Germany's postwar constitution said that anybody with German roots could come back whenever he or she wanted. This clause was written more to needle Stalin than anything else, since most of the 5 million ethnic Germans in Europe were trapped behind the Iron Curtain. Most of them weren't going anywhere. Soviet Bloc refugees were so prized in those days that West Germany even paid Moscow every year or so to release some of these so-called *Aussiedler,* these emigrants. Maybe twenty thousand or so a year. They were greeted in the Fatherland warmly. Their departure was a repudiation of communism.

Hard to believe how rapidly it all changed. First Gorbachev, then the revolutions across the East Bloc, then German unity. Then came the coup d'état in August 1991, the attempt to remove Gorbachev and turn back the clock on the reforms he had unleashed. Gorbachev was taken prisoner at his dacha in the Crimea. A cabal of hardliners declared themselves in control of the country. Boris Yeltsin, the Russian Federation president, climbed atop a tank outside of the parliament building and urged the people to resist. His Homeric moment was spontaneous and spine-tingling. He was instinctively bending history to his will, altering the flow of events simply because it was his nature. Three days later, Gorbachev was freed, the plotters were in custody and the Soviet Union entered the stretch drive of disintegration.

Yeltsin forced a diminished Gorbachev to give more power to the republics, rendering the Soviet Union itself superfluous. An emerging breed of nationalist leaders, often just reconstructed Communists, reached back to a favorite place in history when a particular ethnic group had its own homeland. Never mind that three decades of homicidal gerrymandering by Stalin had repainted the ethnic landscape so many times that no group could occupy any place without infringing on somebody else's historical claim. The forced collectivization of the 1920s, the ideological purges of the 1930s and the ethnic shuffling of perceived Nazi sympathizers during the 1940s had left millions dead. But it was the millions displaced and their descendants who now threatened to exercise some old territorial stake and smash the Soviet Union into a thousand pieces, creating a new and exponentially larger generation of displaced people.

The fissures formed not only along the existing republics, but along overlapping lines that reflected old places that existed only in books or communal memory. The Soviet empire was poised to unravel into contested lands that didn't necessarily reflect the ethnic content of the people within them. If the place broke apart the way it was threatening to, the number of people who would wind up living outside their areas of ethnicity would be roughly one out of every hundred humans on the planet.

Almost daily, the Soviet republics paid less heed to anything pretending to be central Soviet authority. All of them looked inward, at their own ethnicity. The old institutions, the old beliefs, even the names of the cities and the value of a ruble were now as solid as the smog over Sverdlovsk. The August coup attempt seemed to give everyone carte blanche to do what they wanted. They even changed the name of Sverdlovsk back to Yekaterinaburg.

Individual freedoms, once rare and precious things, now were so widely exercised that they almost immediately were taken for granted. Freedom to demand a return to the old days, to turn a piece of land into a new nation, to buy American shampoo with conditioner. Freedom to leave, to just run from the uncertainties of the times. And, every day, more of Schulz's friends and acquaintances came into his office and said they wanted, finally, to leave the Soviet Union and go live in Germany. Ironically, being German in the Soviet Union wasn't such a bad thing anymore. Forget about the blood spilled during past wars. The Soviets loved the Germans in these days. Marrying one might mean a one-way trip out of here, on the train heading West.

This collective loss of equilibrium extended beyond borders, beyond ethnicity, into the soul of each segment of society. Nobody even knew what to think. They wanted communism's constancy, capitalism's cash flow and a homeland that flew a flag that reflected their ancestry. The old wailed about the lack of food in the state stores and the high prices on the free market, while the young peered into an increasingly foggy future and tried to discern the dim outline of their dream. They wanted to own a business that sold products.

College professors who once wrote academic tracts on Marxist economics were racing to the mimeograph machines to copy Western textbooks. Students started skipping useless classes taught by clueless teachers. Administrators stumbled across a wonderfully profitable Western concept: tuition. Socialism — what were we thinking, anyway?

The Evil Empire, in fact, had become something to pity. The republics were becoming less willing to send their farm products into the unprofitable central distribution system, so there were actually food shortages, particularly in the big cities. Some of the farm cooperatives were stealing their own food or funneling it into the more profitable private markets, so the state stores where the poorest shopped had a hard time stocking shelves.

The craftiest people, those most willing to break from old routines and capitalize on the weaknesses of others, fared the best. Stalin had killed millions of peasants during the years he created the system of farm collectives. These collectives, protected from competition and handed a captive market with a subsidized distribution system, had evolved into inefficient factories overstaffed with clock-watching workers. Even with the winter of '91 threatening to bring potentially catastrophic shortages, these indolent workers were still taking only a halfhearted stab at bringing in the harvest, still knocking off at 5 P.M. whether they were finished or not. And some city dwellers realized this. They got off work, caught a bus to the outskirts of town and then foraged the fields that supposedly had been harvested but which, in fact, were still fat with food.

But most people weren't so resourceful, and the world took pity on the struggling superpower. Even impoverished India sent twenty-six tons of food and medical supplies. It became downright chic to feed the Soviets. Berliners who had food stockpiled from the days when the Soviets tried to starve the Allies out of West Berlin in the 1950s wanted to send that emergency food to the Soviets. War in Liberia? Factional fighting in Somalia? Sorry. Nothing was more riveting than a starving superpower.

Some contrarians tried to point out that the situation wasn't that bad, that hunger was worse in other places, but few people listened. Nobody wanted to see the old empire explode, sending the detritus of its population flying out like shrapnel. The Soviet

Union was vanishing like a morning fog. The West stood, transfixed, while the republics and pieces of republics reassembled themselves messily into something akin to sovereign states.

At first, it seemed like the deadliest fissure was developing between the two biggest republics, Russia and Ukraine, both of which had nuclear weapons and seemed destined to emerge as separate nations with unpredictable agendas. But the smaller and more complex cracks in the Caucuses really were more reflective of the times and indicative of the future, of a trend toward little but lethal fights over opposing visions of territorial geometry. A war over a predominately Armenian enclave in Azerbaijan alone had dislodged 200,000 people, a refugee population that would carry a thirst for revenge to the grave, though not before passing it on to the next generation. Fragments of buried history were being unearthed in places such as Dagestan and Kabardia and Balkaria, where some felt the antidote to uncertainty was to become a nation.

Nowhere was this chaos more chaotically illustrated than on the northern slopes of the Caucasus, an oil-refining bit of southern Russia known as Chechen-Ingushetia. The Chechens and Ingush were ethnically identical Turkic people who shared space with a large Russian minority. After the abortive Soviet coup, the Chechens decided to declare a new Chechen nation even though they made up only about 60 percent of the population. The Russians, a quarter of the population, wanted the place to remain in Russia. The Ingush wanted their old homeland in what was now North Ossetia, which was in Russia. But the North Ossetians wanted to unite the land with territory occupied by the *South* Ossetians, who were in northern Georgia. And the South Ossetians waged a guerrilla war of independence

against the Georgians, who already were consumed by conflicts between Muslims and Christians, nationalists and Communists, secessionist provinces and one irate band of paramilitary
horsemen.

These were actual conflicts, real wars of varying intensities.
They were tiny and complex and easily ignored, but they were
sending hundreds of thousands of people scattering, trying to
guess where the new borders would be and whether they could
consider the land within them to be home.

Wild migration patterns were emerging. When a civil war
broke out in Somalia in 1991, thousands of cagey Somalis
headed to the suddenly accessible Soviet Union, where one of
the cheapest flights you could catch was to Finland, a reasonable
facsimile of the West. And the Finns were left wondering how
all these Africans wound up on the Baltic shore.

The world's persecuted or merely poor were using the
porous remains of the Warsaw Pact as transit points to get closest to the culture they all coveted, the sole role model for the
changing world. For decades the United States had one essential
message for its Communist adversaries: Let your people go. And
now they were coming. The West got the world it had demanded, and now it was scrambling to shield itself from it. Italy
began expelling thousands of Albanians within days of their
arrival. Germany ran chopper patrols along its eastern border.
Even Austria, which once welcomed refugees like Michaela
Woike with food and wine, began posting armed soldiers along
its frontier with Hungary.

As 1992 approached, the world agenda was awesome. Cold
War arsenals were finding their way to Third World wars. Bits of
wayward plutonium were turning up on the black market.

Yugoslavia's dissolution had already resulted in bloody conflicts in the breakaway republics of Slovenia and Croatia, and a third seemed possible in Bosnia-Herzegovina. There were conflicts in Africa that burned like tire fires.

With this chaotic new world as his backdrop, Boris Yeltsin made a state visit to Germany in November 1991, three months after he had thwarted the coup. This was his coming-out party, his first trip West since he had seized his country's destiny. There were no Soviet flags flying to greet him, only the white, blue and red of Russia.

He reveled in the shared history of the two countries. He toured the rococo villa where Harry Truman, Josef Stalin and Winston Churchill held the historic 1945 Potsdam Conference that led to the postwar division of Germany and assigned the ascendant superpowers their starter sets of spheres of influence. He made repeated references to "the new Russia and the new Germany."

He had a country bristling with nuclear weapons, ethnic conflict and unhappy people, and he used the implicit threat of world-altering instability as a marketing tool to press for aid and investment. He brought two messages: Deal with *me*. And: *Deal* with me. On behalf of a reborn Russia, he signed a cooperation pact not only with Germany, but with Daimler-Benz, the nation's biggest conglomerate. He went before a group of industrialists in Stuttgart and told them: Let my people go . . . shopping.

"Come and conquer our market," he said. "We are cordially inviting you."

And he brought a gift; he agreed to re-establish an autonomous republic for the roughly 2 million ethnic Germans in

Russia. This was a welcome bit of relief for Germany, which no longer even wanted to let other Germans enter its crowded country.

Viktor Schulz was unimpressed by Boris Yeltsin and his promises. He remembered the old Yeltsin from Sverdlovsk, when he was just a local party functionary. Never did much for the Germans. Not nearly as much as Germany was now doing for the Soviets, hurling billions of dollars at the reeling empire in the hope that people like Viktor Schulz would please stay home.

Toward the end of 1991, leaders of the ethnic German communities from across the Soviet Union gathered in Moscow to talk about the future. Viktor Schulz was among them. Everybody was saying the same thing: Time to go. For years, the West Germans had left a light on for the descendants of the farmers and craftsmen who went off to work for Catherine the Great. And now they were returning, like forgotten comets completing circuits of the sun.

Schulz figured that three-quarters of the 32,000 ethnic Germans in Sverdlovsk — make that Yekaterinaburg — had applied to leave since the August coup attempt. His community was disappearing from under him. Ethnic Germans were leaving at a rate of twenty thousand a month. Entire villages were being emptied.

Schulz figured it was finally time to sit down with his wife and son for a little meeting, time for the family to make its own decision. And Schulz knew what it would be. The Soviet Union would disband in just a few weeks, a little more than a year after Germany had reunited. The breakup would force the migration of 9 million people. Schulz expected to be among them. He had no faith in this proposed new homeland on the Volga. He figured his future was in his past, back in a fatherland he'd never seen. He filled out an application. He couldn't help himself. A powerful force that he couldn't begin to define was beckoning him to take his chances on the road. He peered into the vortex, grabbed his wife and his child and jumped in.

7   fresh orphans

I T TAKES effort to make a connection between a distant event and a stranger on a doorstep, to realize that the difference between an alien and an asylum-seeker is often just a matter of perspective. It's easy to be put off by a group of foreigners standing on a street corner, chattering away, while feeling pity for the same people somewhere else, darting across different streets, heads down, hoping to elude a sniper's fire. It's easy to look with distaste at a pesky youngster begging theatrically for money, yet pray for a kid on television, cowering in a combat zone.

Even in a town like Berlin, just a day's drive from any one of the confusing wars in Yugoslavia, the effects of arrival generally overshadowed the cause of movement. There were, however, occasional exceptions. Sometimes the two sides of the same circumstance would converge in remarkable ways. Sometimes, the connection between what happened there and what happened here would become stunningly clear.

After war broke out in the Yugoslav republic of Bosnia in 1992, after the West's will to stop it proved no match for the combatants' resolve to wage it, a collection of vacant-eyed orphans became something of a symbol of transitional times, of the frustration and helplessness many people felt in an era of inexplicable chaos and cruelty. The children lived in Sarajevo, a city encircled by Serb rebels, and their orphanage was getting shelled on a regular basis. Some of the children had been killed, and others had to live in a laundry room because one of the wings had been blown up. They were sick and wounded and hungry.

Even though worse things were happening to more people throughout Bosnia, these orphans had come to represent, to some, all that had gone uncontrollably wrong with the world. Some influential people in Western countries, including the Austrian chancellor's wife, began talking about carrying out a rescue mission. Officially, no Western government wanted to get involved. The United Nations said such a mission would be too risky and might further provoke the combatants. But a couple of politicians from Germany, old friends, came up with a rough plan of action to save those kids.

These politicians were west Germans who had decided to run for a state legislature in east Germany after the two countries had unified. West German candidates quite regularly won east German elections, since many easterners figured these westerners must know all about free markets and democracy. Though their political mandate was local, these particular politicians were obsessed with doing something about Bosnia, with striking some blow against the war's implacable aggressors and unyielding momentum.

So they plotted a rescue mission. All they needed was somebody with the nerve and the knowledge to carry it out. Somebody who knew the mountains and the lowlands and the fields that overlapped frontiers. Somebody who knew when to avoid certain checkpoints, when to hug the coast, when to scoot inland. Somebody who could find the shifting holes in a war and slip through them quickly without losing or damaging a cargo of kids.

This mix of instinct and expertise, fearlessness and finesse was a valuable skill, no question about it. But far from an exact science.

HERBERT Puchwein made a living off avoiding conflict and chaos. He ran a big security firm in Vienna. He supplied bodyguards, surveillance, technical expertise, professional advice, mostly for rich and powerful people. He even installed traffic lights. Sukarno, Iacocca, sheiks rolling in oil wealth — Puchwein made sure their trips to Austria were safe and uneventful.

He had certain talents. He was pushing sixty but he was still pretty formidable. He was a pilot, a judo expert, a former cop. He was a private eye, but not the solitary sort who sat in a small office, waiting for someone to find him in the phone book. He had two thousand employees. He dealt with logistics, tactics, training, communications. He even did charity work, though his was with the Flying Tigers, a mysterious group of daredevils and doctors that had flown relief missions to war zones in Vietnam and Romania and Armenia, among other places. Most of the time, the Flying Tigers did things quietly. They even used code names. After the war in Bosnia broke out, they began delivering war supplies to the Muslims on behalf of a Saudi sheik who was distressed by the Serbian efforts to ethnically cleanse the country while the rest of the world did little.

They knew where to land, where to drive, how to move without detection. They understood the latticework of frontiers. And they, too, had become fixated on these kids in the orphanage. So the German politicians and the people close to the chancellor and the shadowy group known as the Flying Tigers all came together and organized a team that included doctors, orphanage workers, a Bosnian children's charity and a driver who wasn't afraid to take a busload of kids across a web of war zones.

If everything worked according to plan, if everyone did their jobs, if all the proper permissions were arranged with the warring sides, the bus would be escorted out of Sarajevo, pass through the Serb encirclement and stop in the Croat-held city of Kiseljak just east of the capital. Puchwein would rendezvous with the bus there and then, following a route he had already checked out the day before, shepherd the bus on the fifteen-hour journey to the Adriatic port city of Split, where a plane would be waiting to take the children to an orphanage in Germany.

That was the plan. On an unbearably hot day in July 1992, Puchwein in his favorite bulletproofed truck left Split for the journey toward Sarajevo. But Croat forces launched artillery attacks on Serb positions along the main road linking the two towns. So Puchwein had to carve out a harrowing path over steep and sinuous macadam roads that wound through the mountains like a bewildered snake. Bringing a busload of kids back this way, he thought, would be very dangerous.

He paid his way past the checkpoints with cigarettes and beer and finally made it to Kiseljak after nightfall. But there was no sign of a bus, no sign of an orphan, no sign of anybody from his team to explain why there were no signs of any of them. It turned out that almost all the buses had been commandeered by soldiers, and the Serbs were being stingy about giving permission to let a bus pass through their lines. It took six days of scrounging and cajoling, of going through the official channels of warring factions by day and cruising around at night, trying to get a sense of where the checkpoints were located, before everything came together.

Puchwein's crew got a bus. They finally got some Serb officials to agree to let the orphans cross through the Serb encirclement of the city. They asked the UN Protection Force once again for a little protection, but it refused. The orphanage officials selected fifty of the smallest and sickest orphans, those most in need of getting out of Sarajevo. Almost all of them were less than two years old. Everything was finally in place.

Then, a fresh round of fighting broke out around Sarajevo. More delays. Puchwein had figured that this mission was top secret, but too many people were involved in too many different countries for it to have stayed a secret. Unbeknownst to the people on the ground, every day's delay in the start of the mission was reported around the world. When would the orphans be spirited from Sarajevo?

Finally, after a week of setbacks, the rescuers simply decided: Time to go. The children were brought out from the orphanage and carried onto the bus. They were lashed to their seats with strips of diaper cloth so they wouldn't fly around during the jolting journey over the jagged mountain passes and rugged roads.

"Whatever happens, just don't stop," Puchwein told the driver.

He got in his trusty Jeep Cherokee and the bus full of children followed behind. It was 7 P.M., a time that a UN official would later describe as a "daft" hour to leave the encircled capital. It was the first day of August 1992, a day when nearly six hundred people would be wounded and forty-three killed during fighting that raged mainly in the vicinity of the capital. It was, in other words, a rough Saturday night in Sarajevo.

The bus and the Jeep rumbled all alone down an eerily empty main avenue no longer known by its normal name, but as Sniper Alley. It was a three-mile stretch of road scrutinized by Serb sharpshooters who selectively brought tragedy to random lives. The bus rolled down this road, filled with children, past the scorched high-rise apartment buildings punctured with holes, where cowering families hid behind walls of sandbags. It rolled toward the last Bosnian government checkpoint, toward the first Serb checkpoint. It was motoring along, moving toward freedom. And then the windows began exploding.

Puchwein heard the shots and looked in the mirror. One bullet blew out the left front tire of the bus, but the driver kept driving. The second came in the front window. It went under the steering wheel, right under the armpit of the driver himself and grazed the shoulder of a woman behind him, one of the orphanage workers who was riding along. She started to scream.

The third bullet struck the middle of the bus. It went right through a one-year-old boy, a Muslim lad named Roki. The bullet exited the boy and then came to a stop inside a two-year-old Serb, a mentally retarded girl named Vedrana. They died.

The bus kept moving, thumping madly down the road on one flat tire, rolling to the end of the street, toward a bridge, carrying a cargo of sobs and screams. Puchwein stopped at the bridge and the bus followed suit. The kids on the bus cried hysterically, the wounded woman screamed, and Puchwein and the driver wondered who in the hell would shoot at a busload of orphans.

The bus proceeded to the first Serb checkpoint. The Serbs delayed the bus for six hours. They took the bodies of the two children and turned them over to relief workers. They said that various people would have to be contacted about securing permission to transit Serb territory. And they brought some officials down to take a look at these children. The Serb authorities in the Serb-held suburbs of Sarajevo demanded to see a list of the names of these children. They began to read down the list.

"Muslim . . . Croat . . . Serb!"

Puchwein could not believe it. The names all sounded the same to him. But the first names apparently provided clues to whether somebody was a Serb, a Croat or a Muslim Slav. And then, to the consuming horror of the orphanage workers and the rescue mission organizers, the Serbs pulled aside nine of the children who seemingly had Serb-sounding names, though that wasn't the most foolproof way of assessing ethnicity. Nevertheless, the Serb soldiers took the children away and said these little Serbs would stay behind. They would remain inside this particular section of Bosnia that was being sterilized of non-Serb contaminants.

The bus could move along now. And, after all the logical entreaties and demands and pleas were rebuffed by the superior will of xenophobic righteousness, the bus moved along. Soon, word of what had happened raced around the world. The painstaking progress of these pilgrims was being globally dissected, each tragic step demonstrating the folly of the mission and the cruelty of the combatants, while at the same time wrenching hearts.

The United Nations and the other critics of the mission began the litany. See? It was too dangerous to do such things. Yet back in Sarajevo, even as the bodies of the two dead orphans were returned for burial, hundreds of parents descended on the orphanage, demanding that their children be taken out of the tortured city just like those other kids. And one Croat woman went down to the police station to insist that her child, not an orphan after all, had been mistakenly taken off the bus by the Serbs at their checkpoint outside Sarajevo.

In the meantime, the bus moved along, through Serb territory, still on the edge of Sarajevo, still a long way from the end of the journey. It finally came to what should have been the first stop of the first day: a hotel in Fojnica just twenty-five miles outside the city. Fojnica was in what was considered a safe area under Croat control. The hotel manager had cleared the entire first floor for the children. A doctor from Germany and his crew were there, waiting, and they had toys for the kids. Everyone's agony was eased just a bit by the unexpected smiles of the children.

Puchwein began working the radio, looking for help. He had serious doubts about the ability of this ramshackle bus to make it over the mountains. The August heat was suffocating, and the journey would be difficult for the children. He finally reached a UN general close to midnight, and this general seemed irritated to have been awakened. Children? He told Puchwein to call the UN Children's Fund, so Puchwein did.

"I need two helicopters for the kids to bring them to Split!"

"No problem," said the UNICEF official. "We'll get you what you want."

Puchwein was amazed. The German doctor let out a whoop of joy.

The UNICEF man continued.

"Just send a list with the names of the children and I'll call you back in one month."

Puchwein and the doctor were stunned. "Go to hell!" Puchwein said, slamming down the receiver. Apparently the children would have to travel over the mountains after all.

In the morning they set out, creeping over tortuous terrain, climbing higher, hugging a harrowing, horseshoe-shaped pass that taunted travelers with plunging possibilities. At times the bus literally inched along, feeling its way over the ruts and the rocks, while the children bawled in the heat.

They finally hit the lowlands and cruised through citrus country, past grove after grove of untended oranges on the other side of the mountains. They stopped at a children's hospital on the coast, just as planned, and the kids were fed and cleaned up. They swapped their bus for a new luxury liner with air-conditioning. Then they rolled into the medieval port city of Split, the Adriatic offering them an open view of the Western horizon.

The Soviet airline Aeroflot had donated a paratrooper plane for the final trip to Germany. The children were put up in an orphanage in Split for their final night in the former Yugoslavia. The next day, the two orphans who had died on this trip were buried side by side back in Sarajevo, not far from a battered statue of the lion that symbolized Bosnia. Twenty children who hadn't been chosen for the evacuation mission were among the bereaved. Up in the hills, Serb gunners fixed the position of this funeral and sent four mortar shells thudding into the soft earth, scattering the screaming mourners and sending grave-diggers diving into open plots. Flying shrapnel mangled the arm of an old woman, the grandmother of the dead Serb girl.

And in Split, the orphans who had survived the bus trip were loaded aboard the big Soviet transport. The toddlers were seated on the wooden benches that lined the inside of the fuselage. The infants were tied to mattresses laid in the middle. Fifty kids: two killed, nine seized, thirty-nine en route to a better world. The tiny refugees, at peace at last, clung to their new toys as they left the ground for the trip to Germany.

8 raising the drawbridge

NINA stretched out her arms for a hug and smiled in the sunshine. For the first time in a long time, the tiny two-year-old with the soft brown curls was safe. She wanted to be picked up, held, cradled by big arms. One of the orphanage workers obliged, scooping her up and carrying her to the row of ambulances lined up on the edge of the airstrip.

Some of the children looked dazed, some slept and some chattered brightly, enthralled by the attention of all these people milling around. Some kids were badly dehydrated. A little boy with a face full of sores giggled as he played with a toy hippopotamus. A dark-haired girl with huge brown eyes stared vacantly from the window of an ambulance, fiercely clutching a doll as big as herself. They were emotional wrecks, and psychologists were among the people waiting to greet them.

The planeload of orphans had touched down moments before at an abandoned Soviet air base just outside the sleepy little east German village of Zerbst. Everyone seemed to linger a bit at the airport, to bask in the balmy weather and the serenity of the surrounding countryside. Herbert Puchwein, a gray-haired giant in khakis and safari hat, leaned a big shoulder against the landing gear of the immense Aeroflot AN-26 transport jet. He watched the children being loaded into the ambulances. He chatted with a reporter who had come out to cover the end of a bittersweet mission.

"When we gave them the first toys, it was a terrific feeling," he said with a grin, recalling the lone happy moment of these disturbing last days.

The children who had been so wrenchingly adorable from a distance were still adorable once they landed in Germany. Their sad-eyed expressions led newscasts and newspapers around the world. The German government would be flooded with offers of adoption. The connection between a distant event and strangers on a doorstep had been made with triumphant compassion.

This warm feeling was only fleeting, however. Other Bosnians would continue to pour into the country the rest of the year, and the next, and the next, as the war wore on. Germany in particular would get a little sick of these refugees, so sick that even these thirty-nine little orphans would finally be marched back on a plane and forced to go back to where they came from, back to where they belonged, back to their bombed orphanage in the besieged city of Sarajevo. The kids again would become symbols, this time of the frustration of a nation that figured its hospitality had been exploited. The two German politicians would curse the mood of the moment that put those kids back on a plane bound for Bosnia.

There were just too many people seeking asylum. The leaders of the West decided it was time to take some truly draconian steps to insulate their world from this exodus, time to begin building some impregnable barriers. Time for some serious laws to be passed. Time to begin sealing the portal.

ABABACAR Dene found sanctuary in software. He took pleasure in the pure concentration needed to style a program to fit the personality of a particular business. He was one of technology's tailors, a man who could configure a computer system to mesh with the most idiosyncratic of enterprises. The salesmen sold the hardware at a larcenous markup. The technicians carted the stuff off to the client and plugged the correct cables into the proper ports. Then Dene walked in with his little briefcase and made the machinery indispensable, trained it to balance the books and track sales, inventory and depreciation. He put it to work.

His was a trade that carried a certain amount of prestige in a swampy equatorial backwater like Togo, a coastal slice of West Africa shaped like an extended middle finger. In 1960, after the French ended their control of the government if not their sizable stake in the economy, the nation was left with decent roads, a fairly booming cocoa and coffee trade, and a sultry, stylish ambience that attracted a certain type of European tourist with a taste for potent marijuana, roomy beaches and limber sex with taut young Togolese.

But as with most other African nations, the postcolonial power vacuum was filled by a dictator, in this case General Gnassingbé Eyadema, whose nearly three decades of rule were marked by casual brutality, open corruption and almost slapstick incompetence. He created a system seemingly designed to funnel the nation's resources into the bottomless maw of the military, which sustained its power by winning Western aid in exchange for not embracing Marxism (or threatening French economic interests). It wasn't until the Soviet Union imploded in 1991 that Togo, along with virtually every other developing nation, was forced to confront the fact that it could no longer profit from playing the role of superpower stooge.

Intellectuals like Dene, surreptitiously active in opposition politics, sensed that their moment had arrived. In early 1991, the opposition began organizing peaceful street protests. Opposition newsletters were distributed more openly. A multiparty political system even became a topic of delicate debate in the officially approved press. Even Eyadema seemed unable to slow this strange new momentum that spread across Africa. Under pressure at home and abroad, he agreed to a constitutional convention that would be charged with designing a democracy.

Though he'd had every intention of controlling the process, the constitutional delegates moved too quickly. They appointed a prime minister and stripped Eyadema of all but the ceremonial power of a titular president. They sent him a message: You are obsolete.

Being outmoded wasn't the same as being outgunned, however. Eyadema unshackled his secret police. Newspapers critical of the general were burned. The head of the opposition movement was shot and critically wounded. At least twenty-eight people were beaten to death in a single day, their bodies dumped in the steamy lagoon surrounding the capital, Lomé. Hundreds were murdered by the military in the next few weeks. Opposition leaders were forced to move from house to house to avoid detection. Street protests turned into bloodbaths, sparked mainly by members of Eyadema's tribe, which made up only

15 percent of the country but most of the military. In a three-month span, the military staged four strategic coups against the new prime minister and his Cabinet, each time taking him hostage and shooting a few of his guards. Eyadema insisted he had nothing to do with the violence. But with each negotiated end to each coup, a bit more of his power was restored. In a matter of months, nearly a quarter of a million people had fled the capital for the jungle highlands.

Dene was terrified that he would be caught in the ruthless security net that seemed to be strangling the country. Brutish troops patrolled the streets, stopping and searching cars and pedestrians, arresting anybody regarded suspiciously. Opposition members disappeared almost daily. Bodies bobbed in the lagoon. One Sunday, while Dene was clearing up some work at the office, his wife answered the phone at home.

"Tell your husband to stop working for the opposition," said the voice on the other end, "or he's dead."

Two weeks later, it was with trepidation bordering on terror that Dene reluctantly took a business trip to Cameroon, to the city of Douala, leaving his wife, Susan, and their three children at home. The job itself was a simple programming task for a new client. But on the evening of his second day there, he returned to his hotel to find an urgent message from his mother-in-law. He anticipated the worst even before he dialed her number, before he heard her hysterical voice, before she finished delivering the news: Security men went to your house, looking for you. They raped Susan, killed her, and beat your oldest son when he tried to stop them.

Dene gave in to the paralysis of overwhelming grief, then tried to reach some of his opposition colleagues seeking help, guidance. But his friends were scattered, terrified, reduced to saving themselves. His options were clear. His three children would have to live with his in-laws for the foreseeable future. Returning home was not an option. His existence in Togo was fatal to his family. He had to erase himself from his society for as long as Eyadema ruled the country. He was a forty-year-old man with an excellent education and a sophisticated skill. There would be no simple act of flight, but a well-executed process of bold reinvention. With the same rationality he used to write a program, he designed his escape and drafted the blueprint for a new life.

Dene took a car across the Sahara Desert and into Algeria. From Algiers, he booked passage on a passenger ship across the Strait of Gibraltar to Marseilles. He'd considered seeking asylum in France — he'd studied economics for three years in Paris — but he had a more ambitious and seemingly logical destination: the newly united, suddenly ascendant Federal Republic of Germany. Now, with East Germany absorbed by Europe's most powerful economy, the nation was the continent's undisputed Goliath, a powerful conduit between the wealth of the West and the newly unshackled markets of the East.

Dene hired a car to Paris and then took a train to Strasbourg, right on the German border. He took a cab to the checkpoint outside Freiburg, walked up to a border guard and, in French and English, requested political asylum. The guard gave Dene a paper to fill out. He was taken to a nearby building full of Romanians, Vietnamese, Bosnians and a few other Africans. He was given a blanket, a pillow, a bed and a meal. And he began talking to his fellow exiles.

Dene hadn't understood the depth of the asylum situation in Germany. Half a million alone would register in 1992; probably twice that number arrived illegally. There were Soviet Jews, Romanian Gypsies, countless Kurds from three contiguous countries, four types of Yugoslavs fleeing four shades of conflict. Arabs, Africans, Asians.

Chancellor Helmut Kohl was trying to change the German constitution to tighten the nation's liberal asylum policy, which required it to take in just about anybody who uttered the word *asylum*. The only roadblock was the liberal Social Democratic Union, the number two political party, which refused to give Kohl the two-thirds majority he needed in the Bundestag to tinker with the nation's basic laws.

Dene spent three months in the refugee processing center at the French-German border. Then he was assigned to a shelter. It was a dilapidated one-story motel beneath a highway overpass in Berlin, where Easterner, Westerner, Communist, capitalist, skinhead, anarchist and foreigner all mingled in a combustible stew of conflicting agendas. Skinheads hurled bottles through windows at Dene's refugee home and sprayed graffiti on its walls. Dene, once a respected man of a certain social standing, was relegated to the role of subhuman. Just walking a boulevard, buying coffee at an outdoor café, drew disgusted looks or casual rudeness.

"Isn't it true," an old German man asked him one day as he sat in a café, "that some Africans live in trees?"

He was riding the subway one night in June 1992 when three young men got on and sat across from him. They wore leather jackets and sported shaved heads. They stared at him, muttered, then barked racist profanities. Dene stared grimly ahead. Then they stood and spat at him with such intensity that they'd finally worked themselves into enough of a frenzy to simply kick him to the floor and into unconsciousness. Dene tore ligaments in his right knee. His only pair of glasses was snapped in half. He filed a complaint, but the police never contacted him again.

His asylum application, meanwhile, was running into trouble. The Germans were demanding that he get some proof that he had been a member of the opposition. He contacted a friend in Togo to see if he would write him a letter to that effect, but the friend was noncommittal. These authorities, they didn't realize just how dangerous it was to ask someone to do something like that. There were spies everywhere, at the post office, in the telephone company.

For this reason, Dene contacted his mother-in-law in Togo only in extreme circumstances. He knew that things were bad for her. He and his wife had sent the children to private school, where they took classes that prepared them for college. But now, with no income, his mother-in-law had to move the children to public school, which prepared them for poverty.

All the people in the refugee home, particularly those who had legitimate reason to fear for their lives back home, felt a gnawing sense of transience, a feeling of floating toward some unpleasant end, on a raft bound for a waterfall. The Germans seemed intent on picking them off, nationality by nationality, until they were gone.

One day, for example, the Gypsies disappeared from Dene's refugee home. It turned out that Germany had signed a treaty with Romania that obligated Bucharest to take back Romanian citizens found living in Germany with either incomplete or missing identity papers. Germany's interior minister said that the treaty covered about 70 percent of the Romanians in Germany. Advocates for the Gypsies pointed out that probably 70 percent of the Romanians in Germany were Gypsies, who were less likely to have identity papers than were other Romanians.

Even some advocates of tougher refugee laws were aghast that the Germans would zero in on the Gypsies in such a way, considering that the Nazis murdered them by the hundreds of thousands. The Germans had reluctantly granted blanket amnesty to Soviet Jews. Why not confer the same status on the Gypsies?

For one thing, polls showed that most Germans supported tougher refugee rules, and Kohl was running for re-election. And the worsening economy made everybody meaner. The Gypsies stood out. They made up the biggest group of illegal aliens, the biggest group of official asylum-seekers, the biggest group of foreigners receiving social service benefits. The government had a logical answer for everything. But it had no public relations skills whatsoever. When the treaty was announced, the Baltic coastal town of Wismar was in its fourth day of riots outside a refugee home housing mainly Gypsies. The treaty with Romania was seen as a victory.

Down the hall from Dene lived a tiny woman, her hair wrapped tightly in a psychedelic shawl, named Natalia Muntean. She had come to Berlin in 1990 with the first wave, emerging from the Lichtenberg train station with her ten-year-old son, Fabian. She had declared asylum and had spoken vaguely about political persecution, about how her husband had been jailed for opposing the Communist despot Ceaușescu, who was long dead.

But Germany didn't consider Romania an authoritarian state anymore, and so the woman didn't have much of a case. Gypsies were being beaten up and murdered in Hungary, Czechoslovakia and, of course, Germany. They were being screamed at on buses in Rome and chased away from tourist attractions in Paris because they were presumed to be pickpockets. Mrs. Muntean had to apply a veneer of political oppression to make her story stand out, but it didn't stand up to scrutiny. Her people were disliked by Europeans in general, and that wasn't enough to win asylum in any one European country in particular.

She was here, mainly, because her kid had cancer of the larynx and couldn't talk anymore. She represented what the wealthy West derided most: economic refugees, people who took advantage of laws designed to protect the politically oppressed, when in fact all they were doing was looking to improve their financial situations. And it was true. Natalia Muntean and her kind may have been disliked, even hated and harassed, but her motives were essentially economic. She was one of the poorest people in one of the poorest countries on the continent, a place with a wretched health system that was infamous for the number of healthy people it killed, for the numbers of babies its blood transfusions inflicted with the AIDS virus. Her boy was in danger of dying of cancer and she knew that if she got on a train in Bucharest and got off in Lichtenberg and went to the refugee home in Biesdorf and demanded political asylum, he'd get good treatment at a price she could afford, which was nothing.

Of course she was an economic refugee. Capitalism was the official theology. The West demanded that Third World dictatorships and Soviet-era Stalinist states embrace free markets in exchange for aid from the one-superpower world. Yet many of these abrupt transitions caused crushing economic hardships that forced many people to flee as justifiably as if they had been running from a war. And though the West demanded free trade and open markets and commerce without borders, it wanted to make sure that no undesirable aliens were hiding in the shipping crates.

Which is why countries like Germany pressured countries like Romania to take back people like Natalia Muntean. Which is why Natalia Muntean and the rest of the Gypsies disappeared from Dene's refugee shelter one day, and why Dene and the others feared they were next.

9 losing japanese

DENE was encouraged by some unexpected news. In November 1992, the United States cut off all aid to Togo to protest the government's human rights abuses. This, he figured, would have to help his case. It didn't. Two days later, the famously liberal Social Democrats finally caved in to the will of the people. Lawmakers convened and rewrote the constitution. Just two months after the Gypsies had disappeared, Kohl and his people scored their biggest victory yet in their struggle to close off the country.

The new law required refugees to apply for asylum in the first country they entered that was considered free. Since Germany was now surrounded by countries it considered free, it figured it had built a suitable moat. The rest of the West would soon follow suit.

A reporter went down to the refugee home beneath the highway overpass to find out what people there were saying about this decision. He poked his head into a room with an open door and saw Dene, a slight man who looked older than his thirty-five years, sitting hunched on his bed in his rumpled gray suit, shoulders bunched, hair sticking out. He kept wrinkling his nose to keep his busted glasses, crudely taped at the bridge, from sliding down. A decal that said BERLINERIN SIND FREUNDLICH — Berliners are friendly — was stuck on a wall of his tiny room.

He seemed like a man overboard, shouting at the ship, too overwhelmed by the waves to be seen or heard. He was stuck in a slipstream. He sat there and talked about his predicament until the shadows climbed up the walls. He wondered where in the world he could go.

Then, sometime later, he vanished. People who worked in immigration said they were bound by confidentiality rules from saying where he'd gone, or even whether he had been there at all. He may have gone underground, or moved on to another country. Most likely he was sent back to Africa, a continent that convulsed almost inconspicuously, hemorrhaging people who flowed around the world, lost in the shadow of a dying super-power. A continent on which many people simply dreamed the same modest dreams of the prosperity promised by the new era.

———

YOU work hard, stay out of trouble, try to succeed in a place where the odds favor failure, and then it happens: Somebody notices. Somebody picks up the phone in the big bad city and calls you up in the countryside and says: You have been chosen. You have the brains and the skills and the determination to go to a better world, live a better life, learn a better way to practice your profession.

Schaack hardly knew how to handle the news. A trip to Japan, free of charge. It had never occurred to him to consider the place a part of his future, but there it was: a scholarship to study in Japan, for a year. Just like that.

Kay Schaack — just Joe to some — took every opportunity at his disposal. He was a lanky fellow with salt-and-pepper hair, thinning fast, and a thin Fu Manchu shaped like a frown. He had a round face and crinkly eyes. His skin was light, almost ochre. People said he even looked a little Japanese.

He'd moved to the northern Liberian town of Yekepa in the 1970s, some years after they'd found iron ore in the mountains. It had been, in fact, the biggest discovery of iron ore ever, anywhere. Schaack was a smart young man, worked hard, went to school. He was a little quiet, maybe, but he definitely was easy to be around. He got a job with LAMCO, the Liberian-American-Swedish Minerals Company. Training programs, overtime, extra classes, you name it. He learned welding technology, machining. Then, before you knew it, he was a mechanical engineer.

And now, here was another opportunity: studying mechanical engineering in Japan. He'd always wanted to see someplace else, get out of Liberia for a while. And now, somebody had noticed the truly fine record he'd compiled. Somebody had opened his folder and said: You, Mr. Schaack, are the one. He kissed his wife and children good-bye and off he went, to a strange and exotic place. For a year.

Tokyo suited Schaack more than he could have imagined. He loved the place. He loved the people. He loved the food. He felt like he should have been born Japanese. He studied the language every day. It was part of the package, three months' intensive Japanese. Schaack thought it was fun. He savored each new sentence like sweets after supper. Sure, he missed the family, but he hated to leave. When he did, he brought dozens of

Japanese books back with him. Learning the language was going to be his hobby, going back to Japan his goal.

Schaack came home and picked up where he left off. He got a promotion to the LAMCO vocational and technical school, teaching mechanical engineering. He and his wife, Rosana, had a few more kids. Life was pretty good up in the hills, until the new government of Sam Doe took over the business from the foreigners who ran it. Things sort of went downhill after that. Lots of people got laid off. Salaries got slashed, prices went up, food got expensive.

Schaack had always tried to avoid the echoes of the political dramas in Monrovia, where Doe tortured and killed his enemies, plundered the coffers and rigged the elections. Doe was a semi-literate ex-soldier who had managed to ruin the economy in a decade. He divided the country, exploited ethnic differences and gave his own Krahn people, who constituted a tiny minority, the idea that they were in charge. Schaack always managed to get by, to muddle through by being smart, doing his job.

But nobody could hide from what happened on Christmas Eve of 1989. Not even Doe. Especially not Doe. That was the day that Charles Taylor came back to haunt Liberia. Taylor had been Doe's chief of procurement, but he had gone too far and procured more than his fair share. He had managed to escape before Doe's men got to him. He went to the United States, but was caught and put in jail. He busted out by buying off some guards, or so he claimed. And now he was back, with an army. He invaded from the Ivory Coast, captured some countryside and, just like that, Liberia was in a war.

Word started circulating that the rebels were heading toward Yekepa, and people just started leaving. One day Schaack could

hear the boom of big guns in the distance, and the army began bringing wounded soldiers into the hospital where Rosana
worked as a nurse. That night, he was awakened by a phone call
from one of his friends.

"What're you still doing in Yekepa, brother? Everybody else
is going."

Yekepa was right on the border, just a hike through the hills
to Guinea. Schaack looked out the window and saw the long
line of headlights, snaking through the highlands. He guessed
that people really were getting out.

At daybreak, he loaded the kids and some clothes into the
car and got out of Yekepa. The Guinea border guards took advantage of the flood of refugees by extorting stuff from them as a
condition of entry. They grabbed videocassettes and other
things out of Schaack's car.

He rented a little windowless hut just over the border and
stayed there for a week. He and Rosana wanted to get to Monrovia, where they had friends and family and places to stay until
things quieted down up in Yekepa, something they figured was
inevitable.

Lots of other people must have had the same idea, because
the roads were just filled with people trying to reach the capital.
That's the way it worked. Wars broke out in the countryside
and everybody converged on the big cities, where they figured
there was food and shelter, usually not realizing that the food
sold in the city had come from the farmers who were fleeing the
interior.

Schaack and the family re-entered the country though kind
of a back door and circled wide around the war zone. They
made it to a town outside of Monrovia and stayed at the house of

a missionary couple who had adopted Rosana as a little girl and who were now back in the United States. Then Taylor's rebels stormed the area, and there was fighting all around. Schaack got the idea that maybe he should head up to his sister's house, outside Monrovia near the ore operation called Bong Mines, and see if it was secure.

Rosana Schaack told her husband not to do it, but he insisted. This place was too dangerous, and he had to scout out somewhere safer to stash his family. So he headed up there on foot and damn if he didn't run into a patrol of rebels, Taylor's rebels, along the way. They took Schaack's wedding ring and what little money he had, and one of them put him in a car and started to drive away.

"Where we going?" Schaack asked him.

"I'm gonna kill you," the rebel said, kind of matter-of-factly.

"Why you killing me for?" Schaack asked him.

The rebel wouldn't say. He just drove up to this big old satellite tracking station that the Americans had outside the capital and dragged Schaack out and pushed him up against a low wall and laid that AK-47 barrel right on Schaack's shoulder and just started squeezing off rounds. Schaack heard them as he was going down, slipping into darkness, getting used to the idea of being dead even before he hit the ground.

CHARLES Taylor, back in Liberia, leading a revolution. Nobody could believe it. He was about Schaack's age, but that's where the similarities ended. Schaack liked to blend in with the scenery; Taylor liked to chew on it, steal it, sell it. He was the product of two places, somebody who could trace his ancestry both to the indigenous people of Liberia and the repatriated American slaves who had come home and conquered them. These former slaves founded Liberia in 1847, and their dominance ensured an enduring American influence.

To the Liberians, the United States was the only foreign country that mattered. Their founding documents were based on the Declaration of Independence and the U.S. Constitution. Their currency was a facsimile of the U.S. dollar, their flag a replica of Old Glory with a single star. They named schools after Richard Nixon, John F. Kennedy. Monrovia was named after James Monroe. The cops wore copies of the New York City police uniforms. The Liberians themselves spoke in a euphonious patois that felt like some lost American dialect. Liberia was a tributary of American history, suddenly split off into African rain forest.

Liberia sent more students to the United States than any other African country, and one of them was Charles Taylor. While Joe Schaack was working as a mechanic up in Yekepa in the 1970s, Taylor was working as a mechanic in a Boston plastics factory and studying economics at nearby Bentley College. He was also the head of a group of Liberian students who wanted to end the century-and-a-half monopoly on power by the so-called Americo-Liberians, even though Taylor himself was of their blood.

He came back to Liberia in 1980, right around the time that Doe, then a master sergeant in the army, led a coup that ended the reign of these descendants of freed American slaves. Doe had members of the previous government executed on the beach for all the world to see. And Taylor, armed with brains and ambition and an American economics degree, managed to worm his way into Doe's inner circle.

Doe's indelicate style of governance didn't harm the special place that Liberia had in the U.S. sphere of influence. The United States had used the country as a military base during both world wars and as an ideological staging ground during the Cold War. Despite Doe's indiscreet killing and corruption, Liberia got half a billion dollars in U.S. aid during his dictatorship, more per capita than any other African country. It was the home of a Voice of America transmitter and a satellite tracking station and sophisticated listening post. It was the transit point for shipments of supplies to the anti-Communist rebels whom the Americans bankrolled in Angola during their proxy war with the Soviets in the 1980s. American spies gathered there to undermine Libya to the northeast. Liberia was America's special friend because Liberia was strategic.

Though Taylor would insist that he had invaded Liberia purely to topple a despot and install a democracy, there were all sorts of agendas in play. Taylor's little army, probably for lack of any other benefactor, had been trained and armed by Libya, which was bent on expanding its control over black Africa and at the same time undermining American influence in the region. And the launching pad for the invasion was the Ivory Coast, whose ruler couldn't stand Doe. Among the people Doe had killed when he took power in 1980 was the Liberian president and the president's son, who just happened to have been married at the time to the Ivorian ruler's daughter.

The Ivorian ruler was also something of a French patsy who helped protect that country's substantial economic interests in

West Africa. And he was a fierce rival of English-speaking Nigeria, the former British colony that was eager to expand its own influence in West Africa. After Taylor launched his invasion, Nigeria organized a peacekeeping force that immediately allied itself with Doe, a good friend of Nigeria's dictator. And the French enthusiastically brokered commercial deals with Taylor, whose captured territory included most of the country's mineral resources.

Few of these ulterior motives were apparent in the beginning. Charles Taylor's invasion the day before Christmas didn't even make the holiday papers back in the States. In fact, it would take weeks before anybody would even notice that something serious was going on, and years before anybody would truly care. The Berlin Wall had just tumbled, unrest was spreading across the old Soviet Bloc and the Big Red Machine itself seemed to have thrown a rod. Liberia? Right.

Doe noticed. With his usual deft touch, he sent his army into eastern Liberia and, unable to find Taylor's army, his soldiers just started raping and killing the locals and setting villages on fire. Hundreds of thousands of Liberians fled into the Ivory Coast and Guinea. Many of them joined Taylor's army, which began killing Doe's Krahn people.

Thousands of Krahn fled into Sierra Leone, on Liberia's northwestern border. Taylor's people chased them and wound up falling in with some insurgents in Sierra Leone, triggering an uprising there. Nigeria began bombing both places and at one point dropped a few on the Ivory Coast. The war got so sloppy and convoluted that a group of junior officers in Sierra Leone, all of them in their early twenties, drove to the capital to complain about their lousy wages. The dictator, fearing that a coup was afoot, ran away, leaving these young soldiers totally in charge.

So, thanks to Charles Taylor and what began as his army of mere dozens, a huge piece of the continent was destabilized. Only the Americans were missing. They'd had two ships full of U.S. Marines just off of Monrovia right at the outset, but all they did was bolt in, scoop up the fifty-nine stranded American expatriates and leave. They had enough firepower and commanded enough respect to have stopped the war and saved thousands of lives, won thousands of little loyalties. Instead, the long relationship with Liberia was abandoned to the greed of the warlords and the competing agendas of the regional powers and the economic interests of the Europeans. George Bush had been lashed for invading Panama just a few months before, and he wasn't going to go in to Liberia. Not in 1990, not with German unification unraveling the Warsaw Pact, not with relations with China made fragile by a gangland-style assault on reform in Tiananmen Square, not with land for peace possible in the Middle East, not with monumental changes afoot in world trade and nuclear arms agreements. And definitely not after Iraq invaded Kuwait and endangered U.S. oil prices. Not Liberia, not now.

More than 150,000 died, one out of every seventeen or so people in the country, most of them noncombatants. More than 80 percent of the 2.5 million Liberians were displaced, another million in Sierra Leone. Hundreds of thousands of refugees packed into squalid camps in the Ivory Coast and Guinea, and thousands of others ventured farther out, some making it as far as Europe and the United States. Liberia spun and its citizenry was flung off.

The place was insane. People were tortured, raped, mutilated, murdered. Enemy testicles hung on belts like prized pelts.
Much of the war seemed to be waged by kids, many of them
drunk or stoned on reefer. Taylor's front lines in particular were
manned, so to speak, by what people called SBUs: small boy
units. These kids had no conscience. Age brings something to a
man, cools the blood a bit. These boys, their gyroscopes weren't
quite formed yet, and they could tilt toward lunacy in a heart-
beat, which could be your last.

Right after the invasion, Taylor's army broke in two pieces.
The splinter group was run by another old enemy of Doe's, an
army lieutenant named Prince Johnson. Johnson was one of the
few soldiers who had survived an attempt to topple Doe back in
1985, one of three dozen such attempts that the dictator survived. Now *he* was back from nowhere. All these old characters
kept coming back.

Prince Johnson's army raced to Monrovia, where Doe's army
was holed up. Prince managed to grab a piece of the capital
before the West African intervention force led by Nigeria
arrived in Monrovia to give Doe's army a hand. The two sides
fought to a stalemate.

Taylor's people, meanwhile, wolfed down the rest of the
country.

SCHAACK sprawled on the ground, listening to the soldier's car
take off, thinking about how painless and peaceful death was,
thinking about Rosana and the kids and the life he was leaving
behind. He mulled things over for such a long time that, after a
while, he began to think that maybe he wasn't dead.

He sat up, felt for wounds, blood. Nothing, except a deafening ring in his ears. Maybe that rebel had decided, in the end, just to scare him. Which he certainly had done. Schaack got up and dusted himself off and started to think: What should I do? He decided to continue on to Bong Mines, find his sister's place, finish his mission.

He walked a few miles and came upon another rebel checkpoint. Taylor's people were everywhere. As luck would have it, one of the rebels was an old student of Schaack's from Yekepa.

"Hey brother, how you doin'?"

"Well, you know, just trying to get away from the war, get to Bong Mines and find my sister."

This old student of Schaack's talked to an officer, and he agreed to give Schaack a ride up there. But another officer stopped them on the way, said this wasn't exactly rebel business, so Schaack was abandoned at another checkpoint. After a time, he was able to flag down a bus heading toward Harbel, where Firestone had the world's largest rubber plantation. It was still nowhere near Bong Mines and quite a ways from his family in Monrovia, but at least it was away from this rebel checkpoint.

There were lots of displaced people up in Harbel, which was controlled by Taylor. The refugees all collected in a big camp that was starting to draw some humanitarian assistance. Schaack found himself stuck there for days, weeks, finally months, with no way of getting word back to his family, who assumed he was dead.

Then Prince Johnson's people stormed the area around Harbel and drove out Charles Taylor's troops. They took all the people out of the camp and herded them into a big hospital, probably to keep a better eye on everybody. Schaack and the other refugees just lay on the floor, crying and screaming and belting out old gospel songs while the building shook with explosions and bullets flew in through the windows.

Taylor's people won the battle and took control of the area again. Thousands of refugees decided, silently yet somehow collectively, to flee Harbel and head toward the ocean, to a town called Buchanan. Schaack knew he still couldn't cross the frontier and get back to Monrovia, so he went along. The journey took all day, and it was rough. Rebel soldiers didn't care about winning the hearts of the people, only the people's meager belongings. They'd just pull people out of line at the checkpoints and accuse them of working for the government or something. And the accused would anxiously deny whatever charge was hurled their way. There would be no investigation or anything, though. They just got shot on the spot.

Schaack got to the town and managed to find another old student of his and stayed with him. The next morning, he went down to the train station to catch the train to Yekepa. He figured maybe he could get up there and then go out through Guinea again, circle back and re-enter the country at Monrovia.

When he got to Yekepa, he found out that the rebels had taken over his house. They'd stolen everything, including his Japanese books. One of his friends who knew one of the rebels said he saw Schaack's photo album in the rebel's house. He could have it back, if he wanted. For ten Liberian dollars. Schaack paid, smiling bitterly at the thought of paying for his own photo album, the pictures of his wife and kids.

After they had finished looting and raping everybody up around Yekepa, the rebels decided to make a big show of reopening the schools. Schaack wasn't able to get out of the area, so he wound up going to work at the elementary school teaching math, making a hundred Liberian dollars a month, just enough to live on.

There was certainly no way to get to Monrovia. Doe's army and the Nigerian-led intervention force were holding half the capital, Prince Johnson's group the rest. Taylor's people had most of the countryside and controlled the border with Guinea. Schaack was pretty much confined to Taylor's territory, while his wife was stranded in the capital, which was swollen with refugees from all over the rest of the country.

Those were hard times, man. The Red Cross kept Monrovia alive, after all the dogs disappeared. The dogs ate the corpses that piled up on the beaches, and the people ate the dogs. The relief supplies were a godsend. Rosana stood in lines forever to get the little bit of rice, some cooking oil. Rosana kept moving around, going from her parents' house to Schaack's old house and then to friends' houses and then back to her parents' house, depending on which faction where was fighting which faction when.

Meanwhile, interesting developments ensued at the highest political levels. One day, Samuel Doe made a trip down to the headquarters of the Nigerian peacekeepers in Monrovia. Prince Johnson's men heard about it. They went down there, grabbed him, shot a bunch of his men and took him away while the peacekeepers just stood there, like they didn't know what to do. They took Doe off somewhere, tied him to a chair and, among other things, offered him a snack that consisted of his own severed ear. Doe had about as much fun as a fish getting cleaned. His leisurely death was videotaped for popular distribution later.

Then the peacekeepers did something smart. They appointed a dissident and former university dean, Amos Sawyer, as interim president. Sawyer was Schaack's kind of man, a teacher. Doe had thrown Sawyer in jail for a while, then exiled him. Another old enemy, back in action. Meanwhile, Charles Taylor claimed he was president. Prince Johnson claimed *he* was president. A few more factions split off. Territory was taken, mines were planted, territory changed hands, people forgot where they laid the mines. Soldiers doubled as bandits and vice versa. They raided refugee camps of rival groups, killing all the people, mostly women and children and old people, and stole all the grain.

And, every now and then, the United Nations would negotiate a cease-fire that would last just long enough to allow some people to move just far enough to be stranded somewhere unpleasant when the truce was invariably broken. One such truce went into effect in October 1991, more than a year after Schaack had left his family in Monrovia. He figured this was the time to make a move.

He needed to get to the front, but the rebel commanders wanted three hundred Liberian dollars, and Schaack only had fifty. Schaack, being a good guy, had built up a lot of goodwill among his many friends and students, so it didn't take long to raise what he needed to get approval for a ride to a town near the front, a place called Kakata.

But when he finally got there, the rebels wouldn't let Schaack pass. He spent the day in Kakata, trying to figure out how to get to Monrovia, when he ran across one of his nephews, who happened to be a rebel soldier. He got Schaack a ride to the last rebel checkpoint on the outskirts of the capital. But the rebels wouldn't let him pass through there, either.

Schaack told them he was a math teacher back in Yekepa, working for Charles Taylor's new school system. All he wanted to do was get his family and take them back. His wife was a nurse, he told them, and her skills were needed.

They decided to let him cross. After relieving him of his last fifty dollars.

Schaack walked the rest of the way, from morning to sundown. He made it to the home that his wife's foster parents owned. They were all there, his wife and six children. Right off the bat, Rosana started hollering about how angry she was with him for leaving, about how she went through hell trying to keep six kids alive during this damn war. And then she and Schaack and the kids all started crying and hugging one another, just lamenting how poor they were and how skinny they looked, how scared they had been, how happy they were that they would at least face the rest of this war together.

Rosana's foster parents in the States managed to get them some money that saw the family through some more rough times. Schaack bought a yellow Toyota wagon for three thousand Liberian dollars and turned it into a taxi in downtown Monrovia, which was packed with refugees. He charged a buck-fifty Liberian for a ride, which was a nickel in real dollars. He painted Japanese phrases on the side and used them on his puzzled customers.

"*Ohayo gozaimasu!*"

"Huh?"

"*O-hay-o goz-ai-mas-u.* It means 'good morning!'"

The streets downtown were filled with little markets where Liberians would sell each other things they had stolen from each other, and Schaack pretty much memorized the particular size and look of these bazaars as he cruised around the city all day. Every now and then a new pile of books would catch his eye, and he'd stop to see if maybe one of his Japanese primers had found its way to the capital. He needed to bone up badly. But he couldn't find anything.

The war, meanwhile, just kept getting more complicated. A bunch of the Liberian refugees that Taylor had driven into Sierra Leone formed their own army and began attacking Taylor from the west. And then, in October 1992, Charles Taylor launched Operation Octopus.

Operation Octopus was Taylor's big bid to capture the capital and lay claim to the entire country. Taylor's rebels were crazy. They even murdered five American nuns, which put Liberia on the front pages for the first time, although not for a long time. Schaack and the family just laid low. You know what it's like when you just lie on the floor, barely breathing, listening to gunshots and screams outside, and you're too scared to even light a candle? It was like that.

Taylor's men got pretty close to the capital and overran the headquarters of his old buddy, Prince Johnson, who managed to elude capture. He wound up surrendering to the Nigerians. His army, never very big, pretty much broke up after that. He'd been an interesting guy. Once, he had sat under a tree on a sunny day, playing guitar and singing "By the River Babylon," an old gospel tune. One of his men came roaring up in a jeep and made the mistake of squealing to a stop while the warlord was serenading the frightened onlookers. Prince went over to the jeep, grabbed a rifle and blew the soldier away. Then he went back and picked up the guitar and finished his song. Last anyone heard, he went to live in Nigeria.

The Nigerians, the remnants of Doe's national army and this faction from Sierra Leone all teamed up for a counteroffensive against Taylor. Taylor was driven out of the capital and he lost some land in the countryside.

The Nigerians weren't your typical peacekeepers. They bombed relief convoys, hospitals, schools, refugee camps, you name it. They couldn't pay their Liberian allies, so they'd let them loot whatever villages they'd helped them liberate. It was some sight. People would come out of the forest, see that their village was liberated, and then stand there while their liberators cleaned them out.

"That's my wife," someone would say.

"Oh yeah? Prove it," someone else would say.

Some people saw it as a war between acronyms, all of which had long ago lost their meaning. The Nigerians and their allies came to be known simply as "Ecomog," which hardly anybody remembered stood for the Economic Community of West African States Cease-Fire Monitoring Group. Taylor's group was called the NPFL, the National Patriotic Front of Liberia. There were plenty of others, like the perversely named Liberian Peace Council, one of the war's most wicked participants.

Despite party names and party platforms and other political effluvia, the war in Liberia ultimately became an ethnic feud among the Krahn and the Mandingo and the Mano and the Gio. They all had been riled up by warlords seeking to build followings by appealing to tribal loyalties. Frontiers moved like crazy. Displaced people who had moved into the homes of displaced people kept getting displaced. It was like musical chairs, though when the music stopped, some people found themselves starving to death in the forest.

During yet another cease-fire, Schaack figured it was safe enough to actually head up to Yekepa, check on the place up there. Yekepa had been a nice, modern town, and now it was wrecked. The rebels and even the local Yekepans had looted the vocational school, took all the equipment, everything. All that knowledge, all that expertise, all that gone. The mining operation itself, which had provided 70 percent of Liberia's foreign exchange, was ruined. Underground cables and water pipes had been dug up and sold across the border in Guinea, where they were melted down to make cooking pots.

He went to check on his house and just found timbers. The Nigerians had bombed it during their response to Operation Octopus. Schaack poked around in the ruins, looking for anything, looking for some of his old books. Not a thing. He went back to Monrovia.

The toughest part about life in these times was finding enough food for a big family. The United Nations was heavily engaged in Liberia, but its peacekeepers were powerless and its relief agencies administered aid with a certain bureaucratic selectivity. While many UN people worked hard and risked their lives and grieved deeply over the limits of their resources, a disproportionate amount of assistance went to the Liberians who had fled to surrounding countries, even though the people displaced *within* Liberia were dying of disease and malnutrition at a much higher rate. This was because the internally displaced didn't fit the UN's narrow definition of a refugee.

Private humanitarian groups focused heavily on this internally displaced population, but it was hard to reach the most isolated. Warlords did not want relief aid to cross their lines if it was bound for some other faction. And the United Nations would occasionally find this inhumane attitude somewhat understandable. At one point in 1993, the UN special envoy to Liberia even asked the Ivorian government to stop relief groups from entering Taylor territory through the Ivory Coast. There were tens of thousands of people pinned down near the front lines, and the mortality rate, especially among children, was almost catastrophic. Yet Taylor's enemies had complained about the aid, and the UN didn't want to endanger the latest and so far most promising peace accord. So the aid shipments were blocked, and more people died than was necessary.

For people who weren't starving in the rain forest, though, the peace plan that was reached in the summer of 1993 was cause for considerable optimism. All the factions, at least those that the peace negotiators knew about, had signed the thing. All of them agreed to pick a representative to sit on an interim governing council. All of them had even agreed on a date for elections. Schaack just prayed that this one would work.

Nothing like a little flicker of hope to put a little bounce in the step of the pedestrians whom Schaack swerved to avoid each day as he shuttled his fares in and around downtown Monrovia. He knew every piece of every place he drove past. Past the long narrow road called Wall Street, where people traded currencies. Past the seared ministry buildings and incinerated schoolhouses. Past corner after corner packed with people browsing piles of stuff stolen from every part of the country and spread on the broken concrete of the capital. And every now and then something would catch his eye, a new pile of books, and Schaack would park his yellow Toyota by a curb and take a look. And every time he'd say: Damn. Nothing.

Most poor places in Africa looked like poor places in Africa, but parts of Monrovia looked like some exceptionally tortured piece of urban America. But like the other countries on the continent, Liberia was having a hard time adjusting to the one-superpower world. These countries had few indigenous institutions on which to build a Western-style democracy. Most of them just had generals and dictators and former dictators who had grown rich on superpower patronage and stayed in power by exploiting ethnic distinctions.

But Liberia could have been different. The Americans invented the place and then spent generations manipulating it. Yet when it no longer served a useful purpose, they let it go, let it die, with no more remorse than Liberia's murderous armies.

The peace plan signed that summer wouldn't last. Charles Taylor would again wage war in the capital. Schaack and his family would again have to take their chances on the road, walking seven miles down a beach while soldiers robbed and raped and slaughtered civilians all around them. Dressed in rags, carrying no bags lest they tempt a bandit, Schaack would shepherd his family across the sand as shells exploded and shots rang out, praying that nobody would go to the trouble of killing them. They would finally climb aboard a freighter bound for the Ivory Coast, amazed to be alive.

Liberia's endlessly mutating factions would violate two dozen truces and a dozen formal peace accords before they would finally stop tormenting the country long enough to agree to a free and fair election. Voters would have a wide choice of candidates. But they would pick the person with the most name recognition, the one with the biggest army and the most resources looted from the iron ore and diamond and timber industries in the countryside. The one with the most stolen radio transmitters, and therefore the most effective media campaign. Charles Taylor would win in a landslide. Some Liberians would figure that maybe he'd stop destroying the country if he were finally in charge.

It would take several years of pointless suffering to get to that point, though. Years of lying low while the killers and bandits roamed the streets, years of standing in line to get a little maize from a relief group, years of driving a beat-up Toyota cab during periods of peace, a little pamphlet of religious inspiration entitled "Comfort for the Depressed" resting next to the stick shift between the seats. Years of going through stacks of stuff on the street, looking for a pleasant piece of a fading past.

He kept it up for a while, looking at the piles of books. But he couldn't find what he wanted. The words got harder to remember. One by one, they just disappeared. He wasn't really practicing anymore. Mostly, it was gone.

10 stick people

I T WAS HARD. Take the girl from Tampa, four years old, burned over 80 percent of her body, yet totally coherent. And the nurses in ER talked to her, soothed her and distracted her and told her things, anything except that she would be OK.

"We have to put some medicine in you."

"We have to put a little tube inside your bladder."

"We're here to help you."

"We're doing what we can."

The little girl lay on the table in ER and responded lucidly and quietly, despite the fact that her skin was destroyed, her corneas burned off. Mary peeled off the kid's underpants, and the girl said "Don't touch me there!" It was obviously something her mother had told her, something she said with such strength and conviction that Mary and the pediatrician started to cry. They knew this tough little girl would be dead within three days. And she was. Jesus, that was hard.

How hard? The ups were as harrowing as the downs. Take the twelve-year-old, horsing around with his friend, playing with their parents' guns, for God's sake. And the kid comes into ER with a hole in his head. A hole, in his head. Bits of brain tissue speckled across his hair. You checked him in and did what you could and then shipped him off, figuring he'd check out via the basement morgue. But no: The kid and his leaky head were repaired and sent home. Left without any, as they say, deficit in mental capacity.

Hard? You had to be. Which is why Mary preferred to work in ER. They came in, usually unconscious, and then they were gone. You had a lot of people at once, you could deal with them fast, bang, bang, move on. No follow-up. No time to form a bond or get too hung up on what was going to happen to the wrecked body and the person inside it. But if they woke up, made eye contact, especially a kid, it was tough to be hard.

Part of it was the adrenaline, too. The rush of working fast. It was hard to explain, but for sixteen years Mary chased emergency rooms. She liked to travel, move around. She took advantage of the fact that there was a seemingly eternal shortage of nurses. She joined traveling nurse's associations, which plugged necessary nurses into understaffed urban hospitals across the country. Tampa General. LA Children's. Mount Carmel, North Fulton, St. Mary's, whatever. Three weeks here, six months there. She even spent a year in an ambulance.

And, no matter where she went, if some kid came in with serious damage, somebody would say, "Mary, you take her. It reminds me too much of my own kids." They knew she didn't have kids. They knew she could handle anything. They knew if they asked that she'd say OK. They didn't know how horrible it made her feel.

You had to build a wall. A sense of detachment. When you're crying, sad, you can't think clearly. People figured you were callous and uncaring, but it was just the opposite. You had to be dispassionate to do a good job. The patients and their families didn't always appreciate that. They got rude and sometimes even violent. She got kicked, spat upon, threatened with lawsuits. One time a guy got out of bed and punched her in the face.

The foreigners, Mary found, the people from poor countries, they listened. They showed respect. They came back when they were supposed to. The Latinos, for instance. Mary Lightfine got the idea that she wanted to work overseas. Humanitarian relief. Get away from this country, away from the Americans, who took things for granted and then resented the quality of help they got.

She started to check around, but she couldn't figure it out. Médicins Sans Frontières? Doctors Without Borders? How do you break in? It seemed like just doctors, not nurses. She started taking on short-time tours as a nurse on cruise lines, just to get some overseas experience. It wasn't close to what she wanted. Then, she got an offer to work in Saudi Arabia. Not exactly humanitarian relief, though the money was good and it was overseas. The Saudis always needed Westerners.

She was all set to take the job when she decided to visit her mother on the farm in Ohio, the farm with the horses that her mother had promised the kids if they came with her when she walked out on Dad. While she was there she glanced at a newspaper, *The Columbus Dispatch,* and on the front page of Section B was a story about a local doctor who happened to have just returned from two weeks of doing what Mary wanted to do all the time.

LANCASTER, Ohio — Dr. Henry Hood doesn't remember the name of the little boy in the photograph.

There were too many patients and too few days for Hood to form lasting bonds during the two weeks in December that he volunteered his medical skills in a bloody civil war in Somalia.

Mary read about this war, about how half a million people were displaced, how the number of dead had reached twenty thousand. How this hospital where Dr. Hood had worked would get seventy-five casualties in a single day, how nearly a third of the people who made it into ER never made it out of ER. Speed plus volume equals adrenaline. Whoosh.

"This is for me," she thought. "This is what I'm going to do."

She casually mentioned to her mom that she was thinking about going to work in Somalia, sort of soft-pedaling the situation over there. Back then, in January 1992, nobody knew anything about what was going on in Somalia, except for people like Dr. Henry Hood. Mary tracked him down through Information. She'd already heard about this guy; he was an orthopedic surgeon who sometimes loaned his estimable services to this little hospital where she'd sometimes worked. Supposedly a great guy. A real humanitarian.

"It's not easy," he told her when she called. "It's a war situation."

Mary figured: What could they show me I haven't seen? A new type of gunshot wound, a new kind of stab wound? A carload of crash victims on every table? Hah.

Dr. Henry Hood worked with a small relief organization called the International Medical Corps, and he hooked her up with the right people. They sent her some forms, interviewed her on the telephone, basically decided to take her on without a lot of processing or preparation.

"You realize it's an emergency situation?" they asked her. "Lots of war wounded?"

She figured she knew. That's what she wanted. So four weeks after she'd read that article, she was on a plane to, of all places, Somalia. Obscure and distant Somalia, a place that made it into the papers only if there was some handy local angle.

A little plane had picked her up in Nairobi, just her and this strange freelance pilot who kind of gave her the willies as they soared over the arid scrubland. They landed at the airport in Mogadishu. The place was quiet, desolate almost. It was surrounded by these Islamic-style buildings all shot to pieces. A bunch of skinny guys wearing what looked like dresses were running around with AK-47s, and they ran and grabbed her bags. Were they stealing them? She wasn't sure. Then she noticed a couple of guys in T-shirts on the tarmac, who turned out to be from her new relief group. They welcomed her and led her to their truck, which was packed with more skinny guys carrying guns, hanging out the windows and riding on the roof.

They drove through the city. Mary wasn't prepared for these beautiful old Italian villas, all the marble and ceramic. All bombed out and shot up, framed by blooming bougainvillea. They took her to the group's compound, an exquisite villa with a stone wall around it and guards all over. They sent her to the hospital, Digfer Hospital, and told her to go to work.

She wasn't quite sure what to do. There was garbage all over the place and the exterior was riddled with bullet holes. Patients slept on the floor. There was no equipment; it had all been stolen. And so she just went to work, helping the Somali surgeons as best she could in what turned out to be a factory of open fractures and eviscerations, people lying around with their intestines outside their bodies.

She couldn't figure out these Somali surgeons. Somebody would come in and the surgeon would disappear to go have tea and the victim would die on the table. Or somebody would come in and the surgeons would say they felt sick, their mother was sick, or they had to go to the bathroom, and they'd come back and the patient would be dead.

Gradually, she began to understand. Some of these patients belonged to different clans than the doctors, and the surgeons were afraid of being blamed if a putative enemy died while they worked on him. They knew that the rival clan would kill the doctor's family. So they would try to save face by coming up with excuses for not touching a patient from another clan. After a while, Mary began compiling what she called "101 Excuses Not to Operate."

She even found out that it was too dangerous to screen blood for HIV, because there was no confidentiality in the lab. If someone had the AIDS virus, then word got out, and it tainted not just the victim but his or her family and extended family, which was the clan. She heard that AIDS carriers were often murdered. It was smarter, anyway, if nobody knew whether someone had the virus. What difference would it make? You're going to refuse a transfusion because the blood might kill somebody in five years? What about right now? People died constantly, from disease, from infections, from whatever.

And the rapes. Women in Somalia almost always had their genitals ritualistically mutilated, with the remains of their vaginas sewn together. It supposedly made the women seem more virginal. And sometimes these killers, the people responsible for the war, they'd cut open women from rival clans, gang-rape them and then pour kerosene inside and set them afire.

Mary gritted her teeth every day and took on the wearying task of trying to convince surgeons to operate on people from different clans, or people who had no family. Having no family, no power base, was like having nothing. The families made sure the patients got fed, got treatment. They were your advocates, and if you had no family you lay in the hallway until you died. It was so sad. You couldn't monitor every patient to make sure he or she got that needed amputation, got those antibiotics. You'd go home, come back and the person you thought would have been treated was, instead, just dead.

She'd get outraged by the fact that the doctors and nurses themselves would steal from the hospital. Once, the hospital got a shipment of Valium to relax the muscles of patients who had tetanus. And the doctors and nurses took it all home and zonked out. And they would order extra supplies for fictitious patients and then keep the stuff for themselves, or just sell it.

The pure heartlessness, it took your breath away. One day, one of the peddlers who tried to make a living around Mogadishu, a man who carved little stick figurines and tried to sell them to the relief workers, he made the mistake of trying to push his way through the gate of the compound where Mary lived. One of the guards shot him in the leg. The doctors and nurses ran out, brought him in, patched him up. But he'd lost a lot of blood, and they went to his family and said: We need your blood.

"We will give you blood if you pay us," they said.

Pay for blood to keep your brother, your son, your father alive? Nobody could believe it. So all the relief workers who matched the wounded man's type donated the blood, eleven bags of it. The guy lived, but he lost a leg.

Gradually, she began to understand the callousness all around her, why even the doctors stole and played clan politics and let people die. Everything had broken down. Everything was in lethally short supply. You had to stick with your own kind to survive. These surgeons were in a survival mode, just like the patients. They had to scratch and claw to stay alive, just like everybody else. If you and your family had no food, no shelter, no security, no medical care, you'd do anything you could to get it. Which is why 70 percent of the medicine and supplies donated to the hospital never made it to the patients, but went right back out the front door and was sold brazenly on the street.

Mary understood, perhaps too well. After a few months, she began to realize that the Somalis with the keenest survival skills kept getting stronger, at the increasing expense of a broadening pool of the weak. She began to realize that some of these doctors weren't just coping; they were stealing enough to get rich. She began to realize that most of the people who got treated had cash or connections or simply a gun. She began to realize that most of the people in the hospital beds were soldiers whose only need was a place to sleep. And if you told them to go, they threatened to kill you.

One day, on her perpetual hunt for space, she came across a bed that was unoccupied save for a strange wooden container. She picked it up and walked out into the hallway.

"Bomba! Bomba!" the Somalia nurses screamed when they saw her.

Mary began to realize that sometimes the soldiers would leave what they claimed were little bombs on their beds as a way of reserving them. This bomb didn't explode, and Mary took a post-op patient and put him in the soldier's bed. The soldier came back and threatened to kill Mary, but, fortunately, she managed to talk him into letting her live.

After a while, Mary got even harder, built by far her most formidable wall. Some of the other expatriates, though, they couldn't get a handle on it. They suffered what she called Helping Syndrome. They kept trying to get journalists to adopt babies, or they kept smuggling their own food to a particular patient they decided was somehow special. The hospital had four hundred kids, and this one nurse had an intense need to nurture this one baby girl. Finally, the mother said, "You are in a better position to take care of my child than me. It is yours." The kid was abandoned by her mother, by her clan, all because this nurse had singled the child out. This girl was now a pariah, somebody without a family. The relief group had to place her somewhere, pay for her upbringing.

This is what happened if you went soft. If you tried to do something special for one Somali, you had to do it for all of them. If you hired one clan, you became a target of the other. The jealousy could be fatal. That's why you couldn't let your heart go out to that one particularly pathetic-looking kid. It just made things worse.

The threat of death was part of the workday. Every week somebody stuck a gun in Mary's face. You check the fuel in the generator and someone threatens you, because they're stealing fuel and would rather you not make a fuss about it. You fire a bad driver and he comes back and pumps bullets into the villa. And your guards, they let him on the grounds because he comes from a stronger clan.

The guns, everywhere and in every hand, were unconscious expressions of emphasis. One day, one of the hospital administrators came up to Mary, waving a gun in her face, telling her in broken English that she had to come to his room, right now. Mary was frightened and did as she was told. They went into his room and a few other men were there, waiting, eyeing her. Mary braced herself for the worst. Then the hospital administrator took some powdered milk and poured it into a blender. He made everybody milkshakes. That was it. He was making milkshakes for some people and wanted her to join them.

Some people couldn't take it. One day, after a little bacchanalian R and R in Nairobi, some colleagues were coming back on the plane, heading toward Somalia, when this one guy just flipped out. He tried to open the door of the plane and jump out.

"I gotta get out of here!" he shouted while the other passengers held him back.

Mary worked, not even thinking. The wall held, grew stronger. She stuck tubes in chests and assisted in meatball surgery and basically did all sorts of things that she'd have been sued for back in the States. And then, every now and then, after it seemed as though she'd built a suitable fortress around herself, somebody would come in and manage to put a little crack in the wall, just for a minute.

Like the guy with the foot infection. He was a nomad who'd wandered around with his camels and his family until the civil war forced him to flee to Mogadishu, to the city, where the warlords and looters allowed a little relief to get to the hungry in exchange for huge bribes. Mary and a doctor looked at his foot and told him: Sorry, it's got to come off.

He just sat there for a moment, then started to tell a little story. How he once had 108 camels and how the gangs had come and taken 107. How he and his family grew so hungry that he finally had been forced to slaughter this last camel to feed his four daughters. How the gangs had watched him butcher the camel and then came over, grabbed each of his four daughters and cut their throats while he watched. How they had taken the camel meat and left.

And now, here he was, a nomad, the millennial descendant of Somalia's earliest inhabitants, and he was going to lose a foot. A shepherd who had lost a foot truly had lost everything.

Mary saw the impact of this war on the nomads sometime in May, three months into her mission, when she went with some people from Médicins Sans Frontières out into the Somali countryside. MSF was a very cool relief group founded in France. It sort of set the standard for everybody else. Mary was quite pleased to accompany them on an assessment of the health situation in a town called Baidoa.

Life in Mogadishu was dangerous and hard, but not quite impossible. But out in the countryside, where the fighting had displaced and isolated vast populations, death came at a deeper discount. Baidoa had filled up with refugees, but nobody could get enough food to the place, nobody could get through the gauntlets of terror and extortion that the clans had established. Mary went out to Baidoa with her colleagues and she saw scores, hundreds, thousands of skeletons strewn across the 160 miles of road that linked it to Mogadishu. Places where people had just dropped and died while their relatives went on, too weak to bury their dead. And then inside the town, these stick people, these little leathery sacks of obscenely defined bones, crowding a market where the only thing being sold was charcoal. Mary went to the hospital, and a man greeted her by dying, as if on cue.

She was struck by how the killers and crooks and con artists had seemed to accumulate in Mogadishu, the treacherous capital, while the nomadic herders and farmers out here in the countryside were truly the biggest victims of the war and the cruel migrations it had forced. These people had no food. Rival clans had filled the wells with stones and debris, so they had no water. They were helpless. Totally helpless. They were all dying. That was the assessment. They were all dying. Is anybody listening?

You had to blow off steam. Friday was the day that everybody had off. Mary had never been much of a party animal, but she learned to become one. She'd quit smoking seven years earlier, but she started again in Somalia. People would come here and they'd find themselves doing things they never would have imagined doing back home. They ate, smoked, drank and screwed each other with perfunctory rapacity. They indulged openly and easily and excessively. Last night on earth? Get drunk, get high, get laid, get through it. Reporters seduced nurses, American women had these amazingly explosive chemical reactions with French men, and French men consumed large quantities of tantalizingly exotic Somali women, those biblical beauties with swanlike necks who never said no because they wanted to go away, go West. Instead, they lost their reputations, their virtue, their standing with the clan. Maybe more. Some of these Somali women, after exhausting their male options, even propositioned the expatriate women.

People talked about everything with an easy intimacy that just didn't exist among large groups of people on the outside. They would sit up at night dissecting the most painfully personal parts of their lives. And they'd make jokes about things that weren't really funny, that would have seemed sick to someone who didn't live this life. Mary drew comic strips constantly to entertain her colleagues, morbid stuff that made people both laugh and cringe. Like a comic strip depicting a Somali with a bullet hole in his head, and the doctor telling him to take two aspirin.

To the outsiders, like the occasional journalist who'd drop in for a sniff of Somalia, it looked decadent and callous. But they didn't have to stay here and do what Mary did. They could vent by getting on a plane and leaving.

Sometimes, the French and American doctors and nurses and logisticians that Mary hung out with would take a convoy of minibuses out of the city to the coastline, to a little village where they could hang out on the beach and have a picnic and even buy fish from the fishermen. The hell and the smell of humanity at its worst seemed so far away. She and a bunch of other relief workers decided to head out to the coast one Friday in November 1992, the thirteenth as it turned out.

It wasn't a good day. The sea was rough and churning and the clouds got thick and dark. Everyone, maybe fifteen or twenty people, decided to pile into the buses and head back earlier than usual because the weather was going to make it get dark sooner. Everybody feared the night in Somalia. Nobody wanted to get stuck on a road in the evening.

No one said very much on the trip back to Mogadishu. The clouds roiled and the light was too dim too early. Everyone was edgy. Mary stared at the horizon, the threatening weather, and suddenly she saw four or five figures, crouched down and running across the road just up ahead.

"Something is wrong," she started to say, but things were already happening.

The drivers of the three vehicles carrying the relief workers just stopped. The guards on the roofs jumped off and started to fan out. Mary heard shots. Then the bullets started coming inside the bus.

"I'm getting out of here!" shouted one of the relief workers, an American. He jumped out of the bus and took off. Another guy followed. Mary and a few others flattened themselves on the floor and started shouting questions at the driver.

"What's going on!"

"Why are they shooting at us?"

"Maybe they want to steal our vehicle. How do we tell them they can *have* our vehicle?"

"Jesus, we're all going to die now."

The driver finally just floored it. A girl next to Mary saw a bullet fly over Mary's hairline. It must have hit the guy next to her, because he shouted, "I've been hit!"

He was lying next to Mary. He turned white and broke out in a sweat and put his hands between his legs. Mary thought he must have been hit between the legs and he's going into shock.

The people in the bus finally saw some members of the small contingent of UN observers. The clans routinely bossed the observers around, actually limited how many people the UN could post at the seaport and airport, just so the world body

177

wouldn't get any ideas about interfering with the looting and extortion and blackmail of humanitarian agencies.

In this case, though, the UN escorted the bus back and helped track down the others who'd jumped out. As it turned out, nobody was killed. The one guy who'd been shot just had been hit in the arm. Jesus, what a day.

All this time, Mary Lightfine had no real sense of how the rest of the world felt about this seriously malfunctioning section of it. She didn't know that the world largely ignored the place until sometime around the middle of her tour, when the sheer number of people starving to death began to rouse a lot more humanitarian agencies, a lot more reporters and a lot more film crews who panned across communities of future corpses in towns like Baidoa. She didn't know that the reports they sent back began to bring shame to the Western nations that had the strength to stop this suffering but didn't.

Mary Lightfine was burrowed far too deeply inside Somalia to get a sense of what the world was thinking. She only knew that a day didn't go by when the place didn't threaten and confound her, and that any foreigners who decided to come here had better make a serious effort to understand how it worked, how it got this way, how things just fell apart. Otherwise, terrible surprises would await them.

11 mission creep

THE father was raised to be a carpenter, and his son grew up to be a civil engineer. The grandson? Pure entrepreneur. It was the son who turned his father's humble trade into a construction company that bore his father's name. But it was the grandson who built the Xule Co. into the biggest contractor in town.

One of the keys to the grandson's success could be described in just two words: government contracts. It paid to please the people in charge, particularly if they were in charge of virtually everything in the country. And it paid to perform work for the international agencies, since they came to town with money to spend. And it paid to curry favor with the superpowers because, well, they were in charge of the world.

Pleasing everybody was one of the hardest things to do in Somalia, but the three generations of men who ran the Xule Co. did it pretty well. They hired people from different clans so the staff would reflect the nation, so the company would look like Somalia, if you will.

Well, maybe not exactly. Somalia was, at heart, a nation of lethally quarrelsome goat herders. It was, deep down, not really a nation. In the age of antiquity, the Egyptians knew Somalia as a place called Punt, the land of myrrh trees and little else. The nomads who became Somalis wandered in from Ethiopa a thousand years ago, claiming a harsh land as unforgiving as themselves.

Because the fickle climate and indifferent soil made life rough, these migrants coalesced into various groups that became clans and subclans and sub-subclans ruled by various chiefs and sultans and elders who presided over fiefdoms and independent states that frequently waged arcane and seemingly eternal blood feuds among themselves. They were colonized in the nineteenth century by the Europeans, who coveted the region's long Indian Ocean coastline and lucrative trade route to the Red Sea. The combative Somalis got a lesson in war on a grandly Western scale when the Italians, who controlled the south, and the British, who controlled the north, took turns driving each other out of the place during World War II. The two pieces of what became Somalia were welded together when the colonial masters granted them independence in 1960.

Nationhood was hard, however. The old turf battles seemed insurmountable. The closest any leader came to binding together all the factions, albeit with barbed wire, was Major General Mohamed Siad Barre, a former shepherd who seized power in 1969. He declared the country a socialist state and moved Somalia and its strategic entrée to the Red Sea into the sphere of the Soviets. In return, the Somalis got guns.

And Xule Co. got contracts. Somebody had to build bases

and barracks and homes for Soviet advisers. This relationship lasted until 1977, when Somalia orchestrated an uprising by ethnic Somalis in neighboring Ethiopia. The Soviets sided with the Ethiopians, who had an even more attractive access to the Red Sea. Ethiopia drove the rebels out, along with 2 million refugees. The United States stepped in as Somalia's new patron and took over the Soviets' old naval base. In return, the Somalis got guns.

And Xule Co. got more contracts. Somebody had to remodel those Soviet buildings to suit the Americans and their 110-volt tastes and their preference for fancier bathrooms. By then, the grandson was running the business, and business was good. Mohammed Abdi Abdulli helped lay the concrete for the new U.S. Embassy complex, a very big job. When Siad Barre courted World Bank assistance and International Monetary Fund projects, Xule got contracts to build their offices. And when the civil war broke out in December 1990 and Siad Barre was deposed, business finally went bad.

For two decades Siad Barre had been a master of manipulating clan jealousies to keep his enemies weak and divided, but the old laws of strongman civics didn't work as well in the new world. Like his Cold War counterparts across the continent, he just didn't understand the forces of change, the demands for democracy, the petitions and rallies and complaints of human rights violations. He arrested his critics and had them shot. He went to a soccer match and got booed, and his guards responded by brainlessly pumping bullets into the crowd, killing more than a hundred people. Rebellions broke out in the countryside and then moved into Mogadishu, the capital. Siad Barre ran for his life, and so did Abdulli.

"The city was crazy," Abdulli told people afterward, shaking his big hairy head. "Cannons going off, looting, people killing each other. Crazy."

Abdulli barely got out with his wife and children. He flew to Djibouti, a tiny country on the northern border. He was a relatively wealthy refugee without revenue. He lost a bulldozer, a crane, four cement mixers, eighteen dump trucks, half a million dollars in building materials and the lives of twenty-one of his four hundred employees. He waited for the hostilities to ebb, for somebody to take over and exert control so he could come back. Anybody.

The clans that had toppled Siad Barre began fighting among themselves for control of the capital and the country. The chaos of land changing bloodstained hands triggered even larger mass movements of people. Gangs of looters seized the meager resources. They ripped the tin rooftops off homes and stole electrical wiring so they could sell the stuff in Kenya. They took the pumps that irrigated the crops. They plundered schools and hospitals right down to the light fixtures. They wrecked the factory that made farm tools. Half a million Somalis fled the country, most to neighboring nations such as Kenya, though many made it to Europe and beyond.

More than 700,000 were damned to be displaced inside the country. Most were herders and growers whose existence already had been threatened by serious drought. The larders of food they kept for such times were depleted. They were forced to flee from looters and rival clans. Some formed their own bands and raided other villages, forcing the fresh victims to follow suit. A new type of economy emerged.

Many people journeyed toward places they heard had humanitarian aid, and the roads to those places were littered with bodies. Malnutrition made everyone incrementally more susceptible to the country's copious carte du jour of infectious diseases. The fighting, running, banditry and bad weather formed a compound of circumstances more deadly than the sum of the individual parts. Under the cover of internecine carnage that no outside nation wanted to touch, huge numbers of people began dying, thousands each day. Journalists wrote stories and took pictures. But many editors passed. Fighting and famine in Africa? This is news?

The Americans weren't going to get involved, not with a presidential election in November. Too many other things were going on. It had become more and more obvious that Saddam Hussein was committing something akin to genocide against the abandoned Shiites in southern Iraq, so the United States ordered the Iraqis to keep their aircraft out of their own southern skies. After more than a year of neglecting a region that the Persian Gulf War had left in lethal tumult, the Americans finally dispatched fighter jets to at least limit Saddam's ability to eradicate a portion of his people.

But the numbers in Somalia got so big. This astounding footage of desert vistas filled with living skeletons, dying forlornly. And then President Bush got beat by Bill Clinton and had a couple of months to kill, waiting for his term to run out. With nothing on the agenda but posterity, a lame-duck president willed the rest of the world to rally around an American-led relief effort. To Somalia.

"History is summoning us once again to lead," he said.

After acquiring a UN stamp of approval, the Americans said they would send a fighting force into a sovereign nation that was posing no threat to any other country, but was just quietly off in a corner, mutilating itself. All it was doing to offend other countries was bleeding refugees.

An army was built that was unmatched in its combination of potency and purity of purpose. United States Marines, French Legionnaires, British commandos, Canadian paratroopers and contingents from two dozen other countries were sent to secure safe corridors to eight cities so aid could travel unmolested to the dying. They moved across the flat Somali savanna dotted with scrub and the occasional acacia, cutting a safe trail for convoys carrying food and medicine. They strode like giants among the crowds of people so astoundingly skeletal they seemed a freakish new species spawned by a god gone insane.

Abdulli the builder was back in Mogadishu in an instant. Actually, he had tried to come back several times. Whenever there had been a lull in the three-year orgy of killing, he would slip home, coax workers out of hiding, buy equipment off the black market, root out suppliers, set up an office, ready to start again. Three times, he was driven back into hiding.

Then, when the United States arrived with the thirty-nation army, Abdulli thought: This is my market. He opened a small office. He hunted up workers, bid on contracts. In the beginning, it was just military. But in a matter of weeks, the United Nations began expanding. Its bureaucracy ballooned until it physically overshadowed the military presence. In no time at all, Abdulli was lining up work.

Three weeks into the mission, some dubbed it a success. There were still random murders and occasional hijackings, sure. It seemed as if everybody with a temper had a gun and a pocketful of *khat,* the stimulating shrub that many Somalis chewed for an edgy buzz. Pulling a trigger in anger was as natural as balling a fist. But it was nothing like before.

The mission was going so well that Bush himself decided to visit Somalia, sort of a last hurrah before vacating the Oval Office. He came down to spend New Year's with the troops and survey their impact. The nation was being fed. It was coming back. The warlords and their gangs of thugs and killers had largely slunk to the sidelines, a bit awed and intimidated by the Americans and their allies.

Mary Lightfine and some other refugee workers went down to the U.S. Embassy compound to see the president. They got close as he moved among the troops, almost got a chance to shake his hand. He was wearing desert camouflage, the chocolate-chip design made famous by the Persian Gulf War. The festivity of the moment, the sense of triumph was so overwhelming that even some Somalis declared Bush "the president of Somalia." Reality set in that evening, when two clans waged a battle in the capital.

It was New Year's Eve, and Mary's relief group was hosting a big party inside their compound. They moved banquet tables and marble-topped coffee tables and embroidered Italian love seats out into the courtyard, beneath the palm trees and bougainvillea. They picked flowers and placed eye-catching arrangements all over the party zone. The servants brought out platters of goat and gigantic whole fish. The guests came from all over, from MSF and various UN agencies. Some American soldiers that Mary had met during the Bush visit managed to slip away from their posts for a forbidden taste of sweet intemperance.

When the fighting began in a distant part of the city, the partygoers climbed onto the rooftop. Mary watched the orange and red explosions in the sky and thought about that line, that lyric, the bombs bursting in air, and wondered if this is what Francis Scott Key saw when he scribbled his poem about American fortitude. She took another hit on another joint. It was time to dance. She and the others came back down and returned to their revelry, to their appetites, smoking pot, chewing *khat*, pairing off and passing out. They drank and danced and devoured each other until, at midnight, they opened the cases of champagne that they eventually wound up spraying on each other. They laughed hysterically. They'd made it to 1993. Somebody strummed a guitar. Mary danced while the capital rocked with the thunder of war.

The fighting had been triggered when one clan tried to capture the weapons cache of another clan. They marked the new year with tank, artillery and mortar rounds. The wounded were dragged to the hospital, where doctors from many countries tried to stitch people sliced by shrapnel, many of them noncombatants caught in the crossfire. For the first time since the Americans had arrived, there was combat in the capital, and it raged as the American president slept on an aircraft carrier just offshore, as Western relief workers finally slipped into stupor on the other side of town. The fighting didn't last long, not much past sunrise. But it was not a good sign.

That morning, Bush flew to the famously recovering city of Baidoa. It got the most publicity and therefore the most aid because the misery was highly concentrated, conveniently epic, many of its hundred deaths a day easily filmable in one continuous pan. It became a test case in how to shock-treat mass starvation with a disproportionate influx of assistance, and it was being held up as a model of recovery.

Bush went to an orphanage, where he accepted a red garland of flowers that he wore over his camouflage shirt. He walked among smiling, clapping children, shaking hands with kids and teachers. He came back to the Mogadishu airport and gave one more pep talk to the troops. And then he was gone, off to Moscow to meet with Boris Yeltsin and sign the biggest nuclear arms reduction treaty ever, a document that formally ended the superpower arms race.

Now that he had saved Somalia, what next? Bush was resisting UN pressure for Washington to expand its mandate to include the disarming of the combatants who were bristling with three decades' worth of arms supplied by the superpowers. He resisted assisting the rebuilding of the shattered society, resisted keeping the troops around until a stable government — something Somalia had never really had — was formed. That would be up to the United Nations. As soon as the UN organized its own peacekeeping force, the Americans were *gone*.

On the flight out of Mogadishu, his aides complained to the presidential press corps that the United Nations wasn't getting its act together very quickly. More than a month into the mission, and the bureaucrats still hadn't come up with a good plan for replacing the U.S. military, as if that were possible.

In May 1993, ready or not, the United Nations took over command of the mission itself and the vast grounds of the U.S. Embassy. A new city sprang up behind its high walls. Big international builders got big international contracts.

But Abdulli got a lot of the ancillary stuff, like hauling waste, repairing roads and buildings, building storm sewers, digging sewerage lines. He formed a joint venture with a South Carolina firm that had fixed roads and catered peacekeeper camps in Croatia, Cambodia and Kuwait. Soon, they had twenty contracts worth $3.6 million. The grandson was earning $300,000 a month. And he was on the short list of bidders to build a base camp for a couple of dozen Ukrainian helicopter pilots who were coming in to help save Somalia, now that Ukraine itself was an independent country. Abdulli was on a roll.

He had an office in a trailer on a back lot of the vast U.S. Embassy compound. When the Marines commanded the mission, it was a postapocalyptic encampment, a harsh haven of shelled buildings plundered to the bones. Now, under the United Nations, it was being transformed into some sort of dreamscape of weirdly symmetrical, prefabricated office buildings laid out in lines and right angles and humming with hundreds of air-conditioners. Commissaries from a phalanx of foreign countries sold booze, burgers, CD players, sunscreen and I-survived-Somalia sweatshirts. There were horseshoe rings, volleyball courts, softball diamonds. The place was crawling with people who made a living building and planning and consulting and photocopying in the crisis points on which the UN decided to descend. So much cash was flying around that somebody even managed to pocket $3.9 million from a UN filing cabinet. From November of 1993 until February 1994, the United Nations was budgeted to spend $330 million on *itself*.

And not one bent Somali shilling of this was going to rebuild a building or clear a road used by actual Somalis, who hovered ravenously outside the gates of this surreal global village. Every bit of profit that Abdulli was raking in was being made off the United Nations' efforts to construct for itself a gigantic infrastructure in a country that some people, like the Americans, were beginning to think about abandoning.

Abdulli, the most enterprising of three generations of builders, was a fat and friendly man of forty-eight with a degree in commerce and a mind that could scroll instantly to exact dates, terms of contracts, estimates of earnings, causes of death and degrees of destruction. He sat in his office one day and entertained a visitor. Tons of heavy equipment from dozens of contractors were parked outside in the searing heat. He was preoccupied with the fact that the latest incarnation of the family business was built on something only slightly less transitory than a displaced nomad: global interest in his country. But the alternative — pouring money into Somalia itself — made even less sense.

"I would rather the money goes to the community, the rehabilitation of schools, hospitals, water service," he told his guest, an American reporter. "But right now, it would be a waste. Somalis still can't manage themselves. They kill for power, they kill for looting, they kill for food."

Much of the reluctance to rebuild was the fault of warlords like Mohammed Farah Aidid, who controlled half of Mogadishu. He had tolerated the initial United States–led intervention. The Americans had insisted so loudly that they had no interest in disarming the militias that Aidid must have felt very reassured. And even though the Americans were still manipulating the mission after they had passed titular command to the United Nations, Aidid viewed the changeover as a real threat to his power.

The UN mandate was politically broader and more invasive. The United Nations wanted to disarm and rebuild. It was organizing district governing councils that Aidid viewed as a challenge to his authority. It was trying to form police forces that Aidid saw as competition for his militias. So he organized rallies that turned into riots. He authorized attacks on convoys. He boycotted UN meetings.

When the UN took command of the operation, peacekeepers began hunting for Aidid's arsenals in an attempt to weaken his power. And Aidid responded. On June 5, his men ambushed a patrol of Pakistani peacekeepers out hunting for his guns, killing twenty-four of them.

The UN Security Council ordered Aidid tracked down. A $25,000 price was put on his head. American aircraft and UN troops battered Aidid's house, his headquarters, his various strongholds, killing some innocent Somalis in the process. But Aidid eluded death and capture.

Militiamen began blowing up American convoys with remote-control mines. President Clinton sent in U.S. Army Rangers and members of the elite Delta Force special operations team. Their mission: get Aidid.

A few weeks later, a U.S. Army Cobra fired into a crowd of Somalis, killing indiscriminately. That was it. The saviors had become oppressors, and the level of threat rose. American military commanders wanted to bring in heavy armor, but Defense Secretary Les Aspin wouldn't allow it. Too many critics in Congress were tossing off analogies to Vietnam.

The hunt for Aidid went on without the tanks. And things just got worse. On the night of October 3, nearly a hundred Rangers were pinned down in an ambush while hunting for Aidid. Two choppers were shot down. Soldiers from the Army's Tenth Mountain Division were sent into the white heat of a firefight to rescue the Rangers, through the narrow streets of south Mogadishu, through a nightmare of burning barricades and rockets roaring down alleys and gunfire exploding at them from seemingly every door and window in town.

The battle lasted fifteen hours. Maybe three hundred Somalis got killed. But what resonated back home were the eighteen dead U.S. soldiers, the nearly eighty wounded, the happy Somalis dragging blasted bits of American boys through the streets, hailing their great victory. Four days later, Clinton announced that the United States would pull out of Somalia beginning in December.

Now, a gut feeling was made official: the hell with Somalia. A nation expert in the art of ambush had managed to hijack the biggest humanitarian effort ever and turn it into just another chapter of a pointless war.

The American military hunkered down to wait, steering clear of Aidid's avenues. The looters had a field day, picking off supplies again. Soon, the emphasis switched to diplomacy, to wooing Aidid. But the peace talks went nowhere. All anybody talked about was pulling out, winding down, moving on to someplace else.

One humanitarian group after another quietly moved on. Some complained that the military wasn't protecting them anymore, and the military said: Well, too bad. United Nations officers leaked data showing that a lot of the humanitarian aid, perhaps 30 percent, was going directly to Aidid as a payoff.

Through it all, the UN bureaucracy was operating in overdrive, like a kid obliviously building a sand castle as the tide rolled in. Tractors and cranes rumbled across the vast compound. Functionary after functionary stamped various authorizations, then sent people who wanted to book a relief flight or register a weapon to another office for another stamp, then to another office for another signature, then to another office for word that the first stamp was in the wrong place, meaning that the process had to begin all over again.

UNOSOM, the United Nations Mission in Somalia, was like a car that kept rolling after the engine had blown. The bureaucrats themselves were defensive about this, of course. Here they were, plodding along with their tasks. Procuring UNOSOM-embossed stationery and Christmas cards. Ordering office furniture. Spending a million dollars a day in bottled water. Arranging embalming services for the occasional bandit victim. Snapping up goats by the herd to feed the Somali staff who built the offices for the highly paid consultants who studied the logistics of sustaining the system's logistics after the Americans left with their logistical expertise. All while the diplomatic and humanitarian underpinnings of the mission were eroding away.

The operation was running on fumes. The donors, as they were called, were disgusted. The Americans were going, the French were almost gone, the Belgians and Germans were already eyeing the exits. Pakistan and India were being coaxed in as replacements, but nobody expected them to have the stomach for a long commitment.

Yet even though the signs pointed to an inevitable abandonment of the place, the commotion and the construction and the contracts made it tough for people like Abdulli to think that the UN's elephantine presence would vanish. It didn't seem possible.

"They wouldn't stay here so long, spend so much money and just leave," he told the visitor to his office.

He was in denial. Even when the Americans pulled their aircraft carrier out of the region the next day. Even when the first

U.S. combat troops began pulling out nine days later, beginning with the Tenth Mountain Division that took part in the battle that convinced America to give up on Somalia.

The brass gave some speeches on the airport tarmac. The men were urged to remember that this mission, for all its fatal flaws, had halted hunger of historic magnitude. The American soldiers hoisted their rucksacks and boarded a Boeing 747 for the flight back to Fort Drum, New York. They would catch a last glimpse of the place from the plane. Maybe their final view would be of the fields below, filled with grain. Maybe not.

Many more would follow. The nations that came to save Somalia would slip out of the country. Eventually, they would be followed rather quickly by the grandson of the carpenter, the fat man with the sharp mind who would realize that, for the foreseeable future, Somalia was no place for builders.

MARY Lightfine spent her final months in Somalia working at a small hospital in the outlying town of Belet Uen. Security was provided by the Canadian contingent of the big lifesaving army. Insecurity was provided by the reporters who made Belet Uen a dateline on their tours of Somalia. Every time she turned around some notebook or microphone was asking her intimate questions or eavesdropping on conversations. And she'd get quoted as saying something that sounded mean or unfeeling or callous, and it made her organization look bad. These reporters didn't understand.

With the military here, Somalia had become something of a circus. In fact, a young doctor from Albuquerque spent a month at the hospital as part of his residency. Mary and the others were told to pretend that they had never heard of the guy, who happened to be William Kennedy Smith, the Kennedy spawn who had been acquitted of rape during a sensational trial in Florida in 1991. Everyone played along, pretending they didn't know him, although occasionally clueless officials would stop into town, meet the man and say, "Don't I know you from somewhere?" Mary showed him some comics she'd drawn. He was disgusted.

She appreciated the presence of the Canadian soldiers. They seemed to really care about the humanitarian effort. They were terrific, though a little naive. They had big hearts and wanted to help, but they just created a monster. She told them, "You can't just march in here and start giving things out." After a while, they came to the hospital almost every day, complaining about how the Somalis constantly tested them, taunted them, slipped into their camp and stole whatever they could carry.

One night, some Canadian peacekeepers invited her and some other relief workers to come out to their camp and climb their tower, to look through the night-vision scope and see what goes on in the dark. And Mary peered through the glasses at the Somalis around the compound, trying their damnedest to sneak inside and steal something. She understood the frustration of these peacekeepers.

The Canadians seemed much more involved than the Americans. To her, the American soldiers had seemed uncertain about their mandate and indifferent to the concerns of the aid workers. Still, she dreaded the day when they and the rest of the international army would leave.

"I don't think I want to remain after the troops have gone," she said in a letter to *The Columbus Dispatch*, which wrote a story about the Ohio nurse in Somalia. "I don't know what will become of Somalia, but I think that the people will have to first want to help themselves. I'm not sure that the Somali people will ever learn to dream of a day beyond the present. They have come to expect handouts and help."

She was true to her word. She intended to beat the troops out of this place. When her contract with the International Medical Corps was up, she ended her thirteen months in Somalia. Just a few weeks before her departure, however, one of the Canadian officers came to see her.

"Mary," he said. "The Somalis say we killed someone. I need an objective observer to look at the body."

They went to the village where the body supposedly was, but the family had already buried it, in keeping with Muslim tradition. But word got out and made it into the Canadian papers. People went public, made statements. They said some Canadians had kicked and beaten this sixteen-year-old Somali kid, tortured him with lit cigars, basically just methodically murdered him inside a pit while he was tied up and blindfolded. Took his picture. Word got out that other Somali interlopers had been shot by soldiers who had left "bait" of food and water in an open area of the camp. Allegations were made that some peacekeepers were racists of the worst order, that officers covered up and even tacitly approved of the brutality.

One of the peacekeepers tried to hang himself with a bootlace. He was found before he died, but he had throttled himself long enough to sustain serious brain damage. He didn't have to face prosecution, but others did. A private got five years in prison for manslaughter, a sergeant got ninety days for negligent performance of duty and a major was reprimanded for the same thing. Six others were acquitted of various charges, but an independent commission would conclude that the debacle was the result of bad planning and poor preparation at the highest levels of the military.

Mary couldn't believe it. She wrote a deposition on behalf of one of the officers, attesting to his integrity. The Somalis were so crafty, so brilliantly skillful at outmaneuvering people that she believed they were pinning a rap on the Canadians as a way to extract some compensation. After a while, after more allegations came out and the thing got huge, she didn't know what the truth was. She was just happy to be gone.

She began to think that it had been pointless to do anything in Somalia. The country had just been going through a cyclical change of power. If not one shred of food or medicine had been delivered, the process probably would have been over quickly and with much less impact on the general population. Instead, the outside world just made things worse. People have a war because they want power. They have to kill people, displace people. Yet relief goes to the losing side and the losers get strong enough to respond in kind. So the cycle goes on interminably, agonizingly. The weak and afflicted are aided until they become strong enough to strike back. It was a hard view to accept, but Mary figured that Somalia ultimately would have been better off if it had been left to bleed in the shadows, to heal itself in the harsh ways of nomads.

Mary moved on to yet another new job. She had very much admired Médicins Sans Frontières. She flew to Paris, got a place to stay and enrolled in intensive French-language courses. One week later she walked into the MSF office and applied for a job. Not much French, but a heck of a track record as a trauma nurse.

They asked if she wanted to go work at a refugee camp for Somalis in Kenya. No thanks, she said.

Well, how about Sri Lanka?

Why not?

Mary plunged into her work in Sri Lanka, which was being ripped apart by an insurgency by the minority Tamils against the majority Sinhalese. She worked at a camp for about thirty thousand Tamils who had been driven from their homes in Sinhalese regions. More than a million people were in the same predicament throughout the country.

Even though Tamil guerrillas ranged about and actively recruited inside the camp, the conditions were much more stable. Mary found herself doing a lot of follow-up, seeing the same people again and again to make sure they were responding to treatment, following her instructions. She found herself doing a lot of preventative work, telling people about sanitation and child care and immunization. And she found that these people listened intently to what she said, took her advice and frequently said thank you. And they generally didn't steal everything.

She and some other health workers wound up turning their house into an after-hours emergency room, and every evening Mary found herself caring for somebody even after she'd knocked off for the day. And she didn't mind. She began to think that Somalia had not been a good place to begin a humanitarian career.

One day, an old woman came in with a terrible abscess on her head that must have stood an inch high. A neighbor had cut off all the woman's hair in an attempt to help, and Mary thought this little bald woman looked absolutely adorable. Mary lanced the boil and drained it and packed it with dressing. She had to repeat this procedure for a number of days, and the woman always dutifully returned and patiently waited until Mary finished with her. Finally, the abscess was under control and Mary told her: That's it. All better. No more visits necessary.

This little woman stepped back, put her two hands together and gave Mary a deep bow of thanks. And that dense wall that Mary had built, well, it just crumbled.

12 lost in transit

THE Americans and their allies never rebuilt Somalia or resolved the animosities among the people who lived there. They never seized the guns from the heartless young men who preyed on the weak, never took the rockets from the warlords who shared competing visions of prepotency. They had simply halted the momentum of an epic catastrophe. They had simply given the humanitarian community time to help villages rally back to something resembling stability. They had simply allowed people to *stop,* sink a hoe in the ground and wait for the precious little puffs of clouds that seemed so scarce to maybe drop some rain so the larders could be filled again. Now the Americans were leaving, and everyone knew that the UN mission left behind would dither and whither and blow away without the last superpower to lead it.

The New Year approached, a time for contemplation, particularly about how to dole out the discretionary portions of those 1994 budgets. With the Americans well into their slow-motion withdrawal from Somalia, aid agencies began hinting to world governments that it was time to begin looking for places that might be a bit more worth saving. Even the agency that first warned the world about Somalia, only to be ignored as the country tumbled into hell, had a new message: time to go.

The International Committee of the Red Cross said Somalia had slid down the priority list and now ranked no higher than Liberia, Zaire, Rwanda and a few other places. There were eighteen conflicts in Africa, most the result of a derailed transition from single-party dictatorships to multiparty democracy. They were all ticking.

The Red Cross had been alone in warning about the crisis at the end of 1991. It had made the country its priority, blew a third of its budget on the place, but it wasn't enough. Hundreds of thousands of people died because of global negligence. The spectacle of the Communist world coming undone had been too mesmerizing, too distracting for anybody with the money and power to stop a catastrophe. It took television pictures of mass starvation to wake up the world.

Now, at the end of 1993, it was time to think ahead. There were other Somalias out there, said Max Hadorn, the Red Cross chief in Somalia. He was talking to a small group of reporters who had returned to Somalia to cover the one-year anniversary of the mission and the beginning of its end. They had gathered in the Red Cross conference room for a painfully introspective analysis by a string of aid officials. It was time, he said, to find the next Somalia *before* it became the next Somalia, before it became the lead story on the television news. Is this possible?

"Prevention is much more critical than the cure," Hadorn said, his voice dripping with frustration. "Do we need these horrible pictures before we can have action taken before events?"

Well, maybe so. So much of the global population was fluid that only the occasional epic crash got noticed. *Jane's Defence Weekly,* a publication that tracked the ebb and flow of military conflict, published an itemized list of the decade thus far: twenty-six wars, twenty-three areas of potential conflict and twenty-four areas of tension. Where to begin? The chaotic elements that were at play in so many places had to converge in a particularly horrendous way for the cameras to come calling. A million displaced in Sri Lanka? Sorry. Half of them would have to die for the other half to get noticed. Displaced people weren't news. There were too many of them. They were like a vast, secret society within the known world. The UN Population Fund grabbed a day's worth of headlines in 1993 when it reported that humans in general were moving in unprecedented numbers. A huge migration was underway, between nations and within nations, for reasons political and economic and social. The poorer people were grasping for some sort of prosperity, either in a more developed land abroad or in the most developed part of their own land. The UN report said that the world contained 100 million migrants, people living in places in which they were not citizens. This was a large number. If it were a nation, it would be the tenth most populous. Almost two out of every hundred people on the planet were living outside their countries. And this number was based on fairly dated criteria. It didn't even include the 60 million people suddenly stranded in strange lands when the Soviet Union splintered. It didn't include the tens of millions, maybe hundreds of millions, who were migrating within their own countries, leaving rural areas for urban ones. It didn't include the 10 percent of the Chinese population stuck in a state of perpetual motion, drifting from farms to city after city in search of work. It didn't include the estimated 30 million people who were internally displaced by conflicts in their countries. Achieving prosperity and finding safety were merely two spots on the same scale of human desire. People who ran from a war in Iraq or lethal politics in Togo or empty store shelves in Bulgaria were sharing space in the same Berlin refugee shelters with Romanian mothers seeking medical care for their children that they couldn't get at home. All of them had lost their footing in the great transition that gripped the world. All of them were after the same thing: a slight improvement in their present circumstances. They were part of the same dust storm swirling the planet. If you added all the numbers, collated all the categories, more humans were in motion than at any time in history. Some of them were refugees. Some hadn't quite crossed the threshold of a recognized boundary, hadn't quite vaulted into a clear statistical category. They were just running.

SARINA crouched in the bushes on a cool spring evening and listened to the screams of a community killing itself. Old friends and neighbors were bludgeoning her parents to death. They were disemboweling her schoolteacher inside a classroom where she once studied geography. They were leading pregnant women from a maternity clinic, forcing them to kneel in a circle and then splitting their skulls with machetes.

The killers moved from house to house, building to building, consulting the long lists of names they had compiled. They burst into each dwelling with whoops and screams. They impaled, bludgeoned or shot the men immediately. Nubile women they saved to rape at their leisure later, slashing their

Achilles tendons so they couldn't flee. The killers herded the smallest children into circles and crushed their heads with clubs carefully crafted for this occasion. They looted the tiny clay homes where the dead once lived.

Within hours, thousands of carcasses littered the streets, the schoolhouse, the hospital. In the church, the wreckage of rent bodies stretched from the ornate hardwood altar to a vestibule splashed with blood. In an adjacent anteroom, a couple died in final embrace beneath a picture of a serenely smiling Jesus Christ. In an otherwise empty classroom, a young boy with a stunned expression lay dead amid tumbled desks and chairs.

Sarina Mukagasana abandoned her hiding place and sprinted through the forest, past clumps of bodies among the trees. The tall, sinewy sixteen-year-old kept clear of the chaotically crowded road. Masses of people were on the move. Young men electrified by this sudden explosion of disorder set up checkpoints to screen the panicked crowds surging down the dirt highways. Lines formed at the checkpoints, mere logs and rocks laid across the dirt.

"Your cards! Show us your identity cards!" the young sentries demanded.

Roughly every fourth or fifth card had a stamp that identified the holder as a member of the Tutsi minority. These people were pulled from the line and hacked to death. After a while, some of the killers didn't have time to check everybody's identification. They simply began killing the tall people, since it was believed that Tutsis often were taller than the average Hutu, though that wasn't always the case.

As the hours wore on, more people took to the roads to flee, carrying their clanking cargo of cooking pots and water jugs.

The countryside quaked with violence, terror and confusion. Word spread that opposing armies were girding for battle, that enemy soldiers were only miles away. Vast cordons of people snaked up the hillsides. Civilian militias set up more check-points on the roads, singling out those who by ethnicity or atti-tude seemed somehow aligned with the ethereal other side. The self-appointed sentries swung their machetes until their arms ached. Sloppy stacks of dripping bodies rose high along the roadsides. Creeks of blood soaked deep into the rich auburn soil of Rwanda.

Guided by moonlight, Sarina weaved through the woods, resting in bushes or behind trees, finally reaching the outskirts of a town called Gahini. She waited for daylight. When dawn broke over the velvety terraced hills ringing the town, she drifted warily out of the forest and into the city.

There was no sign of killing in Gahini. Only survival. Tens of thousands of people, all of them fleeing other villages, filled the narrow dirt streets and camped in clearings atop low hills. While Sarina's village stank of fresh death, this one groaned with damaged life. At the end of a dirt road crowded with dazed wanderers, thousands of wounded people thronged the white-washed walls of the single-story hospital, a monument to miss-ing limbs and mortal wounds. The most badly maimed were carried in crude stretchers made of goat hide and tree branches.

Sarina walked into the hospital and looked at the people packed into the halls. She reflexively hunted for the familiar, an aunt, a neighbor, any remnant of kinship. She went outside and roamed among the encampments, studying faces around fires. She stood on the road and watched the new arrivals. She recog-nized no one.

As darkness fell, Sarina returned to the hospital and settled in with the strangers. She stayed on the periphery of what appeared to be a fairly large family. Exhausted, hungry, desperate for a drink of water, Sarina sat on the floor and waited for somebody to come save her.

HE was sleeping on a straw mat in a tent in the woods when he was awakened by the sound of his bellowing commander. Francois and his comrades were being roused with a particular urgency, well before daybreak. The news they heard was breathtaking: Their unit was being mobilized and dispatched to the front. The truce, they were told, had been broken. Broken quite badly.

Francois slipped into his camouflage fatigues and laced up his shoes. He had a long march ahead to the south, to a place where his unit would link up with other elements of the Rwandan Patriotic Front, a quiescent army of rebels now being stirred quickly back to life. The government was in shambles and Hutu extremists were massacring Tutsis. What had been feared was unfolding, a final conflict.

Francois was not happy about this. The president of Rwanda had been under enormous pressure at home and abroad to end four years of civil war, to open his government to the opposition, to hold free elections. There was a signed peace accord. Francois had become obsessed with the idea that he could move on to more personally enriching matters. He wanted to run his own safari tours. He wanted to sit in cafés. He wanted out of the bush. He wanted to go home.

The political officer who was assigned to Francois's unit told the men that there was an enormous number of people on the roads, fleeing. He urged the troops to remember the code they had heard often and ignored only at the risk of death: No matter what you see, no matter what you hear, no matter where you go, there are to be no reprisals of any kind against any civilians, particularly women, especially children. The guilty would be punished later, he said. The political agenda of the Rwandan Patriotic Front was contingent upon its image. The people must not become targets.

Francois hefted his rucksack and moved out. He could not believe this was happening.

LIKE most members of the proud army of nationalists known as the Rwandan Patriotic Front, Francois was not actually raised in Rwanda. He grew up as a refugee in Kenya. His parents had been part of the great Tutsi exodus of the late 1950s and 1960s, when the Hutus finally ended centuries of Tutsi domination by killing many of them and stripping many of the rest of their land, cattle and privileged positions. More than a million fled to the border countries and beyond. Maybe a million remained in Rwanda, where they became scapegoats for whatever went wrong.

Tutsis like Francois's family, educated folk with money, managed to gain a quick foothold in their adopted societies. Many of the refugees had held high positions in government, business and the military, and they promptly used their leadership skills to excel in their new lands. In Uganda, they were part of the force that put Yoweri Museveni in power. Museveni realized the importance of submerging communal rivalries, of building an army that didn't prey on the people. The Tutsis who served

under him learned that there were practical advantages to playing down distinctions. Particularly if you were in the minority.

To Francois, Rwanda was as real as a bedtime story. He was too much a product of an upbringing in Kenya's hustling capital. His French-speaking parents may have christened him Francois, but in English-speaking Nairobi he was simply Frank Rwagasana, a young man who just happened to have REFUGEE stamped on his identity card. Nairobi was a multicultural city, a hub of commerce and tourism and global politics for much of the continent. It was a window to the West, and as the 1980s wore on the West increasingly captured Francois's fancy. He attended the university and studied sociology. He spoke four languages, read avidly and wanted very much to travel the world, to make a successful living and enjoy a bit of luxury. Nairobi had bookstores and movie houses and cafés and nightspots. He moved easily into the coffee-shop milieu of collegiate nightlife, reveling in the seemingly brilliant debates he and his friends had over Africa's future. Democracy was on the horizon everywhere, it seemed, and Francois embraced a new age in which maximizing personal income was both ideology and theology.

Because he was smart and personable, he got a job after graduation as a tour guide with an American outfit that paid him a nice wage to lead Westerners on safaris. He covered the continent from Egypt to South Africa. He knew the way from the Sahara to the Serengeti, from Kilimanjaro to the Kalahari. The place he knew least, though, was the beautiful little country known as the Land of a Thousand Hills, the country that technically he considered home.

Despite the complaints of the countries that reluctantly hosted the Tutsi diaspora, the Hutu president resisted repatriation. The last thing he wanted to do was *double* the Tutsi population in Rwanda. Quite the contrary. President Juvénal Habyarimana had built his career on killing Tutsis in the 1960s. He went from war college graduate to army chief of staff in *three years* because he knew how to beat their soldiers on the battlefield, kill their families in their villages, drive them from the country in fear and horror.

But on October 1, 1990, three decades after the great exodus, thousands of refugee children finally came home. Countless babies raised in foreign countries came back to reclaim a land some had never seen. Only now, they were all grown. They were wearing fatigues, carrying guns. And grudges. The Rwandan Patriotic Front, an army of émigrés, was aiming to break open the border.

Though Tutsi refugees had failed several times previously to barge their way back into the country, this time was different. Now they had the guns, the numbers and the sort of esprit de corps, tactical wit and other intangibles that often are more formidable than mere hardware. They had a pluralistic political platform that could have been written by Museveni himself, which was not surprising: Many of the soldiers and most of the commanders had been Ugandan regulars, Rwandans by ancestry only. They said they wanted a free-market democracy, like everybody else these days. They said they wanted to end the despotic regime of one of Africa's suddenly unfashionable autocrats. They said they wanted to create a society in which ethnicity didn't matter. There were disaffected Hutus in the ranks and

carefully sprinkled in high-profile positions. But the main purpose of the invasion was to repatriate the diaspora.

Francois had known this force was being raised, but he
couldn't relate to the earnest, obsessed expatriates who had tried
to recruit him. When the invasion actually happened, however,
he was riveted. The rebels knifed into the country and confused
the government troops, outflanking them and sometimes attacking from the rear. In two weeks they had captured a tenth of the
country, a foothold in the homeland at last.

Then the French, aiming to protect their economic interests
and political influence in the country and the continent, inter-
vened on the side of the government. The rebel commander was
killed on the battlefront. The rebel advance was halted, and the
war became a brutal chess match.

Francois couldn't stand it anymore. The reports were maddening, incomplete, conflicting. Massacres, advances, defeats. It
was all so . . . exciting. Guerrilla warfare: *the ultimate adventure
tour!* He quit his job — on a lark, really — and went off to join
the rebellion. He was reclaiming the country that had exiled his
parents.

He went to Uganda, where the rebels secretly trained under
the tacit approval of the Ugandan government. He was given a
uniform that was actually surplus from the old East German
army. Boots were in short supply, so he wore Adidas high-tops.

He saw his first action during a big Christmas offensive. His
unit overran a government position. He and the others moved
up carefully and came across a dead government soldier. He
found out that it was time to resupply. His lieutenant raised
the dead man's arms and, with a couple of kicks, snapped them

backward at the elbows. This made it easier to remove the shirt, but the snap and pop of arms bending in the wrong direction, well, it made Francois sick. He watched his commander change into the superior clothing of a warm dead enemy.

"Could I do that?" Francois thought.

Of course he could. He could live in the mud and the rain, so sick with malaria he was certain he was dying and damn glad about it. He could carry twenty kilos of food on his back while smaller men could manage only ten, which meant he had more food for longer. He could plunder the body of a man he had killed. He was thirty-three years old, tall and muscular with a personality that was both expansive and introspective. He was self-conscious enough to marvel not only at his ability to shoot a man, but at his capacity to contemplate somewhat remorsefully his hard-earned lack of remorse.

"Imagine," he'd say later, after he had amassed some war stories. "Imagine coming from a big city like Nairobi, and you find yourself in the bush and you got a gun. People are *shooting* at *you*. Bombs are falling. Imagine."

Imagine learning by rote the mechanics of killing. He came to appreciate the tedium of truces and understand the inevitability of their brevity. He got excited when the rebels and the president and the Rwandan political opposition all agreed in 1993 on a sweeping peace plan that would bring repatriation of the Tutsis and democracy for all. Then he watched it unravel. A burst of murders here, an inflammatory speech there, an assassination of a political figure or two. A radio station urging villagers to be ready to kill.

It was clear that the president had no intention of honoring the accord. Already, there were reports of massacres of Tutsis in the countryside. The government denied complicity, even though the opposition knew it was training secret civilian militias.

Francois had felt it slipping away. And then the peace talks in Tanzania in April 1994. There were no breakthroughs. Habyarimana flew home in his personal jet. He approached the Rwandan capital, Kigali, a city that straddled a mountain ridge and sprawled into the valley below. The plane soared in the direction of a chalet tucked high in the forested hills. It smashed into a banana grove just outside a heavily landscaped estate, barreled through a stone wall and broke apart like a fumbled melon, spilling pieces of plane and passenger as far as the kidney-shaped swimming pool. The wreckage smoked and sizzled on one of the most nicely manicured lawns in town. The president was home from his trip abroad, though the staff need not bother with dinner.

His followers immediately claimed that the rebels had blown the plane out of the sky. But witnesses had heard rocket fire coming from the airport, where his supposedly loyal troops were stationed. This led to speculation that perhaps he was shot down by his own people, many of whom were upset with the generous peace plan he'd reluctantly signed with the insurgents.

What made the crash even more complicated was the fact that he was not traveling alone; his guest was the president of the nation next door, Burundi, a country with internal problems of equal enormity. People in both places were far too polarized to assume that the deaths were merely the result of an error or accident or even an isolated instance of assassination. Nobody took the time to wonder why, of all the places to crash in the capital, his plane had tumbled into his own backyard.

Maybe he had just leaned over to his fellow president, who had only enjoyed a couple of months in office, and told him about his nice mansion and how good it looked all lit up at night, how the trees seemed to cradle it, how the blue of the pool sparkled up at him between the treetops whenever he came home. Maybe he'd told his French pilot to go as low as he could so he could show this new ruler what a perk of power looked like, how maybe the pilot had to execute something a bit too tricky, maybe caught a downdraft in this labyrinthine land of a thousand hills, and then crashed the son of a bitch just a croquet shot away from the presidential gazebo.

Maybe not. Too much history was wound far too tightly into this little land, leaving no room for anything at all resembling reasonable conjecture, let alone rational thought.

The killing began in the capital. Habyarimana's presidential guard murdered the opposition leaders he had been pressured to include in his supposed government of transition, including the prime minister. They tortured and murdered ten UN peacekeepers from Belgium who had tried to protect her.

And then, with all the moderates dead, the hard-line remnants of his government flipped the switch on the citizen militias that had been organized in almost every town. A radio station owned by the president's family exhorted them to begin killing not only the Tutsis, but fellow Hutus who were somehow accommodating to the Tutsi point of view, or who had expressed displeasure with the policies of the now deceased president.

The UN peacekeepers who had been dispatched to oversee the peace accord pulled out of the country. The humanitarian groups complained bitterly about this, then followed suit. The

Americans and their allies, still stung by their debacle in Somalia, insisted almost conspiratorially that the crisis was waning even as it widened, even as it burst breathtakingly into unbridled genocide, even as hundreds of thousands of people let out the same piercing scream.

The killing spread across the countryside, from paved streets of crowded towns to tiny hillside hamlets. Much of the mayhem was carried out with workmanlike rigor by regular townsfolk against people they had considered neighbors, even friends. It was not so easy to kill so many so quickly without weapons of mass destruction handy, so there was much heavy labor required of many people. The awesome breadth of such implacable butchery left many potential victims simply paralyzed by what seemed to be an inescapable tidal wave of annihilation. In many towns, people who were singled out to die just blubbered pathetically as they were led away to their burial pits, where they stood and waited to have their skulls thwacked open by whistling machetes.

But the killings also revived the rebels of the Rwandan Patriotic Front. They drove into government territory. They were superior in every way. They seized town after town. In the time it took a ten-passenger plane to crash into a yard full of peacocks and flamingoes, all the complex divisions and rivalries in Rwanda were reduced to two simple sides, each rallying around its own army and streamlined agenda, squaring off for a final showdown.

THE first town that Francois entered was empty. Except for the bodies, a few dozen, lined up neatly in a field outside town. The living had run away. The second town was the same. And the third. The rebels were trying to stop massacres of civilians in places where their very proximity often unleashed those very massacres. And the killers fled.

"Why don't they fight us?" Francois thought. "Why don't they fight *us?*"

Sometimes the rebels moved quickly enough to engage the army. They almost always won, and the army retreated. And sometimes they came to cities where people still remained. Sometimes the survivors urged the rebels to arrest certain people, and sometimes the rebels would comply. Sometimes they seized a village like Nyatovu and arrested people like Juliana Mukankwaya, a handsome woman of thirty-five, the mother of six children and the murderer of two.

She told the rebels that she was assigned with other women to round up Tutsi children, the fresh orphans. The kids were herded into a circle and the women closed in, swinging clubs. She bludgeoned at least two youngsters, the children of parents she knew as a child.

"They didn't cry, because they knew us," Juliana said. "They just made big eyes. We killed too many to count."

Some of the rebels could not fathom these things. Many were like Francois, educated men from abroad. He realized these people were ignorant peasants, manipulated by their leaders. But he also knew he had relatives in Rwanda, and he knew there was a good chance they were stacked up like cordwood. He found himself referring to the enemy as "the Hutus," even though there were Hutus among his fellow rebels.

Yet he knew there was a strict code, and, with some random exceptions, the rebels generally followed it with almost religious

devotion. Even when they occasionally came to a town like Karubamba, a place they didn't need to capture, but bury.

The buildings were modern and symmetrically arranged, each structure a single story built from the same rust-colored brick. They seemed to defer architecturally to the church, which stood off to one side, its spire towering over everything. In this exceedingly orderly town, only the people seemed out of place. The pregnant women gathered outside the maternity clinic. Families in church, kids in class. All of them were dead.

There was no sound except the spastic chirp of gorgeous little birds and a low roar, the deep vibrato hum of millions of flies as big as june bugs, some so heavy they could hardly stay aloft.

The rebels occupied the nearby city of Gahini. It was filled with thousands of displaced people. The rebels would organize the refugees into sectors, appoint leaders. They would form crews to begin the process of burying the two thousand bodies at Karubamba, but only after they would hunt among the refugees in Gahini, looking for people who could identify the dead.

They would find Sarina in the hospital. She would be led back to find her family amid the human debris of the town. She would identify her geography teacher. And she would, for the first time, feel safe, surrounded by an army of her people.

THE Rwandan Patriotic Front established orphanages and refugee camps in the territories it controlled. It manned checkpoints with a crisp professionalism rarely matched on the continent. It

was conscious of its image. It assigned political officers to lecture people in the camps about the importance of ignoring ethnic or political distinctions. Most of their listeners were Hutus, since most of the Tutsis were dead.

Mostly, though, the rebels chased the government army into a shrinking section of the country. And mostly, the Hutu civilians ran from this Tutsi-dominated rebel force. Three million people, a third of the population, were displaced in less than eight weeks.

Half a million spilled into neighboring Tanzania alone, creating a refugee crisis of epic dimensions. Those refugees were the target of much sympathetic publicity and humanitarian assistance. They were pathetic humans living in horrid conditions that were easy to videotape. Many were murderers with good reason to run.

But larger numbers were displaced within Rwanda. Many were Hutus who had moved into government territory, which was considered violent and forbidding and very difficult for humanitarian agencies to penetrate. Relief agencies were going crazy trying to figure out not only where these people were, but where they were going. They became known as the missing half million.

The international community shrank away from Rwanda like it was spilled plutonium, as three disasters unfolded on interlocking planes: a civil war, a refugee exodus of biblical proportions, and a stunningly successful campaign of genocide.

Six weeks after the president's plane crash, the United Nations finally decided to go back into Rwanda with an expanded security force, but it would take many weeks to put this force together. It would arrive too late and be too weak and

restrained to do any good. It would be a pointless exercise because it would lack the leadership of the United States, which turned in its badge after the Somalia debacle. Let the Europeans play global cop in Rwanda.

They did. The French decided to intervene. They sent 2,500 troops into government territory, ostensibly to protect the displaced who were fleeing the rebels. But the criticism was immediate: The French were going to stop the Tutsis from taking over, just as they did in 1990. They were going to save the remains of an evil government purely to protect their influence in Africa.

The French were greeted wildly when they arrived in the government territory. Cars and shops were festooned with little French flags. Young murderers at the checkpoints shouted "Vive la France" and saluted with their machetes as the French convoys passed.

Despite the dubious nature of the mission, the French intervention also had the effect of bringing a momentary calm to the government side. Though the French force was relatively small, the respect and intimidation factors were enormous. It was almost an ether effect. A well-trained and highly mobile force with superior weaponry and air support had landed, and everybody was transfixed. Nothing commanded respect in these internecine turf battles like the threat of superior firepower. The government-held areas had once been strange and forbidding, sealed and dangerous, with serial killers at every checkpoint almost every kilometer. Now, it was like somebody had pumped nitrous oxide into the territory. As in the opening days of Somalia, it was peace in a bottle. It stayed fresh briefly, but it bought time. And it allowed humanitarian agencies to begin looking for

that missing half million, a mobile multitude that turned out to be much larger than anyone had imagined.

These refugees clung to hillsides and spilled into forests, one vast shifting sea of men in dusty jackets and women carrying babies on their backs. The heaviest masses clustered around the government positions, seeking protection. The army culled them for new recruits, led bodies weakened by hunger and thirst through sloppy sets of jumping jacks. But desertions were high. Nobody wanted to get caught by the rebels. This is why the army was retreating. This was why the missing half million were running.

They would have no time to rest, however. The rebels launched a new offensive against the government stronghold. They captured the capital. The French responded by carving out a safe haven in southern Rwanda so the Hutu killers could hide there. But it wasn't enough. The rebels intended to conquer everything. They intended to drive the government army into oblivion.

Some humanitarian groups, those that were best at anticipating landfall for roving refugee populations, were guessing that much of this careening society of fleeing Hutus might crash across the border into Zaire. Some even thought about positioning relief supplies at what they guessed might be a likely escape hatch: a resort town in the shadow of volcanoes on the shore of Lake Kivu, a city called Goma. But very few did.

13 vicious circles

IMAGINE crossing a river so wide that it seems like the sea. Picture the ragged contours of a white skyline slowly emerging in the distance, like the smudged sketch of an actual city. Focus on the long streak of color that flickers at the base of the buildings and runs along the shore. Watch this wide band take on an undulating definition as the boat chugs closer to port. Closer, and you can see it is actually made up of thousands of specks, dots . . . no . . . heads. People, enough to fill a soccer stadium, are lined up scores deep, waiting for you. They are hoping to carry your luggage, sell you cigarettes, pick your pocket. They are all staring at your boat, at your bags, at your discomfiture as you walk the plank into their murmuring midst on the banks of the Congo River.

Cut through the crowd with a measure of care and good humor. Negotiate the gauntlet of customs agents who come to work only because they get daily opportunities to extort their salaries from travelers like you. Enter the town itself, its buildings shot up and scorched by soldiers who pillage and rape

when too many months pass between paychecks. Look at the hospital, emptied of medicine, housing patients who cannot afford their rotten care and who aren't released until their families pay something.

Imagine a municipality so drained of function that a man stands on an avenue with a shovel in one hand while the other reaches out imploringly to the dented cars that occasionally ramble by. He is taking it upon himself to fill a particular pothole with dirt from the roadside. He is hoping that some motorist will appreciate his effort, stop and pay him. On this particular stretch of street, he has appointed himself the minister of public works in a place where nothing does. He is a civil servant without portfolio, gambling that if he does a bit of civil service someone will supply a wage. Why not? In a place like Kinshasa, a city with nothing left to lose, nothing was not worth trying.

Which is not to say that the capital of Zaire was unrelentingly bleak. Slip inside the sultry corridors of the mazelike Matonge district, a boisterous labyrinth of little shopping stalls and tiny taverns, where Zairian music thumps with thrusting rhythms, where men and women cluster to barter and flirt, where the chestnut brown beer is sometimes mysteriously cool. The gloom fades with the daylight.

Zaire was like a sybarite gone to seed. While places like Somalia or Rwanda just exploded when post–Cold War pressures for democracy collided with old animosities and bad economies and internal power struggles, Zaire went into a slow-motion free fall that was easier to ignore. The United States was like a carouser who awoke from a hangover, in bed with somebody suddenly totally unacceptable. It was too tempting to just

tiptoe out the door. In this case, the head on the pillow was wearing the leopard-skin hat of Mobutu Sese Seko.

Mobutu was a soldier turned journalist turned CIA stooge who, with the spy agency's help, seized power during the political chaos and civil wars that started in 1960, about a week after Belgium granted independence to what was known as the Congo. He expelled the Soviet advisers that his predecessor had invited and pledged allegiance to the other superpower, all the while ruling with outrageous greed and strategic brutality and ethnic selectivity. He changed the name of the country to Zaire and ordered much of the population to change their names, too. He amassed a fortune estimated at $3 billion from the nation's vast copper, cobalt, and diamond industries.

But he did the job he was hired to do. Among other things, he allowed his country to be used as a base for CIA-backed rebels fighting Soviet-backed rebels in Angola in the 1980s. And the U.S. aid just poured in. Mortality rates were dramatically curtailed. Seventy-five percent of the kids went to school. But when Mobutu was no longer needed, he was told to change. And when he wouldn't, the place was abandoned. Once a key square on the chessboard, Zaire was now just a blank space on the map of the new world, more campsite than country.

Mobutu had given democracy the same lip service as had other entrenched African rulers when the Cold War ended. Pressured by the West and unrest at home, he legalized opposition parties in 1990 and formed an interim parliament. He appointed an opposition figure as prime minister, but then fired him. The opposition was powerful enough to obstruct but not take over. Mobutu controlled the banks and paid his presidential guard just enough to make him the strongest man in a leaderless land.

Unfortunately, he occasionally neglected to pay the regular army, so in 1991 the soldiers went on a rampage across the country, killing hundreds of people and destroying much of the industry. This, combined with Mobutu's intransigence, prompted Western donors to cut off aid. The shriveling Soviet empire certainly wasn't in a position to rush in to fill the vacuum. In 1993, the army rioted again, this time after Mobutu paid his troops in a new currency that merchants wouldn't accept. Soldiers killed and raped and stole and generally exacted recompense from the hide of the populace.

Nobody was beaming back TV footage of mass death, but little disaster indicators were creeping upward. Childhood malnutrition was rising fast and decades of progress against tropical disease was being reversed. Every illness that had been slowed by the proceeds of superpower patronage was rallying.

All this collective chaos and neglect was planting the seeds of migration. Competition for shrinking resources increasingly drove people to break into camps separated by ethnicity or geography or class. There was ethnic cleansing on the scale of the former Yugoslavia, but it was unfolding almost unnoticed. There were 40 million people spread out over a country as big as the United States east of the Mississippi. There were more than two hundred ethnic groups, almost all with some claim to a piece of the country.

And it was overrun with generations of refugees from elsewhere. Zaire bordered nine nations, most of them war zones. Sudan, Angola, Mozambique, Burundi, Uganda, Zambia — all of them had swapped hundreds of thousands of refugees with Zaire. Every ripple in one place sent echoes of movement somewhere else, everyone fleeing or chasing some old ancestral concept of rightful home. They traded diseases and disputes. Ugandan refugees brought a meningitis plague that gained a major foothold when Zaire's health system collapsed.

And then there was Rwanda, bubbling on the border. Eastern Zaire always had been a haven for Hutus and Tutsis fleeing centuries of conflicts. In summer of 1993, the competition for land had exploded. Indigenous Zairians began attacking ethnic Rwandans, both Hutu and Tutsis. Then the Hutus and the Tutsis began fighting each other. An estimated 10,000 people were killed and 350,000 were displaced.

None of this drew much attention. The mission to Somalia was unraveling. Europe was convulsed politically over the wars in Yugoslavia. Central Africa stayed off the West's radar screen until six months later, the spring of 1994, when Habyarimana went down in a plane and Rwanda itself exploded, blowing a hole in the foundation of the big country next door.

Isaac Gomez sat in his office in downtown Kinshasa, a thousand miles away from Zaire's border with Rwanda. The apocalypse next door had become another ingredient in a stew of humanitarian concerns for Gomez, the head of the UN Children's Fund operation for Zaire. He worried that even more refugees from yet another war would spill into a country that already was a sponge for the displaced.

"Zaire is a failed state," Gomez told a reporter who visited him one day in June of 1994. "Everybody does what he wants. Children are dying from numerous epidemics. You have looting all over the country, from one city to another. In the regions, all these ethnic conflicts. There is complete confusion."

Zaire was so big, so unnavigable, so riven with intertwined and intractable conflicts that the prospect of refugees from

Rwanda was scary. Already, more than 135,000 Rwandans had fled into eastern Zaire. Gomez figured that number could double.

Yet the humanitarian agencies were in a bind. The more aid they sent to Goma, the more people came. Some stayed in Rwanda but just dined out in Zaire. "In one night you have eight thousand people come in. In one night. Then they go back," Gomez said.

And this was just a trickle. The Rwandan Patriotic Front was driving west. Entire villages were fleeing before it. The missing half million were running out of running room. The number of Rwandans who could stagger into eastern Zaire was huge.

ONE evening, the multitude lost its mind. It began to run, bolting westward in a great wave that was too big even for the horizon to hold. The wave grew with each passing village. It consumed every town in its path, sucked every soul from every hut and every home and rolled them all together into one great churning mass that surged across the countryside. The wave finally crashed against the border and collapsed in great fetid heaps of moaning humanity. The missing half million were no longer missing.

In fact, their numbers had doubled. It didn't seem possible that you could fill a field of vision with so many living, ailing, dying and decaying people. The smell was thick, dense enough to taste. The number was so huge, the need so great, the lack of food and water and medicine so enormous, you would think one would have thought: Where do you begin?

Meggy looked at this writhing multitude and felt very confident, very strong. She saw this town just choked with people in every stage of life and death and thought only about practical things, such as: Where do I hang the IV bottles? How can you drive tent stakes into volcanic rock?

This was the worst place on earth, no doubt. This was the biggest and fastest single movement of refugees of all time, without question. But Meggy was ready. She had been to the desert, been to the bush, been to the malarial backwaters and the arid plateaus. She had treated refugees who populated the TV news and those who literally died of global disregard. She'd been to the mountaintop. She was ready for Goma. She was built for the place.

THE big events in her life had been like a series of lessons, like individual points on an obstacle course designed to toughen her up, sharpen her skills. Meggy Verputten was a nurse from Holland who had decided one day that she wanted to do something different, something really useful. So she enrolled in a course in tropical medicine at an institute in Belgium. While she was studying, Médicins Sans Frontières approached her out of the blue and wanted to know if she wanted to join up. Take the two-week preparation course, they said. See what you think.

She was taking this course as the Persian Gulf War was coming to its quick and booming climax. She was absorbing the latest theories of humanitarian relief just as the Kurds in northern Iraq were staging their ill-fated rebellion. She was just completing the class, in fact, when half a million refugees suddenly materialized on top of the mountains at the Turkish border. By then, it wasn't a question of whether Meggy wanted to join MSF anymore, but how quickly she could pack.

Her first lesson came on a mountain. Meggy had to inch uphill through the muck and the ooze almost to the snow line before she could even get close to the refugees. She looked at the endless expanse of huts made of blue or white plastic that the United Nations had distributed. She looked at the amazing clothes worn by the Kurdish women, these wide dresses and head scarves in these dazzling colors, which seemed so out of place on this stark gray mountain. She looked at all these people, with no sanitation and no water and no food, nothing but a universal case of diarrhea, and thought: Where do you begin?

Scores of people were dying daily, most of them children. This was only the rough draft of a refugee camp, a place where people simply stopped, unable to go on, and waited for someone to come help them. There was nothing here, and relief organizations had to work at extreme speeds to supply essential needs. Meggy's mountaintop was used as a catch point, the place where the new refugees would be immunized against measles before they mingled with the refugees who had already been vaccinated.

Then the Americans and their allies sent an army to intervene. They carved out a safe haven in Iraq and then escorted the refugees back to their homeland. Meggy understood the magnitude of the moment when it came time for her and the other workers to close down their camp and move on. She left the mountain in a helicopter and saw the multitude spilling downward, back toward earth, an endless stream of people being rescued from the road and escorted back to familiar places.

"What will they find when they get home?" Meggy wondered.

Many found their homes destroyed, their villages ravaged by poison gases that had killed all the trees. Many found long stints in transit camps, awaiting repatriation. But they also found the protection of the American-led army of intervention. Refugee after refugee told Meggy that they never would have gone home if the American military hadn't created a safe corridor back to their country.

Meggy moved on to another Kurdish camp in the region, one where the refugees were still waiting their turn to be repatriated. One day a comatose boy was brought into the hospital tent. The grandmother implored Meggy to save this boy. The old woman said he was the last member of her family left alive. The rest had been killed either by Saddam's bombs or by the trek to escape them.

The boy recovered fully, and the grandmother was overjoyed. Meggy felt something special about this child and this grandmother, this fragment of a family clinging desperately together. On the day the boy was released, she walked with the two of them back to the little plastic shelter the old woman had built. The grandmother heated water over a little fire, and the two women sat down for tea. Meggy took some pictures of the boy, awake and smiling.

Meggy promised to send them the pictures. The woman wrote her address in Iraq on a piece of paper. When Meggy returned to Amsterdam, she had the photos developed. She wrote the woman a note and folded it around the photos. Then she carefully copied the Arabic characters of the address onto an envelope and mailed it off.

For years after she had left the mountain, Meggy would wonder: Did the letter make it to the address? Did the old woman and the boy find their way home?

THE next lesson was very different. This camp in Malawi had been around for five years. It was very stable, organized, almost institutionalized. Like a small world, hooked to the outside by a feeding tube.

Meggy felt comfortable walking through it at night. She found small places, little cafés, where you could sit and drink a Coke and listen to music while people danced. Every now and then she eschewed her comfortable MSF compound and slept in a clay hut in the camp, listening to the music and the people laughing, just so she could feel the rhythms of refugee life. And she was impressed by the social swirl, which continued even when diseases such as cholera would make an occasional circuit.

Where there was socializing, of course, there was sex. People had little else to do with their time. As a result, there was not only a high birth rate, but quite a high incidence of sexually transmitted disease. Meggy and the local health care staff organized a little theater group that performed entertaining and instructive lessons on how people got the HIV virus, and how to prevent it.

The camp sheltered about eighty thousand people who had fled the fighting between the Marxist government and a rightist rebel army in neighboring Mozambique. The war had been an ideological struggle sponsored by the Soviets and the West, and it had killed a million people and uprooted nearly 6 million more, nearly a third of the population. With the end of the Cold War, however, the war in Mozambique was quickly waning. Why bother? Even the Marxists ripped up their manifesto in favor of free-market democracy.

After the breathtaking catastrophe in the mountains of Turkey, coming to a camp this old and entrenched was quite a change. Meggy learned that refugee camps always have leaders. They emerge, for better or worse, almost immediately. The longer the camp endures, the more complex and sophisticated the leadership becomes. Since she was the lone MSF medical person, she discussed everything with the camp leaders.

Not long after she got to the camp, she realized that there was a high incidence of childhood malnutrition even though, on paper, an adequate amount of food was being delivered to each family. And, because the children were malnourished, they succumbed more easily to infectious diseases. Childhood mortality was just too high for a camp so well tended.

Meggy followed some food baskets to the huts and watched how the food — mostly maize and beans and cooking oil — was distributed and prepared. She found that mothers almost instinctively gave more food to the healthier child with the bigger appetite, perhaps to strengthen the youngster with the best chance of survival. Meggy weighed the food baskets and found that they sometimes contained less food than they should have, probably through error and theft. And she found that some people had been in the camp so long that their ration cards were outdated, five years old in some cases, and that they had had additional children without getting a commensurate increase in food. Meggy fixed some things, fine-tuned the aid and altered the health education programs.

Meggy spent a year in Malawi. She learned some Portuguese, the official language of Mozambique, and a lot of Chichewa, a tribal language. During her last month there, October 1992, the two factions in Mozambique signed a peace treaty. The United Nations would deploy a peacekeeping force to oversee the accord, but the effort would be poorly prepared and executed and pretty much underfunded, unlike the heavily financed proxy war that preceded it. It would take five months for the United Nations to organize the peacekeeping force. It would take years to repatriate these refugees.

Meggy would be long gone, off somewhere else doing the same thing, learning new lessons.

AS 1992 came to a close, Meggy was assigned to a refugee camp in a dusty and distant section of northern Kenya. The camp was inhabited mainly by an ethnic group from Ethiopia called the Gari. The Gari were nomads who had been driven into Kenya during a grazing land dispute with another ethnic group, the Boran. Neither was the dominant tribe in Ethiopia. They just began fighting over land in the chaos that followed the ouster of Ethiopia's Marxist government in 1991. The Gari lost, so they had to leave.

Unlike the camp in Malawi, this one was terribly poor. Unfortunately for the Gari, their crisis overlapped with the world's sudden awareness of Somalia to the south. Most of the world's available humanitarian resources disappeared into that place. Meggy flew to the Gari refugee camp just as the Americans were landing in Mogadishu. She could not believe how little went to the Gari.

After several months, the UN High Commissioner for Refugees determined that the security situation back in Ethiopia had improved enough for the Gari to go home. But their leaders didn't want them to leave. After all, they were nomads who faced a hardscrabble life back in Ethiopia. At least here there was a little food, a little health care. The healthier the population grew, the less the Gari wanted to leave the camp and the more they wanted to control it.

The UNHCR responded by ordering the relief groups to begin scaling back aid. This heightened tensions considerably between the United Nations and the refugees. Security started to deteriorate. It would take a long time to dislodge these people.

The number of outsiders who cared about the Gari was miniscule. One of them was Meggy's father. He'd spent the past few years worrying about his daughter, off in one terrible place after another. He couldn't understand why she did it, so Meggy finally coaxed him to come out and see what she did for a living. He flew from Amsterdam to Nairobi and took a small plane over the desert to northern Kenya. People had to chase the camels off the dirt airstrip. Many people from the local village, Banissa, came out to greet Meggy's father.

He emerged from the plane in this godforsaken place and spotted the smiling face of his daughter. She led him through the village to the cluster of tents where a handful of humanitarians lived and breathed the unknown plight of the Gari. In the days that followed, he watched as his daughter made the rounds, gave people shots, checked on the ailing. He rode on the back of her Honda dirtbike. He slept in her little tent. He saw how his daughter tried to live close to the needs of the people. It was a good visit.

"Now I think I understand why you do this," he told her.

He learned some things. So did Meggy. Things she would need.

MEGGY spent the summer of 1993 enrolled in a refugee studies program at Oxford University. She was assigned to Liberia the following September. She was posted to the northern stronghold of the Liberian rebel Charles Taylor, and every move her group made was made with the permission and scrutiny of rebel soldiers.

Meggy was in charge of the MSF operation based in Gbarnga, Taylor's headquarters. Her team would prepare a nutritious porridge in town and then fan out to a dozen or so feeding locations out in the bush, where tens of thousands of people had been pinned down by fighting between Taylor and the several other factions in the nation's civil war.

These factions all used the denial of aid as a weapon against each other. Few populations were more vulnerable than the masses of people who were displaced at Taylor's front lines. There was never enough food.

It was one thing to make the porridge in Gbarnga, to try and estimate how many people would be waiting at the feeding stations. It was one thing to drive down dangerous roads prowled by bandits and stacked with checkpoints every ten minutes, where stoned or drunken soldiers carried out larcenous inspections. But it was quite another thing to get to the feeding station and realize that there was not nearly enough food for the people who absolutely needed it and desperately demanded it. Meggy would ask herself: "Who am I to stand at the door to the feeding center and say who can enter and who cannot enter?"

But she did. She stood in doorway after doorway while mothers lined up with their thousands of starving children. These were displaced people. They had nothing except sick kids and the slim hope that they could get a meal if they could just get past this gate. And Meggy had to stand there and look at them and refuse to feed them because, in her estimation, somebody else needed it just a little bit more. And the mothers would be confused, angry, maybe just sad.

Meggy tried to maintain a certain amount of detachment. Yet she still had feelings. She couldn't escape the empathy that came naturally, the ability to comprehend the staggering sensation these mothers must have felt when somebody, your last hope, stands at a gate and refuses food for your child.

That was a hard thing to learn, perhaps the toughest lesson of all. But, like all the others, a grimly valuable one.

EVERY mission ended the same way. First, there was the farewell party. Meggy would wear the local clothing and sing and dance and generally close out a tour with the sweetest memory possible. Then came the difficult morning after, when she would get in the truck and the local staff would stand in the road and wave sad good-byes. It was that way in Liberia.

She went back to Amsterdam in April of 1994 to connect with her other life for a bit, and to await reassignment. She had a mountain of mail waiting for her, and she began to attack it. One letter had an address that was written in Arabic. Meggy was stunned. It was from the old Kurdish woman, the grandmother of the injured boy. The scrap of family she'd met somewhere in the mountains between Turkey and Iraq, years before.

The woman and the boy had made it safely back to northern Iraq. It took a while, but they had been able to return to their town, their house. They had been able to rebuild their lives.

"Thank you for making my grandson better," the grandmother wrote.

Meggy felt an overwhelming sense of relief. The woman and her grandson had made it home. And waiting for them had been the photographs Meggy had taken years earlier, the pictures of a boy recovered from his wounds, smiling, on top of a mountain.

WHERE do you begin? By remembering the lessons. Making a plan. Making a space amid the great heaping pockets of people lying on the ground, making holes in the cooled lava from the volcanoes, putting up a tent. Isolating the people with cholera, building a fence around them. Trying to contain the overlapping outbreaks of infectious diseases, the meningitis, the dysentery, the measles. Organizing mobile teams to wade out into the crowds and vaccinate children. Enlisting community outreach workers among the healthiest refugees. And it's amazing: You see an almost immediate impact. Huge mortality rates begin to plunge. People respond. Populations rally.

Rwanda became real when Goma was overrun. Humanitarian aid poured in from around the world. Reporters who had been covering the transfer of power to a black majority government in South Africa stopped off in Nairobi on their way home, caught a free UN flight to the Goma airport, hired a car outside the terminal and then took a fifteen-minute drive to astonishing scenes of suffering and death.

The human losses were huge, certainly, yet they were still dwarfed by the genocide that had taken place two months earlier, which had been much harder to see, much easier to ignore. Only when the complexities of the Rwandan war were reduced to a single, unthreatening population of dying people packed into an accessible area did the world respond. Only then did the United States intervene, sending two thousand troops to deliver aid to a population of people who had murdered more than half a million.

Charities had a visible target, a tangible image to use as a lightning rod for donations. UNICEF had begged corporations to donate food and medicine when the killings and population upheavals within Rwanda first began, but the response had been poor. When Goma exploded, the sheer volume of televised detail triggered the biggest relief effort in history.

The population began to stabilize. The Hutu army and its fanatical militias began to regroup, to exert control over this massive nation of displaced people. They began to demand control of the huge amounts of food and medicine pouring into the camps. They were like the Gari, writ large.

Meggy was the medical coordinator of the largest camp in Goma, a place called Katale, which housed a quarter of a million people. In the beginning, she didn't have time to think that perhaps the people she was saving were murderers. That came later, when the population grew stronger, when the health threats abated, as the refugee camps became cities, when it got to the point where you could stroll into a shop at the camp and buy a television set. Two months into the mission, and the humanitarian people were asking themselves: Who are we helping? Who are we hiring? Serial killers?

The camps became dangerous. Militiamen seized control of Katale in September. Gangs roamed among the population, stealing aid. All forty relief workers had to be evacuated. Meggy left in the last car. For ten days, health care was crippled. The tensions eased enough for the expatriates to return, but the vanquished Hutu army kept its hold on the people. Soldiers threatened and exhorted the refugees to stay in the camps, telling them that they faced certain death in Tutsi-run Rwanda. Murder and extortion became endemic. Private and UN aid agencies squabbled over whether to repatriate the population, cut off assistance. Meggy and the rest of MSF decided to pull out, but the United Nations and many private agencies decided to keep reviving the monster. France and Zaire secretly began aiding the refugee army, building it up for the day it could go back and reclaim Rwanda from the Tutsis.

Inside Rwanda, the Rwandan Patriotic Front changed its name to the Rwandan Patriotic Army and declared itself in control of the country. A president was installed. He was a Hutu, but the real power rested with General Paul Kagame, now the defense minister, a Tutsi refugee who had grown up in Uganda. The country was wrecked, more than half the population was displaced, hundreds of thousands of bodies needed to be buried, hundreds of thousands of crimes needed to be prosecuted. There were pockets of disease and starvation, but they were isolated and hard to reach, in the hills, far away.

The French sat in their own little colony, which itself had taken on more refugees with the great Tutsi victory. Almost surrounded, inundated with mouths to feed, the French began preparing to pass their ill-advised mission on to the army of UN peacekeepers that was finally starting to come together, half a million lives too late. They wouldn't stay very long or accomplish very much.

Yet the focus of interest and the thrust of assistance remained on Goma, where the defeated government army became the new rebel army, supplied with sustenance by the world at large, a huge chunk of the population at its immediate command. They would create a sort of Hutu world, ready to roll back into Rwanda someday.

But the Tutsis who were already there, they had other plans.

A MAN with a suitcase and a curious look inspected the inside of a heavily damaged store in a Rwandan town called Gitarama. His name was Fred Tagwa. He was a thirty-four-year-old physician from Uganda. He was wearing wire-rim glasses and a white suit. He had the paunch of prosperity.

"My parents come from right over there, from those villages," he told people in town, pointing to a distant spot on a distant hill on the horizon. "But I have no desire to go back there. The militias are hiding in those hills. I think here in Gitarama is a good place to bring my family."

Tagwa's family fled the anti-Tutsi purges in 1959, when he was just a baby. After the Rwandan Patriotic Front captured the country, he came home. He wasn't alone. On the desolate main street, a small van stopped and discharged about fifteen people of all ages. Tagwa watched. "You meet so many coming back," he told a new acquaintance. "A convoy from Burundi. A truck from Uganda."

He figured there would be lots of space in Rwanda, once one of the most crowded countries on earth. He figured the Hutus who fled wouldn't be coming back.

"I don't know," he said. "We keep hearing that these people will come from Goma. But we hear they are being terrorized, that they think we will kill them. I think the ones who committed the atrocities will stay away. They're afraid."

He looked over the town. The silence was strange. There were people on the streets, sandals and shoes crunched on the gravel, but everyone talked in the hushed tones of mourners at a wake. Or maybe newcomers in unfamiliar surroundings. They drifted among the empty buildings, looking for homes.

"I had some cousins here . . . ," Tagwa said, trailing off, then adding quickly: "I lived long enough outside. It's high time we come back."

Across the country, people were coming back. Buses and cars rolled into town after town. Almost all of them carried Tutsis. It seemed easy to believe that it was all part of a plan to repopulate these cruelly cleansed regions. A new Tutsi-dominated government was in place, the French all but gone. The Hutu army and the civilian killers were crammed into squalid camps. The tall people known as the Watutsi were back in control.

Thousands of onetime rebel soldiers resettled in their ancestral villages. And, in many cases, the code of conduct was forgotten. There were reprisal murders, witch-hunts. It wasn't as bad as the original genocide, nowhere close. But the old code wasn't obeyed with the same devotion as before.

The Hutu army and its allied militias staged raids on Rwanda from their camps in Zaire. Finally, the new Tutsi-dominated government of little Rwanda decided to invade gigantic Zaire itself in order to break up the camps. Rwanda enlisted the aid of the Ugandan army and various Zairian rebel groups. They drove the Hutu army the breadth of the country, more than a thousand miles through thick, seemingly impenetrable jungle. They wound up conquering Zaire and scaring the despot Mobutu right out of the country. New leaders renamed the country Congo.

About a third of the refugees in Goma, many of them people who had the most reason to fear a return to Rwanda, fled deep into Zaire and beyond. The Tutsi-sponsored army would chase them down and quietly massacre many, maybe most of them in the distant jungles. Others would keep running, across Africa, around the world.

But the vast majority of the refugees would go back home, to Rwanda, where the Tutsi government would promise to repatriate them without vengeance. It would jail only those who had murdered others. The prisons would fill up quickly.

MSF dispatched Mary Lightfine to check on the health conditions of the thousands of Hutus jammed into prisons. She had some compassion for them. They may have been killers, but they probably were caught up in a frenzy of the moment. She went to some of the women's prisons, places occupied in some instances merely by the spouses of killers. Some women told her sad tales of how they were raped all day.

MSF dispatched Meggy Verputten to assess the health conditions of Hutus from Goma who were seeking to return to their traditional villages in Rwanda. The Tutsis, with trademark efficiency, were indeed processing people coming back, promising them homes. She was impressed with their medical care, their sanitation. But security was bad in the villages where the Hutus had returned. Many of the returning Hutus formed new militias. Some of the Tutsis settled old scores. And there were all these old Tutsis from past generations. The authorities said the right things, seemed to be doing the right things, but things still looked very bleak.

Meggy had always felt that, in principle, it was better if refugees eventually went home. And in Rwanda, most of them eventually did. But Meggy was pretty pessimistic about the place when she finally pulled out of there and went back to Amsterdam. Too many people had too much history of fighting over the same little space. She began to believe that, maybe, some people were just incapable of living together.

14 history lesson

S ENADA was sitting behind the counter, reading a book, when a woman walked into the bakery and began looking around.

"Can I help you?" Senada asked the woman.

The woman didn't say anything. She glanced at the book Senada was reading, did a little double take, and went back to scanning the shelves. She was a nice-looking woman, about forty, very well dressed. But she seemed distracted, a little strange, in fact. Senada went back to her book while the woman looked for whatever it was she was looking for.

"I'd like one of those."

The woman was pointing through the glass counter at a little breakfast roll called a *kisla*. Senada put down the book and got a roll for this slightly weird woman and wrapped it up. The woman paid for it, and then just kept standing there in front of the counter.

"Please," the woman said. "Will you share this with me?"

Senada thought: This woman is craaaa-zzzeeee!

"No, thank you very much," Senada said, spreading her arms to indicate the shelves and bins filled with tortes and tarts and cakes and cookies and leavened loaves and rows and rows of little rolls. "I work in a bakery. I can have anything I want."

The woman trembled. She stared at the book that Senada had been *trying* to read.

"Please, do me a favor," the woman said. "You don't realize how much this means to me.

"When I was a little girl, I went to the elementary school right across the street," she said. "And sometimes I used to come in to this very bakery and buy a *kisla* for breakfast. One day I came in here with my friends and the owner, he grabbed me by the hair and pulled me outside. He said, 'You cannot buy here because you are Jewish!' I just stood there and cried."

The woman and her family eventually had to move away from this town, she told Senada. After the war and its horrors were ended, they returned to Bosnia, to the capital city of Sarajevo. But this was the first time she had been back to her hometown of Banja Luka, back to this bakery, since that day three decades before.

"Ever since my childhood, I dreamed I would come back to this town and just come in to this bakery and buy one of these *kisla*, as a free woman," she said.

Senada stood there and listened, transfixed. She was eighteen years old and her life seemed so . . . so *normal*. Nothing to fear. Nothing to want.

The bakery was owned by Senada's cousin, and she was helping out in the summer of 1976, the summer before her senior year of high school. Since business was slow that day, since she had a required reading list for the summer, and since her area of concentration in high school was history, the book she'd happened to be reading that day was a history book. A historical biography, more precisely. Of Adolf Hitler.

Senada tore off a piece of the *kisla* that the woman had bought and started to chew. She didn't know what to say to this woman who had leaped from the pages of her book and strolled into her shop.

"I am so sorry" was the only thing she could think of. But she would always remember the one thing that ran through her head: Thank God that will never happen to me.

"You have helped me very much," the woman told Senada. "I realized my dream. I don't think I will ever be back in Banja Luka." And then she left.

Senada went home and told her mother and father about this encounter, but their attitude was basically: So what? That's history. Those things happened. Her parents knew that as well as anybody.

But Senada Suljic was drawn to history, even the carefully reconfigured history of the Yugoslavian textbooks that she had grown up reading. She saw films in school about the terrible things the Nazis had done to Jews and Gypsies and the Yugoslavian resistance during World War II, but she read little about what the Yugoslavs had done to themselves. How pro-Nazi Croats and Muslims massacred hundreds of thousands of Serbs, how Serb extremists exacted grisly revenge. How most of the Yugoslavs killed in the war — 10 percent of the population — were murdered by other Yugoslavs.

Instead, she learned about how Marshal Tito's ethnically inclusive Partisans united the country and drove out the Axis occupiers who had dismembered it. Senada's own father had joined the Partisans when he was sixteen years old. He had been wounded twice. He was a hero of the liberation, a soldier in the Yugoslav National Army, a member in good standing of the Communist Party. To Senada, he was what made Yugoslavia great.

Senada went off to college in 1977 to prepare for what she hoped was a career as a lawyer, but things didn't work out. Her mother fell into ill health. Senada was the youngest, the last one left at home, so she quit school and dedicated her life to caring for her parents. She had a boyfriend who wanted to marry her, even after he had moved to Switzerland to take a job, but she kept saying no. She could not imagine leaving her elderly father and her ailing mother, her siblings and friends and the beautiful city of Banja Luka.

Though Senada didn't marry, her family expanded nonetheless. Her sister married a man who owned a paperboard company in town. They had a son they named Ernad. Since Ernad was the first of his generation, Senada was very close to him and interested in his welfare. Her brother married a Serb woman and they had two children. The whole family was very close. Everybody saw one another every day.

When Tito died in 1980, the family was sad. They loved Tito. Maybe because they were taught to love Tito, Senada knew, but she loved him anyway. Yugoslavia's socialist leadership tried to keep together what Tito had wrought, to keep a veneer of unity on the ethnic divisions that Tito had suppressed with force and guile. But as the decade after his death wore on, new leaders arose by exploiting those divisions, by blaming a reeling economy on other ethnic groups.

In 1990, the six Yugoslav republics each held their first open elections. Most of them chose old Communists who had reinvented themselves as nationalists. One would have thought that all the republics would merely have gone their own way, particularly the big republics of Serbia, Croatia and Bosnia. But Croatia had large pockets of Serbs. And Bosnia's biggest group may have been Slavic Muslims like Senada and her family, but the combined population of Serbs and Croats outnumbered them. So one person's nationalism was pretty much another's threat of extermination.

The end began in June 1991, when Croatia and the small republic of Slovenia declared independence. The Yugoslav National Army first attacked Slovenia in an effort to get the Slovenes to reconsider. Senada thought the Slovenes were crazy to secede. She rooted for the army to bring them back. But Slovenia was populated mainly by like-minded Slovenes, and the Yugoslav National Army gave up on the place after just ten days of fighting. Let the damn Slovenes form their little country.

The army instead turned its attention to Croatia, where the ethnic Serb minority already was rebelling against the decision to secede from a Yugoslavia that was dominated by Serbia. When the Yugoslav National Army attacked Croatia, Senada again hoped the soldiers would retrieve a runaway member of the Yugoslav family.

Because Banja Luka was the home of a big Yugoslav army base and strategically located near Croatia, it became an important staging area for the war in Croatia. And because it was located in Bosnia's ethnic Serb heartland, it became something of the emotional core of rising Serb patriotism within Bosnia.

It also began filling up with ethnic Serb refugees fleeing the fighting in Croatia. They brought a measure of resentment with them, to say the least. Many of them were unsophisticated folk from the countryside who hated the Croats for driving them from their land — not to mention killing their families during World War II. They also had an abiding dislike for the Muslims they often denigrated as low-class "Turks," even though these Muslims were Slavs like themselves who just happened to have converted to Islam during the Ottoman occupation of centuries ago.

To gather sufficient support for their wars, the Serb leaders both in Serbia and in Bosnia, in particular Banja Luka, exploited this ethnic mistrust with much propaganda. As the war between Croatia and Serb-dominated Yugoslavia wore on, you could see things changing in Banja Luka, even though Bosnia itself wasn't involved in the war. In workplace cafeterias, people sat together in their own little groups, and sometimes the Serbs would sing nationalistic songs. Serb flags began flying over public buildings. Conversations became stilted between old friends and neighbors who happened to be from different groups.

Senada began to get a sense of the depth of these feelings one morning when she walked out of her parents' home and spotted the neighbor's child, a girl of thirteen. Senada, who always considered good neighbors to be one of life's treasures, said hello.

"You Muslims have to go," the girl said.

Senada was startled. "But why, honey?"

"I don't know," she said sullenly. "You just have to go."

Senada knew that this girl was just repeating something she had heard her parents say at home. People whom Senada had considered good friends, good neighbors.

The whole family began experiencing the same things. Senada's nephew Ernad was sixteen years old when Yugoslavia began unraveling, and shortly afterward his girlfriend came over to his house.

"My mother won't let me go out with you anymore," she told him. "Because you are Muslim."

Everyone could feel the fissures forming. And the outside world, realizing that the country was coming apart in a particularly messy way, responded all wrong. The Germans immediately granted diplomatic recognition to Slovenia and Croatia, an ardent Nazi-era ally, and badgered the European Community to follow suit. This pretty much guaranteed Yugoslavia's demise in its earliest stages. Then the EC set a deadline for the other republics to declare themselves independent to qualify for EC recognition. All this did was trigger more standoffs and confrontations.

Sure, self-determination was a nice concept on paper. Each ethnic group *should* get to decide its particular destiny, shouldn't it? But what happens when these groups share the same space and the same cyclical history of fighting over it? What happens when the record shows that these groups, when allowed to jockey for primacy, when encouraged to agitate for independence, trigger horrible wars and incomprehensible atrocities?

Bosnia's Muslim president was stuck. Bosnian Serbs said if he declared independence from Serbia-dominated Yugoslavia, they would form their own nation and secede, become allies with Serbia. Bosnian Croats said they would form *their* own nation and ally themselves with secessionist Croatia if Bosnia *didn't* secede from Serbia-dominated Yugoslavia.

Faced with this goofy EC ultimatum, however, the Muslim government in Bosnia opted for independence. The capital would be Sarajevo. And the Serb minority declared themselves an independent nation *within* Bosnia. *Their* capital would be Banja Luka. Two nations sharing one space, with blood ties to neighboring countries already at war. Things did not look good.

Banja Luka continued to fill up with Serb refugees who had been dislodged from Croatia. Pretty soon, there were gangs that roamed the city, occasionally beating up Muslims and Croats or breaking into homes and terrorizing the inhabitants into leaving so the Serbs could take it over. Since Serbs were Eastern Orthodox and Croats were Roman Catholics and Muslims were, well, Muslim, the harassment had religious overtones. The Serb gangs burned down Catholic churches and mosques.

The children of these refugees also formed gangs that waited after school, beating up Muslim and Croat children. A kid that Ernad knew, Admir Rakovic, got knocked off his bike by one of these gangs. They took the bike and promised to kill him someday.

Toward the end of the school term, Ernad's homeroom teacher began reading a list of students who wouldn't pass to the next grade. They were all Muslims. When he called Ernad's name, the boy stood up. The teacher said he had failed algebra.

Ernad could not believe it. "But that's my best subject!"

"You failed it. You'll have to stay back."

Ernad lifted his chair in frustration and slammed it to the ground. "It's because I'm Muslim!" he shouted.

The teacher started screaming at him, how Ernad wanted to kill him. Some of the other students started to laugh at this ludicrous charge, but the teacher ran down to the principal's office, told him how Ernad had tried to kill him with a chair.

The principal called Ernad to his office and told him he was being expelled from school forever.

The Muslims started getting fired from their jobs. Admira, the sister of Ernad's friend Admir, had a favorite art teacher who happened to be Muslim. One day someone new was sitting behind the teacher's desk. She told the children that the old instructor wouldn't be coming to school anymore.

Another time, Admira noticed that a new boy in her biology class, a Serb refugee from Croatia, was staring at her in a menacing way.

"What's your name?" he asked her.

"Admira," she said. It was a Muslim name.

"This is not your country anymore," he said. "This is not your city anymore."

He pulled out a gun and showed it to her.

"We have all the power in our hands."

Not long afterward, a gang of kids broke into the home of one of Admira's girlfriends and tied her parents to chairs. Then they gang-raped and killed her as her parents watched. She was fifteen, just like Admira. Admira's parents finally told her that she wouldn't be going to school anymore.

Senada could not believe these things were happening. One day she went downtown to visit one of her friends who worked in an office building. As she entered the lobby, one of the security guards demanded to see her identification.

"You can't come in here," he told her, handing back her card. "You are Muslim."

She just stood there, stunned. All she could think of was that day in the bakery, seventeen years before.

She kept waiting for the Yugoslav National Army, her father's army, Tito's army, the army that had ended the horrors of World War II and had hammered the country back together again. She kept expecting this army to put a stop to this insanity. And the army acted. Now under control of Serbia, the Yugoslav National Army attacked Sarajevo. Soldiers from the great army sat up in the hills, firing on the besieged civilians below, killing women and children waiting in line to buy bread.

When the war broke out, the rulers of the Serb territories began drafting all men to go fight at the front. Muslims and Croats inside the Serb lands wanted to avoid this duty, since the people they would be fighting would be other Muslims and Croats.

Admir and Admira's dad, an electrician for eighteen years, went to work one day and his boss said, "You have to go to fight in the war, Zihad."

"But I don't want to fight in the war," Zihad said. "I don't want to kill people."

"Then you're fired."

A few days later, he got a letter at home saying that he had to pay a fine if he wouldn't fight. He went down to the police station to pay. But a couple of weeks later some Serb soldiers came to his home and took his identity papers. They told him he had to come down to the police station to get them back. When he went to the station, he was told he had to join the army. Instead, he went into hiding. For more than a year, he hid in the rafters and basements of homes.

As the war escalated, the harassment of Muslims and Croats in Banja Luka got worse. One of Ernad's cousins was sitting down by the Vrbas River that ran through the city, fishing, when a gang of Serb kids his own age came up to him and demanded his identification. He knew some of these guys. Before all this nonsense began, he had considered some of them his friends.

"What are you doing!?" they asked him. "Let's see your ID!"

His cousin looked at one of the guys.

"But . . . you *know* me!"

"I don't know you!" the guy said.

Anyway, they killed him.

The war wasn't going too well for the Bosnian Muslims and their uneasy allies, the Bosnian Croats. They were losing territory like crazy. Serbs made up one-third of the population but eventually conquered two-thirds of the territory. The Serbs were better supplied, more heavily armed and seemingly more fiercely driven to spill blood in payment for historical wrongs. They became brutally adept at driving Croats and Muslims from the areas they held by burning down their homes, raping women of all ages, and beating and murdering the men. They stuck thousands in concentration camps and fed them only scraps. The prisoners became skeletal reminders of another era. Sometimes the Serbs just massacred people and buried them in pits.

The United Nations imposed an arms embargo on all of Yugoslavia, but the biggest impact it had was to keep the Bosnian Muslims from effectively arming themselves against the Serb-controlled Yugoslav National Army and the fanatical Serb militias. The UN sent peacekeeping troops to Croatia and then to Bosnia, but they had neither the firepower nor fiat to keep the peace. They couldn't even shoot back at snipers.

The Europeans seemed most concerned about the hundreds of thousands of people who were fleeing the war, the continent's biggest refugee movement since World War II. By the autumn of 1992, there were more than 600,000 Bosnian refugees in Europe and even more in Croatia.

The war was like an endless eviction notice. The roads were filled with people moving, trying to stay ahead of new boundaries drawn in blood across burning villages and broken neighborhoods. Armies drove people from towns and then repopulated them with their own people driven from other towns, and humanitarian groups agonized over whether it was humane to feed and clothe starving and freezing people living in stolen homes. The war moved with an insane, unstoppable momentum immune to the impotent haranguing of the West.

And while the Serb shelling of Sarajevo was well chronicled, less was known about the things happening deep inside Serb-held territory, in places like Banja Luka. Though all the ethnic groups were guilty of atrocities, the Serbs seemed to have perfected the art of tribal-based torment. Every night in Banja Luka, just after curfew, the crimes would begin. Families would huddle in the darkness, listening to the cries and shouts and the gunshots. And every morning, the lucky ones would only *hear* from their neighbors about which girl was raped, which man was killed, which family was beaten and robbed and thrown from its home. The lucky ones would slip out to find food, hoping they wouldn't be noticed or questioned by the gangs or the soldiers or the shadowy death squads that cruised the streets in their unmarked red vans.

One day, a dozen Serb policemen barged into the house where Ernad lived with his parents. Ernad recognized some of these guys as former friends. He remembered his cousin from

just a few weeks earlier, and made it a point not to appeal to
their former friendship.

They had come for his father.

"If you don't want to go to the army, Muslim, you better
die!" they shouted.

They handcuffed his mother to the kitchen table. They
punched and pistol-whipped Ernad and his dad and kicked
them in the head with their boots. They dragged Ernad's dad
away and left the boy lying on the floor, bleeding inside and
out, his skull fractured.

His mother got hysterical and called Senada, who drove
right over. She took Ernad to the hospital emergency room, but
the Serbs who ran the place demanded a hundred German
marks to let him in. Senada paid the money. Ernad lived.

By the time Ernad and his family were ready to go home,
though, they couldn't. The Serb authorities decided to seize the
house and give it to Serb refugees. Ernad and his mother wound
up moving into an apartment the family owned downtown.
Ernad's mother seemed to be flirting with insanity. He prayed
that his father would come home but, deep down, he feared he
was dead.

Tens of thousands of Croats and Muslims fled Banja Luka,
most only after they had signed forms relinquishing their property to the Serbs. But others stayed. Some, like Senada's older
brother, were married to Serbs who didn't want to go. Some
didn't have the money to pay the police and the army for permission to leave a place they were officially being terrorized into
fleeing. Some just did not want to relinquish the home that had
been in their family for generations.

And some just figured the war had to end. There seemed to be so much international interest, so many UN–mediated peace proposals, so much talk of UN peacekeeping missions. It always seemed like a breakthrough was imminent, if you could just survive one more night.

Still others were like Senada's sister and nephew Ernad, people whose loved ones were forced into slave labor. They stayed, hoping to open their doors one day and find what Ernad found months after his father had been seized by soldiers. He was standing in the doorway, a wasted replica of the burly guy who once ran a big paper company in Banja Luka. Ernad's father once weighed 200 pounds, but now was lucky if he was 140. Ernad threw his arms around his sickly father, who spoke like a man gone mad.

He had been forced to build bunkers and trenches at the front. He kept talking about horrible things, how he had seen the Serbs rape children, old women, and laugh to the Muslims and Croats being held in slave labor: "The same thing is going to happen to *your* family!"

He had come home on a fifteen-day leave. He pissed blood and had a knife wound in his arm, a bit of Serb discipline. When the time came to go back, he went to the doctor, who agreed he wouldn't be much use at the front. He could get another fifteen days, but he had to pay three thousand German marks for it.

The bribe kept him from the war a bit, but brought no peace. Serb gangs broke into the apartment three times because they thought Ernad's father had money. Each time they threw everyone against the wall, beat them senseless, and then just took what they wanted — blankets, food, anything they could find. They even assaulted Ernad's mother, whose mental state just continued to worsen.

The family hid in the house, freezing, with no electricity or water. Some sympathetic Serb neighbors sometimes would bring bread and milk. Ernad's father never went back to the army, and after several weeks letters began showing up at the apartment, ordering him to report. Finally, the police came for him. A Serb magistrate heard the case and sentenced him to fifteen years in prison.

The pressures on the family just kept mounting. Senada's mother — Ernad's grandmother — was a diabetic with a bad heart and high blood pressure. She needed medicine but couldn't get it anymore in Banja Luka, thanks to the embargo. Senada decided: This is it. Time to go.

She had a good friend who had fled to Germany the year before. As much as Senada hated the idea of living in Germany — even the sound of the language made her think of the Holocaust — she would go there. A sympathetic Serb neighbor arranged for the family to get on a bus that was going to Austria, via Serbia and Hungary. That was often the only way a Muslim could get anything done; get a Serb to pull some strings.

But her father refused to leave Banja Luka.

"I'm old," he said. "What am I going to do in a strange country? I don't speak that language. All my life I am here."

He told Senada to take her mother to get medical care. He would stay here, keep the home. Maybe, maybe the war would end.

Two days before she left, she walked through the city to see for the last time the things she loved, the beautiful green river that ran through it, the mountains that ringed it. But the people she saw along the wide boulevards were all different. They were refugees from other places, and they had destroyed the town with their hate and vengeance.

The bus to Austria was filled with people. When it arrived at the border checkpoints with Serbia, the guards began checking the passenger lists. They came to Senada and her mother. Because the two women had Muslim-sounding names, a guard said, "You cannot go to Serbia. Muslims cannot enter." They ordered them off the bus.

Senada didn't know what to do. She called the Serb neighbor who had helped her get a place on the bus, and he said he would send somebody to help her. Senada and her mother waited for ten hours at the border before a friend of her neighbor's showed up. He took the two women to the checkpoint in his car and told the guards that they were his sister and mother. The guards believed him. They drove through Serbia, the republic that had started three wars in one year.

And then, finally, they came to Hungary. This was the reformed Communist nation that had stood defiantly alone in 1989, throwing open the door to the free world, making the first breach in the wall that the superpowers had built. Now it was an emerging democracy deep into free-market reforms, eager to build close links to the West.

"You cannot go through," the Hungarian border guard said to the Serb man with the two Bosnian women. "You need a visa."

The Serb slipped the man a hundred German marks, the universal visa of the new world. The border miraculously opened.

They traveled through Hungary and headed for the Austrian border. This was the border through which Michaela Woike and hundreds of thousands of East Germans had poured, ripping open the Iron Curtain, bringing down the Berlin Wall, unleashing torrents of movement across the earth.

"Sorry," said the Austrian guard at the border crossing. "You need a visa. It is now the law."

Senada thought: When did they change the rules?

Not long after the war began. There was a new wall now, one that stretched from Scandinavia to Slovakia, one erected primarily to keep people like Senada and her mother out. Why? Because too many wanted to come. There were 3.5 million displaced Yugoslavs, more than 2 million from Bosnia alone, and most were looking to land elsewhere in Europe. So, in quick succession, each country on the continent began requiring Bosnians to have visas to cross its borders. Europe bolted the doors on the one group of Europeans with the most urgent reason to run.

The United States had waived its responsibility for ending the war in Bosnia, allowing the Europeans and the United Nations to play the role of superpower. They responded with peace talks, peace initiatives, peace plans, but no peace. They were effective only at refusing entry to the tide of refugees that resulted from their ineffectiveness.

The man from Serbia dropped Senada and her mother off at a hotel in Hungary, near the Austrian border. He told Senada to ask her friend in Germany to perhaps arrange for travel documents over there. If she couldn't, he told Senada to call him in Banja Luka, and he would come back for her.

Senada thanked the man and tried to give him some money, but he refused.

"No. If *you* need some money, I will give *you* money," he said. "You are not the first Muslims or Croats I have helped."

Senada called her friend, who promised to find a way to help. Senada got a room for herself and her mother and waited.

The hotel was filled with refugees waiting to find a way across the border, waiting for relatives in Germany to get them some papers, waiting for a miracle to open a new hole in this new wall. Some already had tried to sneak through the woods and had been caught and sent back. Some had hired shady professional escorts, who instead robbed and abandoned them at midnight halfway across a river, or deep inside a forest.

After a week in the hotel a man in a car showed up, looking for Senada. He had been sent by her friend in Germany. He was a Muslim from Bosnia with a German visa, and he was in the business of selling his access to refugees like Senada. The price? Three thousand marks.

"Money, money, money," Senada thought. There was a price for everything. For a hospital to save a dying boy, for police permission to leave a dangerous place, for sanctuary in countries that considered themselves free.

The man took Senada and her mother on a journey without end. They tried half a dozen border crossings, not only into Austria on Hungary's eastern border but into Czechoslovakia to the north. And in each case the guards shook their heads and said, No, sorry, you people can't come in anymore. The border is shut. The rules have changed.

Sometimes the guards just waved them away. One put a stamp in their passports to show other guards that these Bosnians had tried to enter Czechoslovakia without the proper papers. Yet another looked ready to weep. "I am so sorry," he said in a cracking voice. "It is the law. It is the law."

The Bosnian from Germany was running out of ideas. He waited for night and tried one of the Austrian crossings a second time. The guard took the passports and peered into the car. He looked at the face of the sick old woman and the pleading eyes of her frightened daughter. He made a solitary decision in the dead of night on a lonely frontier that still stood, to some, as a doorway not to freedom and prosperity, but simply safety.

"OK," he said. "You can go."

They drove across Austria, toward Germany. They came to the border of a nation cut in two by the Cold War and rebuilt by its end. A country that once bore the guilt of the Holocaust by drafting a postwar constitution that required it to grant asylum to anyone who stood helplessly at its doorstep, whether it was a computer programmer fleeing bad politics in Togo or a mother running from poor health care in Romania. Or an East German girl seeking a livelier life.

Now, it was a country so upset with the number of people who had exercised this constitutional right that it finally had ripped up the damned document.

"Sorry," said the sentry who stood at the portal to the Federal Republic of Germany. "You cannot enter. You must now have a visa."

The Bosnian from Germany implored the guards to let a hypertensive old diabetic come into the country before she died, and they finally said: If she is sick, we will transport her to the hospital. But not her daughter.

Senada had dedicated her life to caring for her mother. She had turned down marriage proposals and a life in Switzerland. "I can't leave my mother," she said.

So the Bosnian from Germany took Senada and her mother to a refugee camp in Austria, on the grounds of a vacant factory. He knew a family there, and they agreed to put up the two women even though they only had one room. The Bosnian from Germany went back to Germany to, he hoped, get two German visas.

He came back a week later. The visas had been denied, but he had a plan anyway. "I have everything," he said. "Tonight we go."

He stopped at a truck stop just before the German border. He had a passport from a German woman — who knew how he got it? — and he told Senada he would take her and her mother across the border one at a time. He left Senada waiting in the little restaurant in the middle of the night. Truckers came in, gave her a look, ordered coffee and left, and she sat there as the help stared at her, wondering who or what she was. She didn't really know this mercenary who had driven off with her mother, crossing illegally into Germany with a borrowed or stolen passport. She thought about her father, alone in Banja Luka. She worried about her brother, a Muslim married to a Serb who didn't want to leave the place where he wasn't wanted. She nursed her coffee for thirty minutes. She stopped caring about it after three hours.

The man came back.

"OK," he said. "Now you."

He took Senada across the border, gave the guard the passports, then drove into the Federal Republic of Germany. Senada took a peek at the photo in the passport and smiled grimly. This woman looked nothing like her, she thought, let alone her mother.

It was like a dream, driving down the autobahn. Arriving in Berlin, the city's Gothic beauty cloaked in shadows. The Germans had made it hard to penetrate the border of this country. Once you were here, though, you could still pursue the process of applying for asylum. The next morning, she registered herself and her mother as refugees. They were put in a very nice building in west Berlin, which was occupied mainly by other Bosnians and some Lebanese. And Senada's mother began receiving medical care.

Several months later, her father showed up. He had been burned out of his house and was able to get on a UN bus out of the city. The Germans let him into the country because his wife and daughter were here.

Senada now had both her parents. But she couldn't relax. Not when the social workers who dealt with the refugees kept saying that this was not permanent, that the day was coming when they would have to leave. Not when she still had blood kin back in Banja Luka.

THE letters showed up exactly as before, only this time they said that it was Ernad's turn to report to the army. He would have to work at the front lines, just as his father did, digging latrines and polishing the boots of Serb soldiers after they had finished that day's raping and killing. His mother couldn't bear the thought of her son following his father into that hell. She sent Ernad into hiding.

He moved into an apartment where a cousin had already holed up. His name was Mursad, and he was twenty-one years old. He was a big guy with a quick temper, and he had a good reason to run: He had fought for a while with the Bosnian army that was trying to keep the Serbs from overrunning the country. He had a reputation as a killer of Serbs. He was a wanted man.

Ernad spent six months inside the apartment. In February 1994, he finally went out one afternoon to buy some bread at a bakery that was two minutes away. He got the bread and then went to buy some cigarettes at a place just a short walk from the apartment.

He was standing in a line at this kiosk on the street when he saw a red van roll by. Ernad felt his knees go weak when it pulled up to the curb nearby. Six or seven cops jumped out of the back and strolled up to the people standing in line.

"What's your name?" one of the cops asked Ernad.

"Nenad," Ernad said. This was considered a Serb name.

They asked for his last name, so Ernad gave them the name of a Serb neighbor who frequently helped his family by bringing them food.

"OK," one of the cops said. "No problem. You're Serbian."

The cops went up to this old guy in a wheelchair in front of Ernad, and you could tell right away he was a Muslim. He had a little hat with a little brim, like old Muslim men wore. The cops asked him his name, and he gave a Muslim one, and they just started beating the hell out of him. An old guy in a wheelchair.

Unbeknownst to Ernad, his hot-tempered cousin had been watching from the house. He saw the commotion and figured that Ernad was in trouble, so he came running out, shouting. One of the cops looked up and, wouldn't you know it, recognized Ernad's cousin as an old school chum.

"Oh, that's Mursad!" the cop shouted. "He was in Kotor Varos! He killed one hundred Serbs!"

Serb-run media always claimed that the Muslims and Croats were massacring Serbs by the truckload, which is how the leaders kept their followers sufficiently dedicated to a truly dubious cause. The purpose and prevalence of propaganda was lost on the cops, who just fell on Mursad and savagely beat the murderer of a hundred Serbs.

Ernad stood there, in shock. "Run!" Mursad shouted. "Run!"

The cops were puzzled. "What's going on?" one of them shouted at Ernad. "You said you were a Serb! What's your name?"

Ernad was flustered. He shook as the Serb cop stalked toward him. Ernad tried to remember the name he'd given them. He couldn't. He just shouted out his own.

"Ernad!

The cop closed in, cursing. "Why did you lie to us?" he said. He raised his pistol and brought it down on Ernad's head, again and again, sending the boy spinning down into the blackness of another barbarous beating.

ERNAD felt like he was indoors somewhere, though not quite. He was lying on the ground. He saw Mursad nearby, unconscious and covered with blood. The old man sprawled next to him. Two other people he didn't recognize were lying nearby, also unconscious. Everybody was soaked in red. They all may have been dead. Maybe even he was dead.

Gradually, Ernad realized he was in an underground parking garage. He tried to move but couldn't budge a muscle. He was numb all over. He could see outside that it was early in the morning, maybe daybreak. But which day?

He saw a man walking from a car.

"Help! Help us!" he shouted weakly.

The man came over, a look of horror on his face as he surveyed the gory sprawl. Only the boy was conscious. "My God, what happened to you!?"

The man went away, and Ernad felt himself slipping back into blackness. He awakened to find his Serb neighbor, the man his family had known forever, coming toward him. Ernad had used this guy's last name when the death squad had questioned him. He was with some other Serbs. They were part of a civilian street patrol. How did they get here? What would they do?

Ernad watched his neighbor bend over him. Then break into tears.

"Oh, my son," he said, cradling Ernad's head.

He lifted Ernad up into his arms and carried him to his car. Ernad could see that his arms and legs were just open wounds. He lay in the car and waited. His neighbor came back and drove toward the hospital. The old man, he said, was dead. The other two, it wasn't clear if they had survived. His cousin, he said, was probably going to be all right. They were all heading to the hospital.

They arrived at the hospital, but a doctor on duty would not let them in.

"No, no, I don't want to take these guys," he said. "They're Muslims."

He pointed at Ernad. "I remember this guy. He was here before."

Ernad's neighbor pulled out a gun. He began firing shots into the air.

"You don't take him, I'll shoot you!" he screamed at the doctor.

"You can kill me! I don't care!" the doctor said. "I don't want to take any Muslims!"

Just then, Ernad's ex-girlfriend and a nurse came by. She was working as a nurse's aide. "Oh my God, what happened?" she shouted.

Ernad couldn't take it anymore. He just passed out. When he came to, he was in a bed and his girlfriend was sitting next to him. There were tears in her eyes. This was the first time he had seen her since before the war.

Soon, the doctor returned with some police officers.

"Listen boy," he told Ernad. "You got to leave tonight."

The Serb neighbor came back, this time with Ernad's mother. They took him back home. He didn't know how long he slept, but at one point he dreamed he heard the voice of his father. He opened his eyes and there he was, standing by his bed, a careless sketch of the man he used to be. The Serb neighbor had gone down to the prison, joshed with the jailers, given them some booze, and got his father out for the night to visit his badly maimed son.

"As soon as I find a way to get him out of here, I will. I promise you," the neighbor said to Ernad's father. Everybody started to cry.

Ernad fell asleep again. He slept for a day and a half. When he woke up, two black guys were shaking him. They were speaking English. He thought: I must be dreaming. His mother said they were with the United Nations. They were trying to help the family get out of Banja Luka. The United Nations didn't have much power here, except to organize some bus convoys for Croats and Muslims, to help them leave the only homes they knew, to helplessly help the Serbs ethnically cleanse the place. The United Nations couldn't make peace, couldn't stop war, couldn't protect people, but it could on occasion make the process of ethnic cleansing occasionally less lethal.

The family applied to the United Nations for a spot on the buses to Croatia. The Serb neighbor went down to the prison and again got Ernad's father out of there, brought him home again. They were waiting for news on the next UN convoy when word got out that his father was no longer in jail. About fifty Serb cops and soldiers showed up outside the building where Ernad's family lived.

The Serb neighbor, who lived downstairs, wouldn't let them inside.

"Nobody's going to leave this building," he said.

"So we're going to shoot up this building just for three Muslims?" one of the soldiers said.

"Nobody is going to leave," the neighbor said.

Ernad's mom called the United Nations. "They're going to kill us!"

Ernad's father got the gun he had been saving for a moment like this. He stood at the door, waiting. And then, something miraculous happened. United Nations peacekeepers showed up. They came inside the building. The Serbs on the street outside hollered at them, threatened them.

"We're going to kill all of you if you take them out!" they shouted.

But these UN soldiers, these powerless Canadian peacekeepers, they were undeterred. They took Ernad and his parents to their headquarters, where many other Muslims and Croats were staying. Ernad saw his cousin, Mursad. Serb soldiers outside shouted that they knew there were a hundred Muslims in the building. They put some bombs under the UN cars to scare the peacekeepers. More UN people showed up the next morning. They met with local Serb commanders, seeking permission to spirit these Muslims away from their country, off to the netherworld of the refugee. The Serbs finally said OK.

At noon on March 8, 1994, the families gathered to board the bus. The people crowded around. Ernad looked everybody over and suddenly spotted an old school acquaintance.

"Admir!" Ernad shouted.

"Ernad!" Admir said.

The boys embraced. They introduced their families. Admira was there, too. So was their dad, the electrician who had lost his job and then went into hiding for a year when he wouldn't report to the army. They eventually did track him down. They made him pick apples every day and then carry them in a box for five miles to a mess hall. He sat down to rest once and the soldiers beat and kicked him until his teeth fell out, until he lost consciousness. He deserted and went into hiding again. While the cops were looking for him, they went to question an eighteen-year-old cousin who was six months pregnant. Maybe they didn't want any more Muslims born in the city, so they shot her to death.

His wife had kept going to the UN office, asking that the family be taken out of the city. Finally, she got permission, but had to get authorization from the Serbian ethnic-cleansing bureaucracy. She had to fill out papers turning over all of the family's property and bank accounts. The family was allowed to take only one bag each. No radios, no tape decks, nothing of value.

The bus carrying Ernad and his friend Admir and their rapidly bonding families finally pulled out of Banja Luka. It stopped at many checkpoints. Finally, it came to one that was larger than the others, and everyone was ordered out. An army patrol approached. Everyone was terrified. They had heard stories about what sometimes happened to these buses, how refugees often were robbed and beaten and raped and killed as they made one last stop at the border.

One of the soldiers approached them.

"Welcome to Croatia," he said. "You have freedom."

The families hugged one another and shouted in exultation. Some fell to their knees and kissed the dirt. Some just stood there and cried uncontrollably. They had abandoned their homes and their homeland, and they couldn't have been happier.

They were taken to a big camp in the countryside called Gasinci, which was near a Croatian army base. They were packed into barracks, trailers and prefabricated houses, sometimes twelve to a room. They slept on triple bunk beds. There were five thousand people at the camp, and in the morning you had to get in a long line to use the toilet. If you wanted a shower when the 3 P.M. showers opened, then you had to get in line by 1 P.M., which meant you had to miss the lunch of macaroni and beans. You had to wait hours to use the one phone, to wash your clothes, to boil the yellow water that came out of the pump. And if you wanted to go into the city, you had to get permission and could only stay for two hours.

Life, in other words, was great. Admir's dad wore out his shoes in five days. He had spent so much time hiding in basements and attics that he couldn't stop walking. And he kept meeting all sorts of people he had known in Banja Luka. Everybody was so nice to one another. They shared things, like clothes. They had endured so much, and now they were free. Conditions were harsh, sure: But the threat of death was gone. Admir's dad counted each holey sole as a blessing.

There was a main street through camp, and a square with a little cantina and a little shop. It became a meeting place, a social center. Ernad had to go to a hospital for twenty days, have surgery on his leg wounds, and he had to wear leg braces for a while, but he recovered quickly. He and Admir became very tight, and their families grew just as close. The refugees formed a soccer league, with teams representing the towns from which they had been driven. Admir and Ernad led the Banja Luka Roosters to the camp championship on the camp soccer field while their families celebrated raucously in the camp bleachers.

There was a place you could watch movies and television shows. The boys loved the latest kickboxing flick, while the girls all raced to the TV room whenever *Beverly Hills 90210* came on.

A disco opened at the camp. Admir and Ernad both found girlfriends. More than one, as a matter of fact. There was just something about this camp, the horrors people had fled, that made people live with a bit more abandon. Everybody reveled in simple human pleasures.

Ernad's family got packages of food, clothing and money from Senada in Berlin. Sometimes, Ernad's family and Admir's family would splurge by going into town for a special lunch.

There were relief workers there. There were Americans teaching people English. Admira picked it up faster than anybody. She always had been a good student. And resettlement agencies set up shop at the camp so people could apply for asylum in different countries. Lots of the Bosnians applied for Germany, Sweden, Austria and Switzerland, where many had relatives.

Both Ernad's and Admir's families decided to try for the same countries, so they both applied for Germany. But they were rejected. Too many Bosnians, they were told. Well. Who wants to go live in a camp in Germany, anyway? All they did was threaten to send people home.

A notice went up one day in the camp kitchen. Ernad read it: Whoever wants to go to America, fill out this paper and send it to the American embassy in Zagreb. We'll let you know.

Ernad's dad had a sister who had lived in the United States for eight years. So they decided to apply. And Admir's family followed suit because, well, they wanted to follow Ernad's family. Admir's dad also had a feeling, maybe, that the United States offered his kids the best chance of building new lives unencumbered by the past.

Two months later, Ernad's family got an interview at the U.S. Embassy in the Croatian capital, Zagreb. A man asked them where this relative lived.

"'New' something," Ernad's father said.

"New York, New Jersey, New Orleans?" said the man.

"Just 'new' something," he said.

The man laughed. He said he'd do some checking. Then, a month later the family got the word: You're going to America. You're flying to New York. You've got a relative in New Jersey. Get ready for a New Life.

Ernad used to see the scenes from New York in the movies. He was happy about going there, but a little scared. "What if we get lost?" he thought.

They flew into Kennedy Airport. A resettlement agency found them an apartment in a town called Clifton. Ernad got a job at a tool company, taking orders on the telephone. His dad got a job at a recycling center.

They called Senada in Germany all the time to find out how she and her parents, Ernad's grandparents, were getting on. They called their Serb neighbor in Banja Luka, and Ernad found out that his old girlfriend had gotten married, had a baby. They called Senada's brother every Sunday, to find out how one of the last Muslims was making out. He apparently got beat up so badly that he couldn't walk anymore. They sent him some immigration papers.

Then, not long after Ernad's family got to the United States, Admir's family followed. They had said they wanted to go to New Jersey, too. They were taken in by an American family who just wanted to help refugees. Admir's dad got a job as a maintenance man at a supermarket, and he worked as a handyman around the upscale neighborhood where they lived, in a bedroom community called Basking Ridge.

This American family put pressure on Admir, who never liked school very much, to finish high school, to finish trade school. And he did. He went to high school during the day and took automotive classes at night. He got a job pumping gas, then got promoted to auto mechanic. His sister, Admira, didn't have to be talked into finishing school. She may have missed more than three and a half years, but she was driven. She mastered English to the point where she pretty much erased her accent. She landed on the honor roll. She got elected to the student council. She started getting scholarship offers from colleges. She began thinking that she might want to work someday helping refugees.

These people were, for the most part, all pretty happy with their new homes, their new lives, their New Jersey. Bosnia? It was history.

SENADA buried her mother in Berlin in 1994. Six months later, her father suffered a massive stroke. He was unconscious for two months. When he awoke, this hero of the great war of unity and liberation could no longer walk, talk or feed himself.

Senada was coming to the end of yet another six-month visa, and she was uncertain whether it would be extended. The threat of repatriation loomed. Once again, it was time to go.

One day, the papers arrived from her sister in New Jersey. She filled them out and sent them off. Word came in the spring of 1995. The world was closing its borders. But Senada's application for asylum had been approved. She could slip through the crack of the closing door.

The plane trip from Berlin to New York was exhausting. Her father needed constant attention. When she arrived at Kennedy Airport, she scarcely recognized the young man waiting at the terminal. Ernad had been a cute boy. Now he was a handsome man. Now, he was known as Ernie.

He hugged his aunt and tended to his grandfather. He took them home to the family, her sister and her brother-in-law and the cousins who had collected in some place called Clifton, the pieces pulling back together. And Senada gave them all a quick kiss, too exhausted to share their excitement over the fact that she was here, wherever, somewhere, home.

"Please," she begged them as they fluttered and fussed. "I just want to rest."

They led her to another strange bed in yet another strange place, and she lay down to sleep. The soft patter of familiar voices drifted through the walls. She felt like she was floating, not quite on earth. It was like a dream. A beautiful dream.

epilogue

THE ambulance was parked inside a compound ringed with razor wire. The crew sat quietly inside, smoking and staring and waiting for the right set of headlights to show up. Almost exactly on time, a four-wheel-drive truck rolled through the gate. The occupants burst from their vehicles, unloaded a stretcher and carried a shouting old man from the truck to the waiting ambulance. It roared away, tires crunching on crusty snow.

Nurses already were waiting at the emergency room entrance when the ambulance arrived at the hospital. The old man on the stretcher was still shouting. Three weeping women were there to greet him, and he tried to tell them everything. "I haven't walked in one month!" he shouted, arms spread beseechingly, as orderlies wheeled him down a corridor.

"Here! Take my bags! I have two bags," he said, holding out two tiny plastic sandwich bags, one with his cigarettes and the other his passport.

He was rolled to the emergency room and lifted onto an

operating table. Doctors and nurses floated around him. His two stocky sisters and one red-eyed niece, a woman named Lejla Petahagic, cried on the periphery. They hadn't seen this man since before the war. They looked at his gray and gaunt body, his shock of white hair, and listened to his desperate declarations. Lejla couldn't believe this was big Uncle Bakir.

"He used to be a *huge* man," she said.

Bakir Drljacic used to be a soldier. He'd fought the Axis conquest of Yugoslavia in World War II. He was wounded in battle and wound up in the Jasenovac concentration camp in the Independent State of Croatia, a Nazi puppet regime created from Croatia and Bosnia. Croat fanatics killed tens of thousands of people in the camp, Jews and Gypsies and occasionally some antifascist Muslims like Uncle Bakir. But, mostly, the Catholic Croats killed those hated schismatics, the Orthodox Serbs. The Croats and their Muslim allies appalled even the Germans and Italians with their enthusiastic appetite for beheading Serb babies and slitting Serb wombs and holding contests to see who could kill how many Serbs with a single bullet or a single knife, how completely one could splatter a Serb head with a sledgehammer blow. Serb extremists took great relish in avenging these atrocities.

These groups would give way to the Partisans of Josip Broz (Tito), whose final version of Yugoslavia would last a couple of generations. Uncle Bakir would walk out of the concentration camp, find a mate and raise a son, and slip into forty years of relative stability and social-ist contentment before the country's flaws and old hatreds would sur-face at the end of Tito's era and the beginning of the new one.

Now, Uncle Bakir was just a shriveled old man, babbling in an emergency room, trying to figure out why he couldn't walk, think straight or keep his bladder from failing. Now he was a refugee. "They stuck a pistol in my mouth and broke my teeth!" the seventy-two-year-old raged as he writhed in the Sarajevo City Hospital. "I ate better in the Nazi concentration camp!"

The Serbs had kicked him out of his apartment because they wanted it for Serbs. A UN doctor made arrangements for him to go elsewhere. And just a few days before the Americans landed on Bosnia to enforce some peace, he was cleansed from the city like blood bleached from a bedsheet.

I had been making the rounds of the relief agencies when a Red Cross worker told me to stop by a certain building at a certain time, and maybe I would see a rare Muslim fished from the purified Serb pool of Banja Luka. And here indeed was Uncle Bakir, a harmless creature living on the margins of a hobbled yet hardened new society, one with a brutally reengineered ethnicity and a fierce intolerance for even a sick old man from another tribe.

I had come to Bosnia at the end of 1995 to cover the arrival of American troops, the spearhead of a 75,000-member NATO force. Despite enormous and nearly successful opposition in Congress, this army of intervention was being dispatched to enforce a peace plan that by most assessments was deeply flawed, even morally wrong. It may stop the war, the argument went, but it endorsed an unholy partitioning of a nation along ethnic lines. It may have called for a united Bosnia in principle, but in reality it sanctified the destruction of a multiethnic society. And its enforcement required the presence of American troops, who supposedly had no business taking part in such wars.

The first Americans were en route to the place even as Uncle Bakir sprawled on the operating table, shouting, even as the nurses started to snip off his big diaper, even as they finally shooed his kin-folk and me through the swinging double doors of the emergency room. I couldn't help but think about the part of the peace plan that sounded more like a wistful hope than a clear stipulation: All refugees could go home again.

Uncle Bakir seemed an example of the reality of Bosnia, Rwanda or any other place defined by a history of hostility between rival factions who claim the same swath of land, places where the very idea of going home is tantamount to an act of war. So vicious, so *personal* were these conflicts that the idea of repatriation had become quietly unthinkable, nice if it happened, but almost superfluous to the fundamental problem of stopping the fighting so the noncombatants could simply stop running, and therefore stop dying.

It was a recurring quandary of modern times: The right of refugees to return home was essential to a long-term solution, yet often a dangerous impediment to short-term progress. Maybe that was one of the reasons why the West so often found itself paralyzed by conflict, afraid to save the occupants of a burning house without first reaching agreement with the arsonists on an acceptable blue-print for building them a new place to burn down.

It didn't make sense. Policy experts kept writing rules for U.S. intervention, but the centerpiece always seemed to be an exit strategy, a way to get out when things fell apart. Analysts clamored for some hard evidence of strategic interest and safeguards against "mission creep," when perhaps the real need was for a freelancing force that was faster, more fluid and much more ferocious than the warmongers. And the humanitarians insisted on preventive measures, formulas for eliminating chaos before it occurred, a technique easier advocated than accomplished. Try to handicap the next Rwanda.

If the great refugee movements of the 1990s were proving anything, it was that no general-purpose principle seemed to make much sense anymore.

The Americans finally rode into Bosnia leading a mighty force after bullying the combatants into signing a peace accord in Dayton, Ohio. This came after years of nuanced diplomacy by UN negotiators, which succeeded only in overcrowding the cemeteries in Sarajevo. Yet matching lines on a map made in America with boundaries drawn in blood in Bosnia seemed daunting. As the huge force made its way into the country, the overwhelming mood in the West was one of pure dread.

But something happened. Roads suddenly became passable. Checkpoints vanished. Relief groups found their jobs a little easier. Buses began running from Sarajevo to the outside world, crossing the frontiers of the three factions and opening doors for people who wanted to risk a return home. The place stayed peaceful for a month, then six months, then a year, then four. Even if the land was officially divided, even if the wounds were still raw and tensions still high, even if Uncle Bakir never made it back to Banja Luka, the plan had worked long enough to have been worth the investment of people and money. The argument that the Dayton accord may stop the fighting but would partition the country was answered with: So what? It was too late and badly flawed, but it was enforced with enough American commitment to have finally frozen the war in its tracks. It gave the innocent a chance to stop running, or reach safer ground. It was an example of what could happen whenever the United States mustered enough courage to halt population upheavals caused by the end of the superpower showdown. Stopping the slaughter of the innocent and the mass movement of the survivors can be considered success enough, without the elusive bonus of rebuilding a society or eliminating old animosities.

Failing to find a perfect, all-encompassing remedy for a conflict is no excuse for failing to act at all. Having the ability to halt a holocaust isn't a burden. It's a gift.

The United States and its allies could have stopped the civil war in Liberia, averted genocide in Rwanda and ended the Bosnian conflict years before they finally did. But they were scared off by high expectations and seduced by the idea that cunning warlords can be swayed at the negotiating table. They were burdened with the attitude that any big intervention that doesn't guarantee the mythical lasting peace is somehow fatally flawed. So in each instance the United States ceded titular control to the inherently weak United Nations, or to regional powers with vested interests or parochial perspectives. And in each instance there was a meltdown. The United Nations continually proved itself conceptually incapable of summoning the strength needed to point a gun at the head of a recalcitrant combatant and just say: Stop it or die.

Maybe there are no reliable long-term solutions, no surefire preventive measures. Maybe too many rival groups are doomed to keep rediscovering and reenacting the worst moments of their history. Maybe the wisest solution is simply to step in fast, break up the fight and separate the combatants before too many people get hurt, rather than agonize over how they can be taught to live together. Because maybe they can't.

FOUR hundred people were herded into a gymnasium and told to wait. They looked tired, disoriented. Armed soldiers stood guard at each door and on the streets outside. Nobody could leave.

Then a woman walked up to a microphone and the audience burst into cheers. She welcomed them, and they roared some more. She praised her husband for bringing them here. She talked about how her country was committed to liberating their homeland. Each short, simple thing that she said was followed by a pregnant pause, and even this haunted group knew it was their cue to add the applause. Even though they had no idea what she was saying.

Some had been raped, some had been maimed, some had watched a loved one die, or left a family or a burning house behind. Some had doctored their IDs or paid a bribe to get to this gymnasium in New Jersey. One woman had been mutilated by soldiers who played catch with a severed breast. All had qualified for salvation, for a ticket on a Boeing 747 bound for America.

None had flown before, and many proved it by puking their way to the promised land. The in-flight movie, a doomsday fantasy called *Armageddon*, didn't help.

Finally, they flew past the Statue of Liberty and landed at an air base outside Fort Dix. They marched off the plane on a hot and muggy day in May and waved wanly to the reporters who stood packed behind the barricades on the tarmac. We clearly outnumbered them. Then the newcomers boarded buses for the short ride to the gym at the army base to meet Hillary Clinton.

Her translator, hastily chosen and out of his league, quickly lost his way and stood helplessly in front of his own microphone. It didn't matter. The sound crews caught her comments and the refugees' cheers for the evening news.

These wanderers were special. They'd managed to find a rare place on the other side of the vineyard, the wall, the checkpoint, a place where the welcome was warm. They found a nation eager to embrace them, indulge them, adopt them, employ them, marry them. I sat on the bleachers behind a rope, with a press pool kept at bay because these refugees were so exceptional. It was the spring of 1999, and these were ethnic Albanians from Kosovo.

The U.S.-led intervention into yet another broken piece of Yugoslavia was a fitting coda to the decade of the displaced. Here was Kosovo, of all places, at center stage. I remembered when it was just another little story popping up on a printer next to my right elbow, when I worked on the foreign desk of the Associated Press. Slobodan Milosovic was using the Serb province's ethnic imbalance — it was more than 85 percent ethnic Albanian and Muslim — to stir dark nationalist passions so he could rule his own country as Yugoslavia broke apart. Indeed, some Kosovo Albanians themselves had the same designs on the province. It was the thing to do.

Milosevic used Kosovo to neutralize his more moderate rivals and got the Serb parliament to declare him president of Serbia. And he stripped Kosovo of the autonomous status that Tito had granted it in 1974.

There were riots, shootings, killings and purges. I watched the place unravel through the dispatches filed from abroad. They usually were short; we made them shorter and sent them to newspapers that simply spiked them. Who could keep up? It was the spring of 1989. So much was happening. Nobody guessed that Milosevic's crusade to cleanse Kosovo was the opening move that would lead to four wars in the former Yugoslavia and five million displaced people over the span of a decade. We couldn't even guess that Hungary's decision to loosen its borders with Austria — which came a few weeks before Milosevic scrapped Kosovo's autonomy — would bring down the Berlin Wall before the year was out.

Kosovo was just part of the cacophony of transitional times. When I went abroad, I kept running into Kosovars in the same shelters that housed Kurds from Iraq and Gypsies from Romania. They were in Berlin when I ran into Hannelore Gensch, in Dresden when I listened to the hate of a skinhead kid called Corpse. The Serbs and the Kosovo Albanians were struggling for primacy even as I caught a cab in Liberia driven by a man named Schaack, chatted on an airstrip with a private eye named Puchwein, stood in a hospital and listened to the story of a girl named Sarina, who helped me reconstruct what had happened in a town occupied only by corpses. Kosovo was *happening* when I sat across the table from a retired Soviet air force general who swore he would go to war with Russia in order to make his vaguely recollected homeland, Chechnya, his own little nation.

News agencies had little fire brigades that careened from one crisis to another, saturating one spot until everybody was sick of it, then moving on to the next place, while ignoring most things altogether. We grabbed people from the fog and got them to tell us their stories as they were happening, then let them drift back into a dimension that one has to inhabit to understand.

I had a fleeting taste of this world once, at the end of the Persian Gulf War. I chanced a quick trip over the Iraqi border to interview Shiite refugees and, with a Kuwaiti translator named Saleh Zamani, got arrested in what the UN had declared a demilitarized zone along the border with Kuwait. Iraqi security men decided to take us up the road, deeper into Iraq, beyond the DMZ. Not a good sign.

Then Saleh and I noticed a little tent surrounded by razor wire, flying the blue-and-white flag of the United Nations. The United States was in the north, protecting the Kurds while ignoring the Shiites, but the UN was here. I threw the truck into a hairpin turn and an Iraqi security man leaped from the backseat and tried to take the wheel. Two Iraqi escort vehicles raced alongside us until we all skidded to a stop on the gravel and sand leading to the gate of the compound.

We all jumped out of our vehicles and raced not at, or away, from each other, but toward this outpost of an organization that seemed more necessary than ever to a fracturing world no longer dominated by a superpower stalemate. The three UN soldiers at the compound — from Ghana, Greece and the imminently collapsing Soviet Union — radioed for their commander, a Colonel Al Feeney of Ireland. He arrived in a glorious entourage of snow-white armored personnel carriers. He held consultations with the Iraqis, disappeared for hours of talks, even took our car keys in a show of good faith that we wouldn't try to escape again. Saleh and I were confident that the colonel would let us join the UN convoy for the half-mile trip back to Kuwait.

Then he emerged from negotiations and approached the truck where we sat. This was a UN observer force, he said. He could do nothing except observe. Well, not exactly nothing. He gave our car keys to the Iraqis. Then he left, leading his white armor out of town. We'd hoped they would have at least done a little bit more observing.

The irritated Iraqis took us on a little trip into Basra and beyond, across the Tigris and Euphrates Rivers, into Baghdad. We were continually interrogated, regularly taunted and somewhat harassed and got, at one point, to hear a man being tortured because he had the phony ID of a higher-ranking officer. We were finally dumped in the desert eight hundred miles from where we'd been captured, at the border with Jordan, which wouldn't let us in. It took a day or two before somebody summoned the will to go find the right entry stamp, and we finally hitched a ride to the capital, Amman, with a passing Palestinian in a Mercedes.

It wasn't much. But for a few days we had a vague sense of the dislocation and abandonment that many endure for years, often a lifetime. We'd felt lost on earth.

And now, out of the ether at the close of the century, Kosovo. I wondered how long it would last. Even Bosnia had managed to vanish, even though it had been one of the most disproportionately covered stories of the decade, even though American soldiers still helped police a peace that remained dangerously fragile. Even though millions remained displaced, and thousands were being resettled every year in the United States because of a special program enacted when Bosnia was, well, special.

Yet it was remarkable how even Bosnia vanished. In 1998, a small humanitarian organization teamed with a big insurance company to buy ninety seconds of time during the opening ceremonies of the Winter Olympics in Nagano, Japan. The point was to raise money to build playgrounds for kids whose only exercise had been dodging sniper fire. Schools and playgrounds and such simple things as traffic police are essential to stabilizing a society. And the Olympics audience seemed like a natural target. Sarajevo, after all, had hosted one of the finer Winter Games back in 1984.

The commercial itself was actually an artful little documentary. Young people talked about how the Games had given them a spirit to survive a war. They spoke against a backdrop of stirring scenes of Olympic sport mixed with horrid images of civilians running from war. Actress Sigourney Weaver provided her potently persuasive voice for the coup de grâce.

"The children of Sarajevo never forgot the Olympics," she said, cool yet plaintive. "Please. Don't forget them."

The American television audience was estimated at close to 56 million people. Hundreds of volunteer operators were standing by. Even the toll-free pledge number was poignant: 1-800-357-KIDS. And the phones began ringing.

How many? Ten thousand? A hundred thousand? By night's end, 145 people had made modest pledges. The organizers were crushed. Bosnia, it seemed, was history.

SERBIA was allowed to compete in those Olympics. The republic of Montenegro was too small and weak to run away from what had been Yugoslavia, so Serbia came to Nagano disguised as Tito's former country. The lifting of such superficial international sanctions was the reward that the United Nations gave Milosevic for taking a break from his decade of destruction and signing the Bosnia peace accords at the end of 1995.

Six days after the Games ended, though, ethnic Albanian separatists killed a couple of Serb cops in Kosovo. This led to furious reprisals, and scores of killings. An army of rebels began taking territory, more than a third of the province by midyear, and Serbia beefed up its military and began driving people out of towns. Then NATO threatened air strikes, and Milosevic pulled back his troops. But the violence continued. Peace talks proved fruitless.

Almost half a million people had fled Kosovo from the end of the Olympics until March of 1999, when the Americans and their eighteen NATO allies decided to intervene. The United States supplied two-thirds of the military resources to this war, but only a fraction of the resolve needed to fight it properly.

The Germans wanted no part of a ground war, even though humanitarian agencies said safe havens and protected corridors had to be carved out to protect the noncombatants who would suffer reprisals for the bombing. And the Americans didn't want to fly too low, lest a battered U.S. pilot turn up paraded on Serb television. French politicians insisted that bridges be bombed only when most everyone in the war zone had gone to bed, and not at all on weekends. Political leaders throughout the alliance kept telling the people who elected them what they *wouldn't* do militarily. This may have pleased the people who hadn't even heard of Kosovo because their newspapers had spent a decade spiking stories about the place. But it did give Milosevic the military intelligence he needed to plunge onward with his ethnic purges.

NATO'S onslaught was so spare, so selective, so surgical, so precise, so carefully constructed to accommodate its members that most people in the war zone wouldn't have known that NATO had entered the fray if they hadn't heard about it on the radio.

Teuta Hyseni felt so distant from this "attack" that she chanced a quick trip into Kosovo's capital, Pristina, so she could pick up some schoolbooks. Her parents told her not to go, but she insisted. She was nineteen. The buses were still running. Pristina was less than half an hour away.

But almost as soon as she got off the bus, she heard that the Serbs had taken her town and were purging it of Albanian blood. Teuta tried to get back home, but bus service was halted. She tried to catch a taxi, but every driver refused to risk the trip. She pleaded and cried and kept flagging taxis until, finally, one agreed to try. Serb soldiers turned them away at two checkpoints on the outskirts of Pristina, and threatened to shoot them at a third.

Teuta got out of the taxi and started to run. She was so scared that she kept off the streets, the sidewalks, stopping to hide in bushes every time she saw a policeman or soldier or member of a Serb militia. She made it to the home of an uncle and pounded on the door. She shouted her name, prayed somebody was home. The door cracked and her uncle pulled her inside.

Teuta and her kinfolk stayed indoors, laying low, hoping the NATO bombing would end the crisis. It only escalated it. Two weeks after the air strikes began, Serb soldiers in black masks drove through the street in cars with loudspeakers. They ordered every Albanian on the block to leave.

Teuta's uncle hustled everybody outside. The family left bread baking in the oven and went to the train station, where mobs of ethnic Albanians were herded into boxcars. The train pulled away. Teuta and the others were dumped at the border and ordered to hike to Macedonia. At the last minute, a Serb soldier snatched Teuta's leather satchel, which contained the diary she'd kept since she was a girl.

The crowd shivered in the mud and rain outside Blace, squeezing under shared blankets. Then relief arrived. American soldiers, logisticians. They brought tents, food, medical care. Private aid agencies finally caught up with the crisis.

Mary Lightfine was there for MSF, and one of her oddest duties involved showing actor Richard Gere around a refugee camp, proof that Kosovo had made it to the top. It didn't hurt that the refugees were European and not African. Humanitarian groups were flooded with offers to help, and many began pulling resources out of Africa so they could fly their flag over Kosovo and, in the process, expand their mailing lists of potential donors.

Yet even the upsurge in aid couldn't keep pace with the sheer number of displaced people. The Europeans didn't want any more asylum-seekers, but somebody had to do something, at least symbolically. The overtaxed camps seemed to signal defeat, bad planning, timid action, and the TV cameras found no easier target than the refugees swelling with each night of NATO bombing.

Teuta was obsessed with the new arrivals, too. She was looking for familiar faces. Anybody from her family, hometown, school. Anybody. She did this every day, for thirty-six straight days, until May 5, 1999. It was the birthday of Karl Marx, the anniversary of the day the United States fired its first man into space in a Cold War contest to conquer the moon. It was the day her uncle and his family found a rare portal to the other side. They climbed aboard a huge jet for the first flight of their lives.

A POPULATION the size of Pittsburgh was being purged in Angola. A rebel group, adopting a psychotic new calling card, was lopping off the arms and hands of random refugees in Sierra Leone. More than a million people were rendered homeless by a rebellion in Colombia. Sudan's civil war between Arabs in the north and blacks in the south hummed at such a steady state of horror that it quietly became the decade's single worst case of mass migration. Yet

Americans and most of the country's media only had eyes for the refugees sleeping on clean sheets in a special army barracks that Washington media handlers had dubbed "The Village," a place with playrooms and prayer rooms, where professional soccer coaches volunteered to form teams, where pop bands entertained in a park, where so many people were sending toys and clothes and food that the army commanders at Fort Dix publicly asked everybody to please stop.

The United States said it would airlift 20,000 people from the camps in Macedonia and give them immediate residency — and, if they wanted to stick around, permanent status and even full citizenship. I was assigned to cover the arrival of the first group, and I made a few calls in advance so I could understand why these people promised to be the most heartily welcomed refugees since the fall of Saigon.

"We've taken calls by the hundreds," said John Kidane, refugee coordinator for the Nationalities Service Center, the Philadelphia branch of a nonprofit refugee group that won the main contract for distributing these immigrants. "We're taking information from American families who want to host a family or two. Rich woman in New York wants some refugees for her mansion."

He sounded tired. I asked about this selective sympathy, and he pointed out that he himself had been a refugee many years ago. He was from Eritrea, which was presently at war with Ethiopia.

Ethiopia was ethnically cleansing people of Eritrean heritage even though they had been born and raised in Ethiopia. Families were being broken up, children orphaned. And the Eritreans were sending these supposedly repatriated countrymen, who couldn't even speak their language, to the front to fight the people who could. "And nobody cares," said Kidane. "We even have refugees from Somalia calling us and asking to take in a Kosovar."

He had a caseworker on his staff, a man named Samuel Joe, who had been a mid-level official of the UN-backed interim government put together during one of the many peace plans that continually collapsed in Liberia. He had been in the West African nation of Ghana, attending peace talks, when fighting flared in 1997 and Charles Taylor once again came after the capital.

Joe couldn't get back home, and his wife only managed to get two of his six children out. The others had been at school, and now were behind enemy lines. Two of his sisters were killed when Charles Taylor's rebels burned down his house. He lost track of much of his family, but many gathered in camps in the Ivory Coast. Joe and his wife took advantage of a special resettlement program, then started to bring over his family.

He was working on bringing over his mother, one of his sons and a brother and a sister when word came down that the Liberian resettlement program was being halted indefinitely. The next week, the Kosovars arrived to an astonishing welcome. Joe sympathized with the Balkan refugees — it was his job to help them settle. He really cared about their plight. But he longed for a camera crew to show up in some other place and report, live, about some other piece of the refugee world.

"Charles Taylor is just as vicious as Milosevic," Samuel Joe told me on the telephone.

Though some hotlines were logging ninety calls an hour from people who wanted to help the Kosovo Albanians bound for America, nobody really realized just how big their arrival would be. The sound, the cameras, the lights. Hillary Clinton, the governor of New Jersey.

Teuta was somewhere in those sections of the bleachers roped off from the press, listening to Hillary Clinton give her brief speech. I was among a pool of reporters allowed to stand by a side door in case the First Lady and her State Department entourage decided to field some questions. Indeed, out they came, but nobody seemed to ask anything that began with anything other than "how did you feel," and Mrs. Clinton lobbed the banalities back. Nothing was appearing in my notebook. Frustrated, pushed back from the barricade by the wall of wide-bodied camera crews that had pride of place for such staged moments, I shouted more loudly than I'd intended.

"Mrs. Clinton! Mrs. Clinton!" The frosty smile tilted up, toward the back of the little press pool pack.

"The number of refugees allowed to resettle in this country has fallen from 132,000 to 78,000 during the course of your husband's administration. Does the arrival of these refugees signal a change in attitude?"

The frosty smile tilted away toward a State Department official, who stepped to the mike and said that the numbers of refugees let into this country reflected the need at the moment. This was almost true: The West didn't *need* any more refugees climbing the walls to get into the prosperous places that were dictating the shape of the global economy. The West didn't need to use refugees as political currency. Well, except for this token contingent of Kosovars, since it took attention away from the shackled bombing campaign and the squalid camps. These refugees probably got the heaviest amount of sympathetic press coverage, per capita, since Moses led the Israelites to the promised land.

I didn't get to pursue this topic with Mrs. Clinton, however.

Mine was the final question, and the group moved on. The spotlight followed, squeezed into its limo and was gone.

TEUTA and I sat on the bench of a picnic table in a grassy area just outside The Village, and she told me her story. She was a morose young woman with light brown hair who couldn't summon a smile when we first talked. It was springtime in the countryside of rural New Jersey, and the sun was warm and the breeze pleasant. The park was a hum of festive chatter, squealing children and intensely whispered conversations among groups with furrowed brows, leaning in intently as they listened to each other's stories. There were counselors around to deal with trauma, to teach people about life in America. And the press surge had already virtually vanished.

But it wasn't enough. Many of the uprooted remained numb to their surroundings, depressed, withdrawn, unable to enjoy or even fathom the concerts and volleyball games and rolling soda vendors that the Americans had given them. Yet I'd spoken to a lot of refugees in this country, and many who had come from Kosovo during the past decade. They all said the same thing: Give them time. Once they get used to life here, they'll never go back.

Even Teuta was able to think beyond the breadth of the ocean that still separated her from her family, wherever they were. "The welcome we have received is very unbelievable," she said. "If my family was here, I would like to stay here."

She spoke through one of the volunteer translators, a man named Bashkim Tolaj. Like many of the volunteers, he was a refugee himself. He'd been arrested seventeen times and beaten even more for his role in the demonstrations against Milosevic's crackdown on the province in 1988.

His route was long and creative and, he hinted, not all quite legal. "Let's just say I didn't have a welcome like this," he said, gesturing to the trim redbrick buildings and neat, well-shaded lawns of Fort Dix.

Nobody did. I came back to the camp a week later to talk to Teuta some more, and she had some remarkable news. The Americans had opened up a PX for the refugees and given each of them fifty dollars. Teuta walked into The Village's newly opened convenience store and browsed through the junk food, disposable cameras and stuffed Snoopy dolls in fighter-pilot outfits. Something caught her eye: a prepaid phone card.

She went to a bank of pay phones and began calling numbers in Pristina, punching in thirty-seven digits' worth of access codes and exchanges each time. One time she heard shooting when somebody picked up the phone but didn't say anything. Other calls didn't go through, or were unanswered. Finally, she called the post office near her old home, and a man answered. Teuta asked if anybody knew where her family night be.

"Right here!" the man said.

Her father came on and both he and Teuta screamed deliriously, then began crying. Her mother was fine, her father said, though her brother was missing. Young men of fighting age were the most likely to get singled out for death in Kosovo. Teuta's parents had holed up in the post office with other ethnic Albanians, hoping to get a large enough group to flee the country. Only small groups are systematically killed, he told her.

"Where are *you*?" he asked his daughter.

"The USA!" she said.

Her father was flabbergasted. "Where?" he asked, over and over. "Fort Dix," she said. "I think . . . New Jersey!"

Seven minutes later, the card ran out and the line went dead. But she knew that her parents were alive. She ran to the commissary to buy another card.

ONCE the bombing campaign got stronger, lower and more devastating, Milosevic finally pulled his troops out of Kosovo. Many refugees came home to burned houses and unmarked graves. Many would bring vengeance down on any Serb they could find, even murdering a UN worker from Bulgaria, a Slav who spoke what sounded like Serbian.

Kosovo was liberated, but the place was a mess. The United States and its allies could have saved more lives if they had acted more decisively. There is something almost chemical about the effect the arrival of a formidable Western army can have on the viscera of an internecine war zone — the militias, the checkpoints, the roads through which aid flows. Yet aggressive intervention in faraway wars is a tough concept to sell to a generation raised on Vietnam. The mother of all quagmires inflicted the country with paralyzing self-doubt and a reflexive opposition to anything that might cause American military casualties. The utter dread of slipping into another such slough made the Americans pull out of Somalia, skip Rwanda and arrive way too late in Bosnia and Kosovo. It prompted enormous congressional resistance to the Persian Gulf War. Vietnam's jungles became Bosnia's frigid mountains, the Vietnamese army Saddam's battle-hardened fighters.

But Vietnam was armed by the other side, just as the Red Army's misadventures in Afghanistan were prolonged by U.S. aid to the enemy. There isn't an other side any more; there is only one nation with the raw power to halt mass upheaval.

The only thing the Americans lack, besides resolve, is speed. The country needs a special military branch to enforce peace agreements, end wars with regional potential and stop conflicts to avert massive refugee crises. The times demand a freestanding and multi-purpose army, composed of volunteers from the other branches, working with comparable units from other nations willing to operate under U.S. command. It would stand as the global police force of the paramount power, halting catastrophic crimes against humanity with lightning speed and ferocious efficiency.

Why not? After an era in which the superpowers remade the world in their quest to one-up each other's redundant abilities to incinerate it, such a force seems a modest and sensible accommodation of the new order. The United States is already overworking the same handful of divisions across the service branches for such missions. Why not just embrace the responsibility, and wear the badge proudly?

Instead, the first instinct is to bolt the doors and stop the spillover from reaching our borders. Refugees are now, more than ever, likely to be stranded in nations that border their own, and which are too poor to care for them. The wealthy nations that took part in creating the dynamics of the old era should assume the responsibility for accepting people uprooted by the transition to the new one. Instead, since 1990 the United States and virtually all of Europe have made it more difficult for people to enter their countries. The West has responded to the most crushing refugee tide by restricting asylum, when it would be better off punishing nations that attack their own.

Internal displacement often leads to external displacement, a ripple effect that can span generations. Only quick and courageous intervention by the last superpower can keep great numbers of people from taking to the road. Because once lives are set in motion, momentum can carry them anywhere.

The last time I spoke to Teuta, she had begun a new diary. A tiny bit of fog had begun to lift on her future. A plan was taking shape. Learn English, get an apartment, get a job, get a green card, go to medical school. Get her parents to New Jersey.

Kosovo? It was history.

acknowledgments

R EPORTERS get paid to invade the lives of people who are in the midst of their most miserable moments. We like to think that we're doing something noble, but usually we're just working. I owe this book to the people on the road who agreed to stop.

I'm also grateful to my friend and colleague, Ralf Neukirch, for conducting additional research in Europe, finding and interviewing people I'd met long ago and new ones who became essential parts of this story. His assistance was generous and insight invaluable.

My editors at Routledge, Eric Nelson, and Little, Brown, Bill Phillips, helped guide me to the finished work. My agent, Sloan Harris, found publishers who believed in this book as much as he did. Little, Brown's Nicole Hirsh made my life easier, walking me through the logistics of publishing; and Steve Lamont made it harder (in a good way) with his keen copy editing.

Bryan Gruley gave me guidance on writing the book proposal, helped me find an agent and read my earliest efforts. Chip Scanlan,

Paul Raeburn, David Beard and David Laventhol also offered strategic counsel or endorsements, and I'm indebted to Tony Fritz, Diane Prager, Larry Thorson and Jim Reindl for offering their opinions of various sections.

The book is very much the product of some editors who trusted me enough to send me places, in particular Frank Crepeau, Kevin Noblet and Lane Wick. My current boss at the *Los Angeles Times*, Scott Kraft, was particularly generous in letting me mix my day job with various things related to this book, and the *Times*' Gloria Lopez got me some large forums for calling attention to it. I am also indebted to some instructors, Judy Rose, Phil Pirages and Paul Tocco, for nudging me toward my trade.

Among my occasional traveling companions, from photographers to translators, I have special thanks for Olga Fedina, Saleh Zamani, Chris Clark, Jean-Marc Bouju, Ricardo Mazalan, Javier Bauluz, Hans Edinger and my old bar-hopping buddy from Berlin, the late Hansi Krauss. I'm also grateful for the continuous support of my parents, Anthony and Dorothy Fritz, particularly for their tireless promotional efforts.

Finally, the person to whom I owe the most is my wife, Karyn, my constructive critic, understanding confidante and very best friend. And, well, my dog, Keeper, simply for greeting me with stunned hysteria after every trip.

index